ALSO BY JOE MENZER

Cavs: From Fitch to Fratello

*Carolina Panthers: The First Season of the Most Successful
Expansion Franchise in NFL History*

*Four Corners: How UNC, N.C. State, Duke and Wake Forest
Made North Carolina the Center of the Basketball Universe*

The
Wildest Ride

A History of NASCAR
(or How a Bunch of Good Ol' Boys
Built a Billion-Dollar Industry out of Wrecking Cars)

Joe Menzer

A Touchstone Book
Published by Simon & Schuster
NEW YORK LONDON TORONTO SYDNEY

TOUCHSTONE
Rockefeller Center
1230 Avenue of the Americas
New York, NY 10020

First Touchstone Edition 2002

TOUCHSTONE and colophon are registered trademarks
of Simon & Schuster Inc.

For information regarding special discounts for bulk purchases,
please contact Simon & Schuster Special Sales at 1-800-456-6798 or
business@simonandschuster.com

Designed by Charles B. Hames
Manufactured in the United States of America

5   7   9   10   8   6   4

The Library of Congress has cataloged the Simon & Schuster edition as follows:
Menzer, Joe.
The wildest ride : a history of NASCAR (or, how a bunch of good ol' boys built a
billion-dollar industry out of wrecking cars) / Joe Menzer.
p. cm.
Includes bibliographical references and index.
1. Stock car racing—United States—History.   2. NASCAR (Association)—History.
1. Title.
GV1029.9.S74 M46 2001
769.72'0973—dc21
2001031088

ISBN-13: 978-0-7432-0507-8
ISBN-10:   0-7432-0507-3
ISBN-13: 978-0-7432-2625-7 (Pbk)
ISBN-10:   0-7432-2625-9 (Pbk)

Acknowledgments

Imagine being NASCAR driver Jimmy Spencer winding through the mountains somewhere between Bristol, Tennessee, and Charlotte, on your way home from a Winston Cup race, and you'll quickly understand the appeal of this sport. As long as you don't hit anything (which, admittedly, isn't Spencer's style behind the wheel), it's a great way to pass the time. I did it for several hours while driving home after attending last spring's Food City 500 at Bristol Motor Speedway. Driving is part of NASCAR's connection with the common man: in what other sport can you envision yourself being a participant while motoring along in a 1993 Ford Taurus station wagon with a baby's seat in the back?

Being a North Carolina transplant from Ohio, it took me a little while to understand the considerable role that NASCAR plays in southern sporting society. The sport has, in fact, grown so much in recent years that its influence is spreading across the nation as fans everywhere begin to realize the raw, pulsating excitement that surrounds most Winston Cup events.

I could not have taken the enjoyable stroll through the history of the sport that I did over the last several months without the help of many folks. As always, writing a book is a team effort much like putting a Winston Cup car in Victory Lane, involving many people behind the scenes who deserve mention even though they unselfishly toil while asking for no recognition.

The Menzer pit crew could not function on any level without the leadership, understanding and devotion of my wife Sarah, who puts up with more from me as deadlines approach than even the most temperamental of drivers (are you listening, Tony Stewart?) could possibly dish out. I don't tell her enough that I love her dearly as wife, secretary, scheduler and in-house (literally) editor alike. And I would be remiss not to thank my son Andrew and daughters Elizabeth and Emma for generally staying out of my office and off my computer when they were supposed to as I struggled to put the manuscript together. Finally, the book contract from the fine people at Simon & Schuster was agreed upon on the very day that Michael, our youngest, was born. It must be an omen of some sort, and I hope that he will grow up to appreciate all sports as I have tried to do over time. It was August 3, 1999 when I took the call at the hospital from Shari Lesser Wenk, whom I am privileged to call my literary agent and friend even though we rarely see each other.

My extended family who helped put this book together also included Jim Vogel, another alleged redneck (in an endearing sort of way) from Hamilton, Ohio. He assisted with some of the photography, was a valuable on-site companion at the Food City 500 in Bristol and offered suggestions for the manuscript at every left turn in the journey, which at times seemed would never draw the checkered flag at the finish line. As best man in my wedding so many years ago, I'm sure neither of us envisioned one day sharing the passion for NASCAR that we now possess. In many ways it is because of him and another Hamiltonian, hard-core racing fan Chris Barrett, that this book came to be.

I also want to thank the editing team at Simon & Schuster, headed up by Jeff Neuman and including Jon Malki. I'm sure they know by now that I really do believe I'll hit every deadline, self-imposed or otherwise. Sometimes, with four lively children and so many other of life's unpredictable elements thrown into the mix, it just doesn't happen. Thanks to them, the books always seem to get published anyway.

Speaking of editors, as always I want to thank sports editor Terry Oberle and Ed Campbell of the *Winston-Salem Journal,* and Zack Albert, formerly of the *Journal* and now with *USA Today.* Their advice, input and guidance is always appreciated.

The book would not be anywhere close to complete without the wonderful photographs that were provided by John Clark of the *Gaston Gazette,* Harold Hinson of Lowe's Motor Speedway and Tom Copeland of the Greensboro *News & Record.* I hope they all realize how deeply I appreciated their assistance. Clark is Mr. Reliable when it comes to shooting photos for my books and the many older photos provided by Hinson accurately portray the gritty determination and unabashed spirit of the sport in its early days. Copeland contributed the historically significant shot of the Petty family that graces page 11. It captures the spirit of four generations of racers in one snapshot, and it took place only after Copeland spent seven months trying to set it up. He dutifully arrived two hours before the shoot was to begin to make certain the lighting conditions were just right, only to have Petty family patriarch Lee lean forward after the photographer had snapped ten or twelve frames and announce, "That's it, we're done. I'm out of here." At that instant, the other three generations of Pettys cracked up—and Copeland captured the magical moment. It can never be duplicated, as Lee, then eighty-six years old, and young Adam, the last in the line of the famous family drivers in the photograph, both passed away shortly thereafter.

Hinson, incidentally, is part of a public relations arm at LMS that is a dream. Quite simply, this book could not have come off without the repeated assistance of Jerry Gappens, Scott Cooper and Humpy Wheeler at the LMS track, which is an impressive facility that is spectacularly run by the irrepressible Wheeler under sometimes difficult circumstances. Scott Cooper in particular was kind enough to introduce me to a small corner of the racing world when I first began researching the book and had little or no idea of how to begin or where to start. I appreciate this more than I can put into words.

There were so many people who gave of their time in one-on-one and group interviews or otherwise assisted that it is difficult to list them all, lest some be left out. But my thanks go out to all of them, especially Ned Jarrett (described as the "nicest man" in Winston Cup racing, he more than lived up to this billing during a visit to his home in Newton, North Carolina), Junior Johnson, Richard Petty, David Pearson, Cale Yarborough, Leonard Wood, Ray Evernham, Jeff Gordon, Darrell Waltrip, Dale Inman, Bobby Labonte, Tony Stewart, Joe Gibbs, Rick Hendrick, Dale Earnhardt, Dale Earnhardt Jr., Benny Parsons, Hill Overton Jr., Karl Patraroja, Max Muhleman, General Thom Sadler, Bruton Smith, Jimmy Spencer (of course), Pete Wright, Doc Brewer, Dave King, Eddie Grist, Al Shuford, Sam Belnavis, Willy T. Ribbs, Ken Schrader, Michael Waltrip, Randy Lajoie, Elliott Sadler and Dale Jarrett. It also was my pleasure to interview Adam Petty before his tragic death. The class with which the entire Petty racing family handled the untimely deaths of both heir apparent Adam and patriarch Lee within months of each other was further testimony to their legacy as racing royalty, and was matched by the extended Earnhardt racing family in the wake of the Intimidator's shocking death at Daytona only nine months later.

Among those of my media brethren who assisted in countless ways on repeated occasions were Ed Hardin of the Greensboro *News & Record,* Joe Macenka of NASCAR Online and David Newton of the Columbia *State.* Hardin and Macenka were the answer men on my many racing related questions, and Newton's contributions late in the project on many fronts helped me complete the manuscript. Along with Steve Reed of the *Gaston Gazette* and Darin Gantt of the *Rock Hill Herald,* Newton also assisted in the tedious task of transcribing hours upon hours of taped interviews. Doug Rice, Alicia Lingerfeldt and Brett McMillan of Performance Racing Network were helpful, as were Terry Hanson, John Isley and Billy James of the infamous, wickedly funny, NASCAR-heavy

John Boy & Billy Radio Network—and my own radio family at WFNZ in Charlotte, which includes *Prime Time* host and devout Earnhardt fan Mark Packer, general manager Mike Kellogg, program director D. J. Stout and, of course, the biggest redneck of them all, the man known as Hayseed, who swaps favorite drivers more than anyone else I know. I also would be remiss if I didn't mention the education I continue to receive by reading the likes of Mike Mulhern of the *Winston-Salem Journal* and David Poole of the *Charlotte Observer,* beat writers who are in the pit boxes and garage areas every race day trying to sort it all out.

Finally, I want to thank Erin Dominianni of the Cotter Group for inviting me to the induction ceremonies of Junior Johnson, William H.G. France and Dale Inman into the North Carolina Auto Racing Hall of Fame at the Charlotte Convention Center. Even though I had to rent a tuxedo, it was well worth it.

JOE MENZER

For the best pit crew any man could hope to be blessed with: crew chief Sarah, Andrew, Elizabeth, Emma, Michael and even Sparky.

Also, for Dale Earnhardt, Adam Petty, Kenny Irwin and Tony Roper, who died doing what they loved to do for a living.

Contents

The Wildest Ride

Foreword

The invitation came via e-mail, which seemed strange enough. Junior Johnson, a legendary figure in stock car driving circles, was being inducted into the North Carolina Auto Racing Hall of Fame. There was no such thing as e-mail when Johnson unknowingly launched his driving career as a young man, trying to outrun federal agents with his illegal loads of moonshine.

Then came the kicker: The Hall dinner and ceremony that also would include induction of William H.G. France, the father of stock car racing, and Dale Inman, one of the sport's master mechanics, would be a black-tie affair.

A black-tie affair? For a guy from the hills who used to drive in a T-shirt and overalls? In yet another illustration of how far this sport has come in the last fifty years, a lavish affair was put on at the Charlotte Convention Center in downtown Charlotte, arguably the epicenter of the National Association of Stock Car Auto Racing, or NASCAR. Sure, there is Daytona Beach, Florida, which can make the same argument and has racing roots that sink deep into the sandy beaches that run along the Atlantic coast. But Charlotte and its outlying areas, particularly Mooresville, where the North Carolina Auto Racing Hall of Fame is located, relies more heavily on NASCAR as a vital cog in its local economy than any other region in America.

According to an economic impact study unveiled in September of 2000, Lowe's Motor Speedway in Concord, North Carolina, located on the outskirts of Charlotte, generates more than $276 million annually in three surrounding counties. Humpy Wheeler, president of the facility, estimated that motorsports was a one-billion-dollar industry in the state of North Carolina, with $750 million of that being generated within a seventy-five-mile radius of his track—where some three hundred race teams and two hundred additional race-related companies are based.

Not that other regions of the United States have been ignored by NASCAR. With the addition in the year 2001 of tracks and Winston Cup races in two more large metropolitan areas—Kansas City and Chicago—stock car racing continues to be this nation's fastest-growing major sport, ranging well beyond its southeastern birthplaces.

The sport has exploded not only in the nineteen states where NASCAR Winston Cup races are now being run, but also in homes across the country as new fans tune in and discover NASCAR's unique appeal. And it is readily apparent to those getting acquainted with the sport that stock car racing is overwhelmingly corporate, to be sure, but in a fashion more *Dukes of Hazard* than Madison Avenue. Winston Cup teams will sell to sponsors any portion of their car or space on their race day uniforms, and the minute they have the dollars committed from that sponsor they are intensely loyal—at least until the second the sponsor drops them.

Take driver Jimmy Spencer, for instance. There isn't a more likable guy to interview on the circuit. So what if he hasn't won since 1994? He still knows how to push his latest sponsor's product. He hopped into cars sponsored by Kmart for the 2000 season, and was asked to assess his chances and those of Kmart teammate Darrell Waltrip prior to the first race.

"I'm excited about the Kmart deal because of the two thousand two hundred stores, and the amount of employees that we have. The people that go to NASCAR races in the Winston Cup series, there's no question they shop at Kmart stores. I think that's special for me and for Darrell," Spencer said.

Then he was asked about 2000 being the flamboyant Waltrip's final season as a driver.

"We're going to be looking for a guy to replace Darrell next year . . . and hopefully we'll find someone who can push the pedal and get the job done for Kmart," Spencer said.

Drivers slide the sponsor's name into interviews so smoothly that it becomes second nature, and the consumers identify them with the corporations they're pushing. In the first two years of an annual survey done by *Street & Smith's Sports Business Journal,* NASCAR blew away all other professional sports leagues in the detailed opinions of sports sponsors. In seventeen of the twenty characteristics measured by the survey, NASCAR graded out best—including in the three areas sponsors said were most important to them in determining where their marketing dollars went: whether the sport has a strong future, whether it is responsive to its customers and whether it offers good value for the money. Ninety-five percent said the sport had a strong future, as opposed to 67 percent for Major League baseball, 49 percent for the National Basketball Association and 37 percent for the National Hockey League. Ninety-six percent said that NASCAR enjoys a strong relationship with its fans, compared to 63 percent for the NFL, 57 percent for the NHL, 45 percent for Major League baseball and 37 percent for the NBA. The sponsors have spoken loudly about their level of satisfaction and long ago determined that NASCAR fans will buy products based on what they see at the tracks, and that's where many of this nation's richest and most influential companies are funneling large portions of their advertising dollars.

The sport wasn't always this corporate and cutting edge, but its history is rich and colorful and full of entertaining stories. It is in NASCAR's birthplaces such as Charlotte and Daytona and Darlington, South Carolina, that grand memories were forged and the foundation was laid for a future so compelling that even Bill France Sr. (nicknamed "Big Bill"), could not have possibly envisioned it. The memories remain firmly ingrained in the minds and souls of the legions who grew up pulling for Johnson or David Pearson or any of the Pettys, stock car racing's first family that includes the King, Richard Petty. This book is their story, but it isn't only for them. It's for the many new fans that today are embracing NASCAR for the first time, those who know little of its history and the men who made it.

In the South, fans and foes of NASCAR alike call it redneck racin'. Antagonists mean that to be derogatory, but fans of the sport take it as a compliment. That isn't quite in tune with today's whacked-out politically correct society, but that's what they do.

Talking with Johnson after his induction ceremony that night in Charlotte, I was left with an idea of what it is like to be an insider in this large, lovable but undeniably dysfunctional family. Speaking in his slow southern drawl, Johnson said, "You want to be remembered for what you've done for the sport and how you treated people and what you contributed to it. You certainly don't want to be remembered as someone that nobody could get along with. You would like to feel like you've treated your fellow mechanics and drivers and everyone else like you would have wanted to have been treated yourself. As far as everything you've contributed, sometimes you're the only one who'll know exactly what all that was. That's why I think the people thing, being remembered for how you treated everyone, is the one thing that your memory can be most honored by."

Research for this book first began in May 1999, but really didn't take flight in earnest until January of 2000 during the annual press tour sponsored by the accommodating folks at Lowe's Motor Speedway—without whose generous help the book could not have been completed. It was on the first day of that tour that Adam Petty offered evidence that he was a special young man, and he had to be, for he was the chosen one to carry on the famed

Petty racing legacy. Flashing an infectious grin, he talked that day about how he hoped to do just that in a way that would make his great-grandfather Lee, his grandfather Richard and his father Kyle proud.

Two days later, during a seminar on the future of NASCAR, word trickled down that another well-respected athlete in the Charlotte community had died in an automobile accident; Bobby Phills, a guard with the Charlotte Hornets of the NBA. Phills, it turned out, had been killed while drag racing with a teammate on a public road. A police investigation subsequently put his speed at an estimated 107 miles per hour at the time of the accident. It was a sobering reminder that even good guys can perish on account of bad judgment or bad luck.

Yet in the occasionally surreal world of NASCAR, where everyone knows the inherent dangers of racing but almost universally chooses to ignore them, speeds of nearly twice that are regularly attained and always sought. Yes, the stock car folks do it on sanctioned tracks in cars that are designed for safety while wearing the latest in sponsor-plastered fireproof suits designed to protect them head to toe from harm. Sadly, though, these safety measures are sometimes inadequate. The reality is always there, lurking: Speed can kill.

Oddly, that contributes largely to the lure of the sport. Attending a NASCAR race is like watching a circus where the high-wire acrobats operate without a net. Make it too safe and maybe folks aren't as interested in coming to see them perform. Remove the net, or at least make it smaller and lower to the ground to increase the suspense, and the interest of the paying and often adoring public is likely to increase. Move the high wire farther off the ground and take away the net completely, and interest surely will increase. The danger of someone falling to their death is part of the public's fascination with the event, and so it is with NASCAR.

Officials with NASCAR don't promote this morbid fascination with their sport. Improving safety is now and always has been their top priority, or so they will tell anyone within earshot. But without the ever-looming specter of wrecks—and possibly deaths as an unfortunate byproduct of them—the sport would lose much of its appeal with the millions who are tuning in.

Why risk the dance with death? Ask any driver and he will tell you that it's not going to happen to him. It might happen to another guy, but not to him. Meanwhile, they chase fame and fortune beyond the wildest dreams of Junior Johnson, once a moonshine runner simply looking to make a little extra pocket money when he first started out. But they don't do it solely for the purpose of chasing glory and mountains of cash. David Blaine, a renowned magician who once buried himself alive for seven days and on another occasion had himself encased in a block of ice for fifty-eight straight hours, was asked why he would perform such outlandish, life-threatening stunts. His reply was, "There's a certain euphoria you get by pushing yourself to a place you normally wouldn't and achieving that." He could have been talking about what NASCAR drivers experience every time they circle a track.

The riches rewarded today are substantial for the top racers. Bobby Labonte earned in excess of three million dollars from NASCAR and R.J. Reynolds Tobacco Company for taking the 2000 Winston Cup points title. For Labonte, Rusty Wallace, Dale Jarrett, Jeff Gordon, Tony Stewart and all the current drivers endangering their lives thirty-eight weekends out of the year, the risk was long ago deemed acceptable. So it was with their predecessors—wonderful characters like the Flock brothers, Ned Jarrett and Fireball Roberts, Curtis Turner and Joe Weatherly.

Today's racing is big business, as demonstrated by the new television contract that kicked in for the 2001 season, paying nearly three *billion* dollars for the right to televise NASCAR for the next six years. But in the early days, folks raced for purses that barely covered the cost of running a car and sometimes didn't add up to even that. Crews consisted of family, friends or drinking buddies who happened to have nothing better to do that day. It became more specialized as the years went by, but it was only in the last decade or so that putting together a quality crew became as high a priority as putting a top driver in the car.

"When I first got in Cup racing [in 1989], you had five or six people working on a race car," said Spencer, who earned his only two Winston Cup victories in 1994 driving for Junior Johnson, then a successful car owner. "Now you walk into these shops and Joe Gibbs has one hundred and forty people working at his facility. Dale Earnhardt Inc. has one hundred and thirty or whatever working at their facility. That's a major, major difference."

Today there are an abundance of operations like the one run by Gibbs, the former National Football League coach who guided the Washington Redskins to three Super Bowl championships. Gibbs owns and operates the teams of Bobby Labonte, the reigning points champion, and Tony Stewart, who won more races than anyone else in 2000 and appears to be one of the sport's budding superstars of the future. Listen to Gibbs explain why he switched from the NFL to NASCAR and one gets a feel for where this sport is headed.

"I told everybody if you're good in football you'd be good in this," Gibbs said. "It's exactly the same. Somebody who is on a race team would be very good in football, because you win with people. It's a people business. It's not technology, Xs and Os. It's getting the best people together and the best chemistry. I think it's exactly the same. I've been shocked. Everything that happened to me in football has happened to me here. It's kind of like reliving something. I'll bring up a football analogy just because it's happened to me. Lots of times the guys on the race teams laugh."

Gibbs is part of a growing movement that has been taking the sport mainstream over the last decade. He talked prior to winning last year's championship about how difficult it is to do just that, comparing it to winning a Super Bowl in football.

"I've got to tell you the truth," Gibbs said then. "It certainly wasn't easy, but by this time in football we'd won a couple of Super Bowls. So this is a superhard deal. It's the hardest thing I've ever tried to do. You've got to do it all. You've got to have sales, you've got to have PR, you've got to have a front office, you've got to have [body] fabrication, you've got to have engineering and you've got to be able to do every single bit of it. It's the hardest thing I've ever tried to do. I think that's the reason why we're in it. It's extremely hard and the best in the world are trying to do it."

It's extremely hard, but the folks trying to accomplish it are extremely talented—from the driver down to the guy who changes the tires or works on the engine—and the circuit is booming. As the new TV contract kicks in and exposure to the sport's many personalities increases, Gibbs said the average fan soon will begin to understand just how much it is like football and other sports.

"Crew chiefs are exactly like football coaches. They're going to get more and more visible as time goes by. TV is going to help that," Gibbs said. "[Crew chiefs] have developed an expertise. They didn't get it by going to school, just like a coach doesn't get how to run a football team from going to school. They learn it on the job and they work their way up to these positions. They are very highly paid and the positions are filled by highly sought-after people.

"It's going to continue to improve for them financially and in other ways too. They've got to do a lot. They've got to be able to handle all the people around them, set up the racing car, get along with the driver and also handle the press and a lot of other people issues."

Gibbs said that NASCAR's meteoric rise in popularity is the direct result of a fan base that has always been able to stay close to the stars in its sport, certainly a unique arrangement that will be put to the test in coming years as growth continues.

"This is a much better atmosphere for the media, for instance," Gibbs said. "In football, for example, the last year I coached in the Super Bowl, the only time I talked to the media was in a huge meeting on a Tuesday and Wednesday morning for one hour. You're insulated and isolated from them. I sit down at the Daytona 500 and the first day I must have done fifty interviews. Guys are grabbing you and talking to you.

"That's one thing about motorsports that is a neat deal. Fans can still get close to the stars and drivers. If I were covering [athletes] I'd rather be in motorsports. You grab somebody, get them off to one side and talk to them. If you tried to talk to Troy Aikman on game day you'd be arrested. This deal right here is the way to have things in sports, where people can still get close to it. That's one thing motorsports has and I hope keeps."

Humpy Wheeler thinks there are other compelling reasons NASCAR Winston Cup racing has caught on among a growing number of fans from all walks of life over the last decade, believing stock car racing's increased popularity is at least partly due to growing disenchantment with professional athletes from many of the other major sports.

"Americans love big things, and they love contact," Wheeler said. "They like football instead of soccer. Again, big guys running into each other. They like basketball. What's bigger than NBA players? Only NFL offensive linemen. They like heavyweights instead of featherweights. They like Mark McGwire, a great big guy, more than they like the rest of the baseball players.

"Why is soccer the greatest sport in the world but it's not in the United States? It tells you something about the American public. We're a violent society, we like contact in our sport. The NFL is the most violent sport in the world when you take the veneer off of it. Pete Rozelle wrapped it up in a beautiful red-white-and-blue package and made it the number one sport in the United States. But only in the United States. Why? I never talked to him about this but I think he understood what we're talking about.

"The other thing is obviously the overall behavior of the drivers. I think there's a disgust, particularly in the heartland of America, over the behavior of athletes. And it's affected the very sports they're in. Race drivers, because they can't have toxicity in their system today and do anything in a race car, have had to keep their noses clean to stay in the sport. Plus, they're more tied to some company than most athletes, so they've got to behave. It's simple."

It could create problems down the road, however, Wheeler admitted.

"The problem with good behavior is sometimes it's boring. It's great for kids, but sometimes you take all the juice out of somebody when they're trying to behave. I'm not suggesting that misbehaving is something they ought to be doing, but certainly creating some drama on the racetrack is what's got to be done to keep us on this climb."

The increased television exposure is sure to bring about changes in NASCAR. Some desirable, some not so desirable.

"Having come over from another sport, I can tell you this: in an NFL meeting, whenever TV says it wants something, the NFL does it," Gibbs said. "There's a lot of money and a lot of power there. The reason for it is everybody in the country is paying to watch our races. We've got a lot of things that a lot of other sports don't have. We've got a ten-month season. Every one of our races is televised live to every house. You don't have delays. You have all the stars of the sport competing against each other every week. You don't have a situation where a fan is sitting at home complaining because he can't get the Raiders, or he can't get the Giants. He gets Bobby Labonte and Tony Stewart and Gordon every week, and he gets them live. We've got a lot of real positives. As soon as you get all of the markets, the Northwest and Denver and Chicago, I think you're going to see this thing explode."

The television money also will lead to increased purses that will continue to help fuel growth, according to Gibbs.

"As far as the added purses, I think the last time we won at Atlanta [in 1999] we won $125,000 to $130,000 [actually the first-place purse for Bobby Labonte was $174,300]. It probably cost us $250,000 to go race that race. The golfer that week I think won $320,000. You've got him and his golf clubs. We've got twenty-six people down there [on the race team]," Gibbs said. "So we've got a lot of catching up to do from the standpoint of the purses and a lot of other things. Hopefully, this will help us out. I think more than anything else is the popularity of the sport and the fact they're going to be doing a lot of half-hour shows to bring a lot of the stories to life. There are so many great stories. The history, in particular, of NASCAR. What I'm excited about are those pregame shows, those one-hour shows and the follow-up shows that will help bring all of this to life and make it such a real story for all the fans out there. Our sport needs that, and I think it's going to be neat to see that happen. Certainly with the networks making that kind of investment, they're going to put the extra resources into it."

Adam Petty, unfortunately, will not be around to see it. He died at age nineteen in an accident when his car slammed into an outside wall during practice for a Busch Series race at New Hampshire International Speedway in May of 2000. Only two months later, driver Kenny Irwin died during qualifying for a Winston Cup race at the same track. And later in the tragedy-filled 2000 racing season, driver Tony Roper of the NASCAR truck series perished during a race at Texas Motor Speedway.

As stunning as each of those deaths was in 2000, nothing could have prepared race fans or the sport's elite for the passing of Dale Earnhardt on the final lap of the Daytona 500 in February of 2001. Earnhardt was the sport's bigger-than-life star with a swagger and a daredevil's air of invincibility seemingly surrounding him like some kind of force field. Other drivers might suffer a terrible fate, but surely not the Intimidator. Surely not the Man in Black. Surely not Earnhardt. The legions who thought that found out how wrong they could be when Earnhardt crashed head-on into turn four at Daytona International Speedway, making it four NASCAR deaths in nine months and moving the issue of safety, always worth debating in the sport, front and center like perhaps never before.

Perhaps Earnhardt's legacy will be improved safety, much like it became part of Fireball Roberts's legacy following his death that was the result of burns suffered during a terrible accident at Charlotte Motor Speedway in 1964. Fuel cells and improved flameproof clothing came about immediately as a result of Roberts's demise (racing pioneer Ralph Moody claimed he had made the fuel-cell technology available to NASCAR even before Roberts's fiery wreck and that it might have saved the sport's first superstar). The hope here is that some lasting safety innovations will result from Earnhardt's passing. Surely NASCAR must and will do more in the immediate future to protect its greatest assets: the drivers.

Each of the recent driver deaths was a violent reminder of what is at stake each time a race is run. But the racing goes on. Why? Because it enriches the lives of so many who are involved in the sport, and many more who only now are beginning to latch onto it.

Despite the official invite to Junior Johnson's induction ceremony, stock car racing is not a black-tie world. It's a blue-collar deal that these days is beginning to appeal to blue-collar and white-collar fans alike. Folks who have followed it for years or studied its history would be pleased to know that upon entering the Charlotte Convention Center for Junior's big day, standing near the door were two of his oldest friends, Willie Clay Call and Millard Ashley. Years ago, they used to run moonshine with him. Johnson has never forgotten them, and history shouldn't either.

Amidst all the wandering tuxedos, Call and Ashley stood tall that night next to a honest-to-goodness, old-fashioned moonshine still and a car that once was used to transport it to thirsty customers. There they told stories that helped explain not only the roads they had traveled, but also how the sport had evolved over more than half a century.

That is what this book attempts to do on a larger scale. Hopefully, it will not disappoint. Jimmy Spencer, for one, thinks it is a story that begs to be told.

"People have no clue what Junior Johnson and the Wood brothers have done or guys like [former driver and owner] Bud Moore," Jimmy Spencer said. "I hear so many things about all the new guys. But everyone has to realize that those boys only made it because of the veterans in this sport. Bobby Allison and Donnie Allison. Fred Lorenzen. Ned Jarrett. I mean, those guys raced for three and four hundred dollars to win. These guys today are making good money. Those guys were risking their life for next to nothing.

"Dale Earnhardt, the same way. It's because of those people that the sport is what it is today. [Now] maybe fans are starting to look for new guys to latch onto—and they're going to look at the cars that are running up front. But fans have so much to learn. There are a lot of new people coming into our sport, with the TV and media coverage we've been receiving, and there are a lot of people who don't know how all this got started."

And Spencer's goal in all this?

"I just want my little piece of the action, that's all," he answered honestly.

Doesn't everyone?

Wrigley Field

Dawn did not beat the paint crew to Bristol Motor Speedway, tucked away in the foothills of the Cherokee National Forest that spill into the Great Smoky Mountains in the northeast corner of Tennessee. A great serenity settles over the area at dawn and at dusk each day, but it would be shattered in a few hours by the roar of forty-three race cars. The paint crew had work to accomplish before then. Less than twenty-four hours earlier, during the running of the Cheez-It 250 NASCAR Busch series race, the outside retaining walls of the .533-mile track had taken a serious beating.

Black marks were everywhere. It gave the place a certain character that bespoke the type of side-by-side, bumper-to-bumper racing the track engenders, but it wouldn't do for television. Not, at least, at the start of the race that was to come. And in the modern era of stock car racing, which only is beginning to dawn, appearances on television are of paramount importance.

Barely five months earlier, an intense bidding war for the television rights to the hottest ticket in major league sports produced staggering results: The FOX and NBC-TBS networks struck a deal according to which they will fork over $2.8 billion over the next six years to televise NASCAR's races, beginning in 2001. That averages out to more than $466 million per year. Only fifteen years

33

earlier, NASCAR received a paltry $3 million for the TV rights to twenty-eight races during the 1985 season.

So the painters were there to paint a prettier picture. It was time to clean up the sport's image a little bit before it was deliberately soiled again. The painters splashed bright white paint over all the scuff marks on the walls, temporarily erasing the ugly reminders that make stock car racing at Bristol the fun that it is for NASCAR fans—and the nightmare it can be for drivers attempting to negotiate what has been billed as the "world's fastest half mile." It is racing in tight quarters at frighteningly high speeds. It is the type of racing that has helped the National Association of Stock Car Auto Racing—more commonly referred to by its NASCAR acronym—become the fastest-growing, most exciting spectator sport in America as it barrels into the new millennium.

"This is the only place to see racin' the way it oughta be," is the way track owner Bruton Smith, chairman and chief operating officer of Speedway Motorsports, Inc., puts it. Those are his very own words, written out in exactly that manner in an open letter to the fans inside the program for the events of this particular sunny weekend at the end of March 2000. Correct grammar? Who needs it? Wreck-free racing? Who wants it?

The black scuff marks would return soon enough on the walls. Smith was sure of that.

He had been counting on it since the day in early 1996 when he purchased Bristol Motor Speedway and immediately began expanding and renovating it. The place seated 71,000 when Smith bought it. Now it seats 147,000 and includes a hundred luxury skyboxes—all sold out for both this race and the even more wildly popular night race in August of 2000.

"We have so many people on the waiting list to come to Bristol, we just stopped taking orders," Smith said. "I mean, it was foolish. We stopped at eighty-four thousand people. They think they're going to get 'em someday. But with a waiting list of eighty-four thousand people, for most of them it's not likely in their lifetime."

No doubt Daytona International Speedway remains the most

famous of all NASCAR tracks. And none has more overall racing tradition than Indianapolis Motor Speedway, where NASCAR's Brickyard 400 is run every August and seems to have rivaled if not surged past open-wheel racing's famed Indy 500 in popularity. There also are other outstanding venues, each unique in its own way . . . particularly places such as Darlington Raceway in South Carolina, Talladega Superspeedway in Alabama and Lowe's Motor Speedway in Charlotte, North Carolina.

But Bristol is stock car racing's Wrigley Field. Its Fenway Park. Its Yankee Stadium.

Why? Because it has character. It has seats perilously close to the action. It even has seats a long, long way from the action that seem great because fans sitting in them can see the entire track, including the pit areas, where much of the action in any race takes place. It isn't the biggest or the fastest track; in fact, it is the antithesis of the superspeedway ovals at places like Daytona, Talladega and Charlotte. It is a short track, one of the few left in a dying breed. Whereas racers get their cars up to close to two hundred miles per hour on the straightaways at the bigger tracks, here the average speed for a lap (taking into account slowdowns for cautions) is a modest eighty-two miles per hour—a speed that would make most of NASCAR's drivers blush in embarrassment on their local interstate highways.

Bristol has nearly 150,000 fans bearing down on the tiny oval where the cars zoom around, banging into one another and brushing against the walls. The place bursts with energy—from hours before the race until it finally begins to dissipate about an hour after the race is over and the last of the sponsor's hats has been deposited on the heads of the winning team members in Victory Lane.

The track can even be rented out for feature film production ($4,500 per day), television commercials ($3,000 per day) and, of course, all-important NASCAR testing ($1,500 per day). Can't get a ticket to one of Smith's precious races, but you still want to see the place? Just throw a party. Depending on the number of guests you want to invite, Bristol can be had for anywhere from $1,000 per day (up to a hundred guests) to $2,500 per day (five hundred guests or more). There are miscellaneous charges, such as emergency services ($600 per day) and for firing up the lighting system ($750 for the infield only, $1,850 to have the whole place lit up like a Christmas tree). And there is a $500 per day surcharge for weekend events. But heck, racing fans, why not plan your next company outing there?

Fans from two-thirds of the nation's fifty states will flock here to see a NASCAR race, and some all the way from Canada too. They will battle horrendous traffic jams and sometimes even each other throughout the course of a long day.

But before the day is through, they will have had what they swear to be one of the greatest days of their lives, especially if their racer has a good showing. Every real fan picks out one guy to root for, and remains loyal to him no matter what happens. Before this day under the unseasonably hot sun is done, they will have announced their allegiance to Earnhardt or Gordon or Wallace hundreds of times and in hundreds of different ways. To them, though, it will be Dale, Jeff and Rusty . . . for in no other sport do fans seem to identify with their heroes as much as they do in this one.

Earnhardt shirts are plentiful. The man in the black No. 3 Goodwrench Chevrolet Monte Carlo—nicknamed "the Intimidator" and "Ol' Ironhead" for his no-nonsense, hard-charging, win-at-all-costs driving style—is like the local sportscaster with the highest ratings. Surveys, if NASCAR commissioned them, in all likelihood would show him to be both the most beloved and most hated of all drivers. Love him or hate him, but few have no opinion of him. And that, plus the fact that he has won seventy-five races over the years, makes him highly marketable.

One Earnhardt fan arrives driving a black Chevy truck with a T-shirt that blares, BADASS BOYS DRIVE BADASS TOYS. It's the kind of T-shirt that no doubt would make the old man smile. Another Earnhardt fan strolls into the infield wearing a T-shirt emblazoned with a huge Confederate flag across his chest and the words *Tommy Hellraiser*. It is an obvious mocking of the Tommy Hilfiger designer clothes preferred by a different crowd, but it means even more than that to its owner. It describes his way of life, and that includes his deep-felt passion for the way the man behind the wheel in the black No. 3 car operates during a race.

"That's me," the fan states proudly, showing off tattoos on each arm. "I'm Tommy Hellraiser."

Like Earnhardt, Gordon is immensely successful and extremely popular. He sort of wears the white hat to Earnhardt's black garb in racing circles, but in this twisted world that makes him the target of abuse rather than the other way around. Racing fans like to root for the guy in black; the guy in white—or in Gordon's case, the guy in the rainbow colors of DuPont, his main sponsor—becomes an object of derision all too often. There perhaps is no more widely debated subject at a track than Gordon on most Sundays.

And if Bristol is the antithesis to the high-speed tracks at Daytona and Talladega, then Gordon is the antithesis to Earnhardt amongst the drivers. Earnhardt is the self-proclaimed outlaw who will do anything to win. Gordon is the self-proclaimed Christian who openly wept at the Winston Cup awards banquet in 1997 after picking up his second driving points championship. While Gordon was gaining in the career win column from 1995 through much of 1999, Earnhardt and his legions of fans were getting steamed.

There are others, of course, who stir the emotions and loyalties of a growing number of fans. Rusty Wallace. Dale Jarrett. Aging veteran Darrell Waltrip. The Labonte brothers, Terry and Bobby. Dale Earnhardt Jr., Dale's son (he doesn't like to be called Dale Sr.), who fancies himself the "rock 'n' roll racer" in a sport that has grown up on country. Even lesser-known guys such as Jimmy Spencer, dubbed Mr. Excitement for his perceived bad habit of getting into too many wrecks, have developed sort of a cultlike following.

Fans love these guys because they see themselves in them. That could be because they've heard the stories. About how Ernie Irvan was a welder, working on the seats at the track in Charlotte and dreaming of becoming a NASCAR driver long before, well, that's exactly what he became. About how Bobby Labonte, currently one of the series' top driving stars, once pushed a broom and emptied trash cans at a shop while waiting for his chance to be noticed and put behind the wheel of anything at all on four wheels. If a welder and a shop janitor can live out their dreams, why can't I? It is a question Everyman asks himself often while munching on fried chicken and gulping beer as racers tear around NASCAR tracks each weekend.

Even now, hours before the Food City 500 at Bristol, the pageantry had begun. The fans are as much a part of it as the players, who include not only drivers and crew chiefs, but car owners and gas men, tire changers, jackmen and body fabricators. They all dress the part of half-gladiator, half-billboard. The drivers are always the last to put on their uniforms, but eventually all team members don their colorful, ad-stained, fire-resistant suits and strut around the tiny Bristol infield mingling with one another and making small talk. They occasionally chat with strangers who happen to have pit infield passes and wander by to offer best wishes. Many of these fans hope for, and almost always receive, a smile, a handshake or an autograph—or even all three—from even the biggest of NASCAR's names. Accessibility to the stars by the common man and woman is another of NASCAR's great appeal to the masses. The players in the game that is about to unfold are waiting . . . waiting . . . waiting for the moment when the mayhem will begin.

They push their cars through inspection, hoping to pass without much trouble. Once they do pass, they are forbidden to touch their cars again before the race begins. The pushing of the mighty car to the inspection site is pure theater in itself. Faces are tense. Anticipation drips in the form of sweat from the foreheads of those surrounding the car. This is the calm before the storm, a touch of its own kind of madness before the mayhem. Every racing team looks for that little edge that might win a race—or perhaps be the difference between finishing seventh and ninth, thereby affecting their position in the all-important driving points championship standings. Dale Earnhardt's crew has been known to push the envelope more than most.

One of the first things visitors to Bristol's infield notice is that there is no way out. Once inside the infield, the interior of the track's stunningly small oval, the only way to leave is to walk back across the track itself. This can't be done once the race begins and stock cars are screaming by in close quarters at speeds that reach more than 125 miles per hour on the straightaways.

Once, not so long ago, a driver was injured in a wreck and could not be treated properly at the infield care center. The race had to be halted so he could be removed from the infield and rushed to an area hospital. In racing, stuff like that happens. Drivers go on about their business figuring it's always going to be another guy. At Bristol, ninety minutes before this latest race was to start, they were all thinking about the same thing: survival.

One day earlier, much of the talk around the garage area—if it could be called that in the tight infield at Bristol, where cars are crammed in right next to one another and worked on under makeshift tents—centered not around racing but around basketball. Dale Jarrett, the 1999 Winston Cup points champion, is a huge fan of the North Carolina Tar Heels. One night earlier, the Tar Heels beat Tennessee to earn a spot in the Elite Eight of the NCAA basketball tournament. His dilemma was that on Sunday, when the Food City 500 was to be run, the Heels would be facing Tulsa for the right to go to the Final Four. How would he be able to keep abreast of what was going on with his beloved Heels?

His big worry was that his spotter—the important team member who sits perched high atop the track on race day and radios the driver with advice on where to avoid trouble—was Bob Jeffrey, a Tennessee fan.

"Bob's mad at me. I'm not sure he's going to give me much of an update," Jarrett joked.

In the Bristol infield media center, Jarrett was all smiles. He spotted his father, Ned, a NASCAR driving legend in his own day and currently one of the sport's most respected television analysts. Ned's other son and Dale's older brother Glenn was the one who actually attended North Carolina, but the driver obviously adopted allegiance to the school.

"How 'bout my Heels?" said the younger Jarrett, smiling and slapping his father on the back. "Everyone said they couldn't beat Missouri in the first round of the tournament. Then they didn't stand a chance against Stanford—and surely they couldn't beat Tennessee. But they're still standin'!"

Another rabid Carolina fan is Elliott Sadler, driver of the No. 21 Citgo Taurus, which puts him in the same Ford family as Jarrett if not the same class because of the superior funding of Jarrett's No. 88 Quality Care Taurus. (Remember, in NASCAR the lingo in simple terms is that Sadler drives the 21 and Jarrett the 88 car— but when they're being interviewed, they're always quick to slide in the names of their main sponsors.) Sadler sat talking nearby with reporters about his own basketball experiences, which included attending many games at North Carolina when Michael Jordan and other big names played there.

"I got Michael Jordan's autograph when I was in college and I still have it today," Sadler said. "I can tell everybody I knew Michael way back when, before he was big-time."

Sadler was a pretty fair basketball player in his own right. He played briefly for Coach Lefty Driesell at James Madison in Virginia.

"I wanted to go and try to play basketball in college and I knew I couldn't play for the Tar Heels, so I tried to go to a smaller school," Sadler said. "Then I tore my knee all to pieces and quit college so I could come back and race and work at home and learn the family business."

The family business was racing. Sadler had been racing since the age of seven, when he began driving two-cycle go-carts near his hometown in Emporia, Virginia. He claimed to remember watching his uncle, Bud Elliott, run in late-model Sportsman cars when he was only three. His older brother, Hermie Sadler, also was a driver.

Racing as a family affair hardly was anything new. This is a sport built upon the tradition of families, even if its participants often feud like the Hatfields and McCoys (sometimes even when they're related).

The first family of racing is the Petty family, and they too were in Bristol in full force. Lee Petty, the family patriarch, was back home in North Carolina, fighting to stay alive at age eighty-six. There were whispers that he was losing the fight at the moment. Richard Petty, the winningest driver in NASCAR history, had stayed behind to be with his ailing father, who was struggling to recover from a stomach aneurysm six weeks earlier.

But Kyle Petty, Richard's son, and Kyle Petty's own son Adam were in attendance. Adam Petty was running in the Busch series race (the Busch series is roughly equivalent to Triple-A Minor League baseball) in his final tuneup before becoming the fourth-generation Petty to run in a Winston Cup race one week later in the DirecTV 500 at the Texas Motor Speedway just outside Dallas-Fort Worth. Adam Petty was nineteen and restless to get to the big-time. He was pretty sure, but not certain, that he was ready.

Sometimes, though, he felt as if the Petty legacy—Lee, Richard and Kyle already had combined for 273 wins at the sport's highest level of racing—was a heavy load to burden.

"With my name comes a lot of hype," he had said only weeks earlier.

Richard Petty admitted that he was a little apprehensive about Adam's pending Winston Cup debut in Texas. Asked shortly before Bristol what made him think that Adam was ready at this point, and the racer known as the King paused before replying, "We don't know if he's ready. The deal is, in order to play with the best in the long run, you need to play with the best when you're learning. It's a learning process. You don't learn with people who are no better than you are. You learn by playing with people better than you.

"My father told me a long time ago, 'If you want to play golf, always play with somebody better than you because you can learn.' Winning is not the name of the game for Adam right now. Learning is the name of the game for him right now."

Pressed about Adam Petty's plans to run five Winston Cup races in 2000 and then run a full schedule in 2001, the elder Petty grinned.

"What will it be like? Well, it's expensive," he said. "It's just a continuation of what we've been doing all these years. We're not trying to push anything or make him do anything. It's a natural progression of the Petty name.

"And hey, it might not stop with him. He might get married and have some kids. If they want to continue to race, fine. If they don't want to, well, I guess that'll be fine too."

Another of the famous families in racing was the Earnhardt clan. It ran three generations deep, one short on that scale to the Petty family, but included former dirt-track champion Ralph Earnhardt and his feisty son Dale. The elder Dale long ago made his name for himself, but Dale Jr., known as "Little E," had stormed onto the scene like a cyclone two years earlier. After winning back-to-back Busch series Grand National driving championships, Little E was running at the Winston Cup level exclusively for the first time.

So far, he had met with mixed success. Little E qualified second in Atlanta and led for eight laps, but eventually finished twenty-ninth. His top finishes were tenth at Las Vegas and thirteenth in the season-opening Daytona 500, but he was beginning to hunger for more. At the same time, Little E wasn't moping about. He was having the time of his life. He had signed a $50 million deal to have Budweiser be his sponsor—and back home in Charlotte, North Carolina, he had designed his basement around a cooler that fit a whopping eleven cases of his sponsor's finest stuff. Some nights at the happenin' place he and his friends called "Club E," they would stay up partying late enough to drink the cooler dry.

The talk may have been about basketball and family traditions early in the day, but by midafternoon, when the Busch series race was in the books and the Winston Cup guys were gearing up for Happy Hour, it was all business. Happy Hour is the frantic time when drivers can run fast laps on the track and confer with their team members to try and correct any problems before the actual race commences the following afternoon.

Among the Happy Hour participants is Dick Trickle, still making laps at age fifty-nine. Trickle is legendary for his habit of smoking cigarettes in the car, in the pit areas . . . just about anywhere when the urge hits him. He has even smoked cigarettes during caution laps in the middle of actual races. NASCAR officials once fined him for having a butane lighter in his car, fearing that he might blow himself and the car up while enjoying one of his patented smoke breaks. Trickle was in the right sport. The sponsor of the circuit was the R.J. Reynolds Tobacco Company, makers of the Winston brand of cigarette and numerous others. Walk into media rooms at tracks across the country and there along with reams of information about the sport's participants you will find carton upon carton of various cigarette brands, there for the taking.

Trickle also had quite a reputation for staying out late to party with whomever was available, if not that great a reputation for finishing high in Winston Cup races. He once ran into a Charlotte radio personality very early in the morning on the date of an afternoon race in Martinsville, Virginia, a woman on each arm and a drink in hand.

"How can you stay out so late before a race? Don't you need to get some sleep?" Trickle was asked.

"I got it all figured out. I need one hour of sleep for every hundred miles we run. If it's a five-hundred-mile race, five hours of sleep will do just fine," Trickle replied.

"I'll tell you what, though. When we run at Sears Point in California, they measure it out in kilometers. That fucks me all up."

On this day, Trickle was working as a substitute driver for the No. 14 Conseco team, which is owned by A. J. Foyt. The impatient Foyt fired rookie driver Mike Bliss after the first three races of the season when Bliss failed to make the field in two of them. Never mind that Trickle looks older than Foyt, who was more than a fair driver in his own day. Trickle was trying to get the Pontiac Grand Prix right for the run at Bristol, one of his favorite tracks, but he was having trouble.

After only a few Happy Hour laps, he pulled into the garage area, narrowly missing some spectators who lingered too close and moved a little too slowly, and lit up while staying put in his driver's seat and conferring intently with crew chief Terry Wooten. A flurry of activity took place around them as the Conseco crew repeatedly jacked up the car, fooled with this and that in the front, then moved around and messed with the back.

Then Trickle was off again to make two or three laps before pulling in and lighting up as the entire process repeated itself. This took place three times before Foyt, who had been trying to stay out of the way and let his crew do its job without his intervention, could stand it no longer. He stuck his head in and started barking out suggestions.

It might have reminded Wooten of how he first met Trickle nearly twenty years earlier. Wooten and a friend were attending an American Speed Association race in Cincinnati, Ohio, and Trickle had wrecked his car during practice. Wooten and his buddy wandered up, and Trickle immediately put the pair to work helping him fix the car. Trickle went on to win the race, and for the next four years Wooten served as a member of Trickle's road crew.

After Happy Hour at Bristol concluded and Trickle conferred some more with Wooten and Foyt, the day was done. Trickle, who usually is very accommodating, was approached by a reporter.

"Got a minute, Dick?"

"Can't talk. Got to go to some banquet the sponsor has set up," Trickle said. "Catch me tomorrow, before the race."

Trickle stands five foot six and weighs maybe 165 pounds. He could be described as ruggedly handsome for his age, but tends to look somewhat disheveled even after he has showered up and headed away from the track. He has never won a Winston Cup race in nearly three hundred starts, although he has earned more than five million dollars in career winnings. Yes, even Dick Trickle is a hot commodity on the NASCAR banquet circuit these days.

The fastest car during Happy Hour? It's Elliott Sadler's No. 21 car, which leaves him beaming and, for the moment at least, forgetting about Carolina basketball. He already had qualified ninth for the following day's Food City 500. Qualifying well at Bristol, where the pits are divided between the frontstretch and the backstretch, is more important than at many other tracks where all the pits are on one side of the track. And now Sadler knew he had a car with a setup that should allow him to compete with the big boys.

Maybe he'd even begin to make a name for himself like that Jordan fellow he once stalked for an autograph.

"We're so happy to be on the frontstretch here," Sadler said. "That's a big plus. To start in the top ten, we might be out of some of the mess."

There was going to be some mess on the track. Of that, everyone seemed certain.

The next morning, after the paint crew had made its quick and silent appearance to restore the walls to their former state, drivers and crew chiefs huddled for the mandatory prerace drivers' meeting under a tent at one end of the infield. Miss the meeting or be late to it and you will be penalized by being sent to the back of the field for the start of the race.

Jeff Gordon and Kyle Petty sat toward the back on metal folding chairs, swapping stories that resulted in repeated rounds of deep laughter. They sat near Bobby Labonte, who mainly just listened and smiled and nodded. Soon John Andretti, the nephew of former driving great Mario Andretti, who now drives the Petty blue STP No. 43 Pontiac Grand Prix made famous by Richard Petty himself, joined them in the animated storytelling.

Dale Earnhardt sat closer to the front, looking like he was all business. His son Dale Jr. also was in attendance as he prepped for his first Winston Cup race at Bristol.

Also sitting near the front and talking quietly were Ward Burton, Darrell Waltrip and Rusty Wallace.

David Hoots, the race director of NASCAR who conducts the drivers' meetings each week, stepped to a small podium and announced, "Welcome to Bristol, where it's a beautiful day and I'm sure we'll have a great race. Drivers' introductions will be at twelve twenty and will be staged in the third turn, after which we'll drive the pickups around [the track, with the drivers waving to fans from the back of the trucks]. Crew chiefs, remove your generators at twelve fifty. Invocation is at twelve fifty-four, the national anthem is at twelve fifty-six and the command to start your engines will be at one oh six. "

Then Hoots leaned forward a bit and made what he felt was his most important point.

"Bristol is an aggravating place. For five hundred laps, we're all going to be aggravated," he told the drivers and their crew chiefs. "I want you to take that into consideration. Take a deep breath before you start the race and we'll all be around for the finish, running for the win."

Not everyone in the room believed that. But they listened intently nonetheless.

"On the pace laps, get your pit-road speed reading," Hoots continued. "Stay on top of it and on the official start, stay in line until you cross the start-finish line. Use your hand signals as much as you can today, drivers. During the yellow flag [brought out under caution when there is debris on the track], it's very important that you stay closed up. It's the only way we can clean up the race track. It's the only way we can expedite the movement of emergency equipment.

"You must stay up. This is your warning. If you don't stay up, we'll call down and have you passed by another car. . . . Your spotters are up there to help you. Think about what you can gain versus what you can lose.

"Y'all know what the gentlemen's agreement is about riding across single file and going above the scene of an accident. If you can do so, please do that. The caution car is parked up in turn one. Keep your speed up on the front and slow down on the back on the first two laps of the yellow flag. It's important, again, that you stay closed up on the car in front of you."

Hoots went on to explain where tires were permitted to be placed in pit-stall areas and warned that it would be important for crew members to pick up the right rear tire after changing it. In races earlier in the year, particularly at the Daytona 500, failure to do so had caused some serious problems for cars trying to rush out of the pits and back onto the track. He warned the pit-road speed limit was thirty-five miles per hour, no doubt a difficult speed to achieve when drivers are used to pushing their cars to another kind of limit.

Finally, Hoots laid down the bottom line.

"If you get in an accident and you're a bunch of laps down, lay over to the inside and let cars who have a legitimate opportunity to get their lap back do so. If you're thirty laps down, you don't have that opportunity," Hoots told the drivers. "If you're in an accident, take the time to fix the car before you go back out there.

"Watch the emergency equipment. These people are out there to help you. Look for the track workers. If you're in a fire, get out of the car as quick as you can. If not, stay in there and an ambulance will be dispatched out to you. Ride in and let the doctor take a look at you. . . . Good luck to each and every one of you."

It was a sobering reminder that this is a dangerous sport, as if anyone needed it. A month earlier, driver Geoffrey Bodine felt fortunate to survive a fiery crash during a truck race at Daytona. Bodine already was plotting his comeback to Cup racing, but the horrific accident served as the latest example of what can happen when things go wrong at the speeds these guys race at.

As Hoots wrapped up the drivers' meeting, Dale Beaver, a minister with the Motor Racing Outreach group, stepped forward and said, "Let's pray together." Thus began the weekly chapel services that take place at tracks around the country at each NASCAR venue. Everyone is welcome, even fans wearing the proper credentials, although they are warned beforehand that this is neither the time nor the place for pictures and autographs. Several racers are joined by their wives and children for the service, which includes one prayer that states: "You are an awesome God. Please protect us not only in the race today, but in the race of life." One song that is performed during the service includes the verse: "In heaven's eyes, there are no losers."

Most of the drivers who stayed, and there were many, sat silently. They did not sing despite being implored to do so. When Beaver began to wrap up the brief ceremony with a story from the Bible, he was soon drowned out first by some Legends cars that roared by on the nearby track and finally by a live country & western band that suddenly resumed playing for fans after earlier taking a break. Two huge loudspeakers loom right behind Beaver, and Darrell Waltrip, winner of eighty-four Winston Cup races, hustled off to see what he could do about getting the music turned down. When he didn't return immediately and the din only increased, Beaver shrugged and mumbled, "I guess we'll end this early today." He sent the rest of the guys off with a blessing and a wish for a safe, clean race.

Outside, some of the drivers lingered. Ken Schrader, driver of the M&M's Pontiac Grand Prix, was asked if he felt nostalgic about Bristol like so many other drivers. He quickly shook his head no.

"It's not one of my favorite places," Schrader admitted. "It would be good if it was a good surface to move around on, but it's not."

The Bristol track was a concrete surface. Most NASCAR tracks are asphalt and drivers believe you can move around on them better.

"You saw it yesterday during the Busch race," Schrader continued. "It was like follow the leader all day long."

"Yeah, until someone hits the wall," Schrader was reminded. The veteran driver smiled and shook his head again.

"Believe me, the walls will be scarred up again today," he said.

A fan sauntered up and asked the Missouri native if he enjoyed the Super Bowl championship season put together by the St. Louis Rams, who hail from near his hometown of Fenton, Missouri.

"I don't like no other sports. I just like racin'," was Schrader's reply.

Indeed, unlike Dale Jarrett and Elliott Sadler, many racing insiders only know and love racing. Bruton Smith, for instance, often talked about how he didn't care for those other "stick-and-ball" sports—even though Smith later would purchase a minor-league baseball franchise in Kannapolis with its most famous native, Dale Earnhardt.

But others shared neither Schrader's disdain for Bristol or other sports. Jimmy Spencer was one. Mr. Excitement loved Bristol because, well, it was so damn exciting.

"I think the fans come here because they know they're going to see an exciting race," Spencer said. "The big thing here is that of all the race tracks that fans go to, they can always anticipate certain things. Here, you're going to anticipate that there's going to be an accident. They know there's going to be fenders rubbing, there's going to be tempers flaring. It might be bad to say that, but that's the bottom line. People love it.

"The one thing this sport was raised on was good, close competition. And you can't pick any better, tougher track to have that than Bristol. And the fans, they go wild at this place. As for the drivers, there are two ways of leaving this event: you're either pretty happy or you're very upset. I've been there and I can tell you there's no other way. You don't say, 'Yeah, we had a decent day.' You're either like, 'Yeah, we're happy. We survived and we came out of this thing pretty good,' or you're like, 'Sonofabitch, Bristol! I mean, gawd.' Those are the only two ways of looking at this event."

Spencer said that the bumping and grinding that goes on at Bristol usually is not done on purpose.

"What happens at this racetrack is a lot of bumper-to-bumper racing. If a guy is a little bit better here or not quite so good here and he slips, a guy bumps him. A lot of that stuff at this track is not intentional. It's just bred into the racetrack. By the end of the race, there are a lot of bumper marks and other marks on the cars that weren't intended to be there," Spencer said.

"But you know—the drivers know—when it's intentional or not. You know if a guy is giving you room or not, and that doesn't happen very often. If it does, NASCAR usually catches it and penalizes the cars for doing it. I don't think you'll see any penalties today because we all know it."

Finally, Spencer took a good look around. The seats were filled. It was time to head to his trailer and change into his driver's suit.

"If anybody was building a new facility, this is it. The only thing I would do is maybe make it a little bit wider. But all in all, if I was building any type of racetrack, I would look hard at this racetrack and Richmond. This is like our Yankee Stadium, our Wrigley Field."

No one was feeling better than Rusty Wallace after the invocation at 12:54 concluded with a prayer imploring everyone "to be thankful to God for this track, this race—and our great sponsors." The National Anthem, sung by country & western star Lee Greenwood, was preceded by his hit song, "God Bless the USA," in which the popular refrain is "I'm proud to be an American."

Yessir, NASCAR racin' is 100 percent made in the good ol' USA, and its fans feel good about it.

Wallace was feeling great as he rode in the back of a Chevrolet pickup truck during driver introductions and conducted a radio interview with Brett McMillan of Performance Racing Network.

"We ran real well during Happy Hour yesterday, so we're feeling good about our chances," Wallace told McMillan.

Wallace had at least seven other reasons to feel good about his chances. In thirty-two career starts at Bristol, he had won seven times, finished in the top five sixteen times and in the top ten an astounding twenty-one times. He had six poles to his credit in qualifying at Bristol. He went into this race ranking second only to Earnhardt in career winnings at the track, and third behind only Earnhardt (ten wins in forty-one races) and Darrell Waltrip (twelve wins in fifty races) in victories there. Besides, Wallace was the defending champ—and always one of the favorites on a short track, where more than half of his career forty-nine victories had taken place.

During the 1990s, Wallace had five wins and Jeff Gordon four at Bristol. Earnhardt had two, as did the late Alan Kulwicki—the former Winston Cup driving champion for whom Bristol's new 13,000-seat addition was named. No other driver had more than one, despite the fact that both a spring and fall race was run at the venue.

Wallace, in fact, had logged the very first victory of his Winston Cup career at Bristol back in 1986. His memory of that event was how it was no big deal at the time. After that race, he actually fell asleep in the back of a 1978 Trans Am on the ride back to High Point, North Carolina, where he lived in a modest home. Since then, he had not only won forty-eight more races but also pulled in more than nineteen million dollars in winnings and upgraded his quality of life significantly.

He wouldn't be taking a '78 Trans Am home after this one, win or lose. He and many other competitors who live close enough to do so took private helicopters to the event—illustrating again how far Rusty Wallace, and the sport in which he thrives, had come in the last fourteen years.

The command to start their engines was given to the drivers at precisely 1:06 by Virginia Tech football coach Frank Beamer. The ensuing roar of forty-three engines simultaneously firing up thrilled the crowd and sent it into a frenzy, as usual. But it isn't until the caution car pulls off onto pit road and the green flag is dropped that the real fun begins. And then it is nonstop for more than three hours.

"It's an assault on the senses," nodded longtime racing writer and editor Joe Macenka as the flag was dropped at Birstol.

On the very first green-flag lap, the mess began and the bright white walls took their first hits of the afternoon. Word spread quickly that Dale Earnhardt got into the back of his son Dale Jr., and then Little E was pushed up into Elliott Sadler's 21 car. Another victim of the incident was Darrell Waltrip, the legend who would retire at the end of the year and wanted so desperately to make one last good showing at Bristol. Now, just one lap into it, it looked like he would have to wait until the fall night race to have one more shot at it.

None of the cars was damaged badly enough to leave the race for good, but in some ways it was worse. Their crews had to work like crazy just to get them back on the track, knowing that any chance they had for a good finish in all likelihood was already gone.

Spencer battled his car early and all day, barely able to stay out of trouble. He kept complaining about a chronic "push" in the car's handling as he tried to negotiate through the tight turns.

"It feels like I've got two flat tires in the front," Spencer said to his crew over the radio. "The car won't roll through the corner like it needs to. It's just too tight."

Near the end of the race, car owner Travis Carter finally came on the radio and said, "We've struggled with it all day. Let's just finish the race and get home in one piece."

Sometimes, especially at Bristol, that's the best a team can do.

Earnhardt survived the early scrape with his son between turns three and four and eventually overtook Gordon for the lead on lap 206 of the five-hundred-lap event. Then he got a dose of his own medicine in the same spot where he touched off the earlier incident, as rookie driver Matt Kenseth hit Kenny Irwin and sent Irwin's car spinning up the track. At almost the same instant, Earnhardt's spotter shouted at him to go low on the track to avoid the mess.

"[Irwin] hit the wall and I saw his car up there," Earnhardt said later. "If he had just held the brakes on, I would have been all right. I'd done committed myself to the low side—and that's where I had to go. That's all I could do, go low."

So he went low.

"I went down there and I got whacked. It was a whack," Earnhardt said.

Earnhardt spun into the wall on impact and ended up facing the wrong way on the track. When he tried to get his crippled car righted and onto pit road, his right rear wheel fell completely off and rolled away—taking along with it any hopes he had of winning the race.

The Intimidator's misfortune left the spoils of victory seemingly in Gordon's hands. Like Wallace, Gordon was searching for career victory number fifty. Prior to his split the previous spring with crew chief Ray Evernham, few had doubted that Gordon would reach the milestone long before Wallace, who had been struggling. But without Evernham, Gordon no longer seemed the dominant force he was only a year earlier.

Something, it seemed, always seemed to go wrong even when he thought it was time for something to go right. That proved to be the case again when Gordon, then the leader, hit a tire in Steve Park's pit stall as he was trying to get back on the track after a pit stop during a caution period on lap 385.

"I drove right into it," Gordon said. "I blasted it and it ruined our day."

By the time he returned to the pits for repairs to his car caused by slamming into the tire, Gordon had fallen from first to seventeenth in his No. 24 Chevrolet Monte Carlo.

That left Wallace in control. Pit-road problems had been plaguing his own team all year to such an extent that the driver had let his crew members have a tongue-lashing earlier in the week.

"I was brutal. I was rough on them. I told them I didn't want any excuses or problems," he said.

There was one, however. One pit stop was delayed when a photographer inadvertently stood on an air hose that powered one of the team's wrenches. Eventually the photographer was shoved out of the way, but it cost Wallace's No. 2 Lite Beer Ford Taurus a few valuable seconds—which can mean everything in the course of even a five-hundred-lap event.

"I think that guy is still in the air," Wallace joked later, when he could. "I think they beat the hell out of that guy.

"That would be something . . . a real crucial pit stop, and you've got a photographer standing on your air hose."

It could only happen in NASCAR, where the human element is prevalent in everything that is done—despite the fact that men rely on machines to take them where they want to go. That would be Victory Lane, which is where Wallace ended up at the end of the day.

Others weren't so fortunate. Sadler's early problems limited him to just 325 laps and a forty-first-place finish, which is not what he had in mind after driving the fastest car during Happy Hour the previous afternoon.

"I went from one of the best days of my life to one of the worst," Sadler moaned.

Jarrett ran strong for a while, staying around the top five. But then a tire started to go bad and he faded to twenty-first.

Spencer started sixteenth, finished nineteenth and survived. But he still went home cursing.

Trickle, by far the oldest competitor in the event, climbed out of his car after the race, mopped his brow with a towel and sighed, "Whew! That's a whole lot of circles."

He completed 496 of them to finish twenty-seventh and collect $27,545 in earnings.

Wallace, meanwhile, won $87,585 for getting to Victory Lane.

He had talked to his crew about getting there prior to the race. A year earlier, he thought his win at Bristol was the fiftieth of his career—only to be informed in Victory Lane by Tom Roberts, his right-hand public relations man, that it was only number forty-nine.

"This is ridiculous now. It really is," Wallace told his crew, which likewise had tired of waiting on win number fifty. "I've won races all over the place—but I've won seven times at Bristol. I've got four car dealerships down the street. It's the site of my very first win. There are a hundred and forty-seven thousand people in the grandstand and it's the number one most exciting track on the circuit. Let's put a big bull's-eye right on this racetrack."

Two nights earlier, Wallace had attended a banquet to honor Darrell Waltrip at a Holiday Inn about ten miles from the Bristol track. He arrived via helicopter and chauffeured limousine and spent a good bit of the night talking about the good ol' days with the man known simply as "DW," as well as racing legends Junior Johnson, Ned Jarrett and Bobby Allison.

"We just kept having flashbacks," Wallace said. "Everything was a little bit more fun back in those days."

True enough, it was different now. Corporate sponsorships for a team ran into the millions. After his win at Bristol, Wallace had to change hats twenty-two times, posing for a different picture each time in an effort to satisfy all his sponsors, *plus* commitments to Winston Cup and the track itself. The drivers were huge stars now, celebrities everywhere they went. Wallace himself had vacationed the previous off-season in Monte Carlo, Monaco, and he even ran into fans there who knew him and wanted his autograph. It was far, far removed from the earliest days of the sport, when guys like Junior Johnson ran moonshine out of the mountains and raced only because they wanted to prove to everybody that they had the fastest car. The only folks who knew most of them were agents from the Internal Revenue Service who wanted to bust them for failing to pay taxes on the illegal whiskey they hauled.

Or was it that different? Someone asked Wallace how big a party he planned to throw to celebrate his fiftieth win, which tied him for eighth on the all-time list for driving victories with Johnson and Ned Jarrett, just five behind one of the men widely credited with making NASCAR what it is today—Lee Petty, father of Richard, who headed the list with a remarkable two hundred wins.

"Are you kidding? My sponsor is a beer company, man," replied Wallace, grinning widely.

Modest Beginnings

History often becomes muddled with time. Conflicting versions of the same event are recorded, and memories of those involved in the making of history are rewritten. But Richard Petty once said that there is no doubt about precisely when folks began racing each other in automobiles.

"It was," said Petty, "the day they built the second automobile."

Stock car racing began to develop in the 1930s in the Southeast, where moonshine runners—or "whiskey trippers" as they were known at the time—took great pleasure in trying to outrun federal agents from the Internal Revenue Service, known simply as revenuers. There was Georgia Highway 9, the old Whiskey Trail, which covered the sixty miles of switchback curves through the Appalachian foothills from sleepy Dawsonville to the bright lights of Atlanta. There was U.S. Highway 421, which originated in the hills and backwoods where the home brew was churned out in makeshift stills and winded through places like Ingle Hollow, Yadkinville and North Wilkesboro before it meandered its way to the big cities of Winston-Salem and Greensboro. There were other well-traveled roads leading to Charlotte where the stuff was in heavy demand, and some whiskey trippers like the legendary Junior Johnson made daily trips to deliver the goods, sometimes making more than one trip a day.

There was, of course, no meandering at all if the revenuers were on your tail. In the early days, whiskey haulers typically would load twenty-four five-gallon jugs of the white lightning, or 120 total gallons of the stuff into their cars. Each jug was placed in its own individual wooden liner, so that they wouldn't rattle against one another during a trip and make loud noises that could tip off cops, who might be listening and lying in wait on a darkened country road. In the 1930s, the stuff would fetch ten dollars per five-gallon jug—meaning one trip would be worth $240. That was a whole lot of money in those days in places where the economy was depressed or virtually nonexistent. Johnson was a native of a tiny little place called Ronda, North Carolina, that, like Ingle Hollow and Dawsonville and hundreds of tiny communities in backwoods country, never made the state maps. Along with his family and friends, he helped churn out and deliver as much moonshine as possible—calling it Wilkes County champagne and eventually adopting a slogan that stated simply, "Those who refuse it are few."

"Just about everyone in Wilkes County messed with it one way or another," said Willie Clay Call, one of Junior Johnson's closest friends, who figures he ran illegal moonshine for about forty years, from the early 1930s until around 1971. "In the 1930s and forties, there were only three places you could work around where we lived—at the sawmill or at one of two small furniture factories. The chicken farm businesses didn't come until later. And the pay wasn't no good at them places anyway.

"If you wanted to have a little money in your pocket, you had to mess with moonshine. It was a way of life for us. You split the profits with the folks who made it, but the hauler made extra. The hauler always made a little extra."

Johnson has never apologized for where he came from, nor for what he did for a living during his formative years.

"It was hard, dangerous and scary work," Johnson said. "It was how we made our living back then. That's all. It ain't nothin' to be ashamed of. Makin' moonshine was a hand-me-down trade that was passed down through the generations where I came from."

Junior was the fourth of seven children raised by Robert and Lora Belle Johnson. As he was growing up, Junior saw his father hauled off to jail many times for running illegal liquor. The senior Johnson ultimately would spend nearly twenty of his sixty-three years in prison, but he would resume the trade again as soon as he got out, figuring it was all he knew and it was the best way to make a living in Ronda.

Robert Johnson never made it past third grade, but Junior once told a reporter of his father: "He was one of the smartest people I've ever known. . . . He wanted to make sure his family was taken care of and he didn't care if he went to the penitentiary doing it. As a kid, you don't appreciate things like that until you're older. Then you look back and see everything he did for you."

Thus, the Johnsons lived in constant fear of the law. Junior's mother made the best of it. Their house was raided so often that she occasionally offered the visiting revenuers a cup of coffee and perhaps a piece of pie as they took a break from hauling out stashes of illegal liquor.

Despite these circumstances, Robert Johnson taught his children certain values. He was a very generous man, often helping out others. He taught Junior to treat others with respect and not to lie or steal.

Junior Johnson would soon be put to the test. Once, running out of gas during a midnight run, he had to siphon gas from a nearby farmer's tractor. Thinking back to what his father had told him and feeling bad that the farmer would find his tractor's gas tank empty the following morning, Junior left $200 cash on the seat of the tractor. He would need to make an extra run or two to make it up, but he felt good about doing the right thing.

Another of Johnson's close friends was Millard Ashley, who attended elementary school with Johnson. That is, until Johnson dropped out of school after the eighth grade to spend more time helping out with the family whiskey business. Ashley lasted one more year before he quit school.

"There wasn't no work in Wilkes County," Ashley said. "Runnin' moonshine was just the difference between walkin' around with no money in your pocket or havin' a little somethin' to jingle around in there."

Ashley said many of the stories about running moonshine have been embellished over the years. But then he tells some goods ones himself.

"What people don't realize is that a lot of times you wouldn't run into nobody. There was maybe only one time out of a thousand when you really ran into a serious problem," Ashley said. "Think about it. There wasn't no traffic back then. There weren't no other cars on the road. We would drive down Four twenty-one to Winston and see maybe one car most trips, and that was about forty miles. And if you met anyone on the roads we traveled, you knew it was either another moonshiner or it was the law. It would be so dark on those roads. You could see the reflection of headlights in the sky a long time before you actually saw another car, so you usually had a pretty good sense of when someone was comin'."

That would give the whiskey runners time to react. They usually had the faster cars, ones that could go nearly 100 miles per hour in first gear and up to 115 in second. This was no coincidence. They all knew that very few police cars could go more than 95 miles per hour, giving them the edge over the cops. Fellows like Junior Johnson also became experts on figuring out how to get extra power out of their cars and how to get them to handle better, inserting special springs and shocks to make them turn corners more sharply.

Local sheriffs, at least the ones who weren't paid off by the bootleggers in advance, wanted to help the revenuers catch the whiskey runners not so much so they could bust them for making illegal liquor that otherwise went untaxed, but because they stood to make a bundle if they impounded a bootlegger's souped-up ride. Sheriffs typically sold such automobiles at auctions and pocketed half or more of the money for themselves. They weren't above selling the cars back to the very folks they had impounded them from, which would then get the cycle rolling again.

"It was a cat-and-mouse game all the time between them and us," Johnson said.

Others accepted the moonshiners for what they were; locals trying to make a living. Ashley remembers making regular runs through one small town that was fortunate enough to have a Krispy Kreme doughnut shop.

"We used to be so regular through there that they let us have doughnuts right out of the oven," Ashley said. "They would be waitin' for us and we would stop and they would just give us those doughnuts every time. You know, if you eat those while they're still hot and you drive too fast, it can make you sick to your stomach."

Still, Ashley insists that driving illegal whiskey through the hills was usually more like making a trip to the local bank than a scene from *The Dukes of Hazzard*.

"I remember telling someone that it wasn't much more wear and tear on my car than if I drove it regular," Ashley said. "I could make my tires last about as long as they would just drivin' around town. You didn't have to run wide open all the time like some people seem to think. You only had to do it from time to time to try to get away from the law."

Except, of course, for Junior Johnson.

"Junior? Hell, he'd run wide open all the time," Ashley said, shaking his head. "Yeah, he was pretty bad about that. He was always blowing a head gasket or somethin'."

It was in his blood.

Those who ran moonshine didn't do it for the glamour or because they thought it would lead to a big paycheck in auto racing, for there was none of that back then. They did it as a means of survival; as a way of carving out a living in the rough-and-tumble backwoods of Virginia and North Carolina and Georgia. Lots of folks were running illegal liquor in the 1930s, from Kentucky and Tennessee on down through the Carolinas and Georgia and Florida.

When they weren't running from the law in their fast cars filled with illegal booty, they soon began running against each other in a number of loosely organized races in a largely futile attempt to prove who was the fastest. There was money to be earned in running moonshine; there was extra money to be won in the races that were held on the side with increasing frequency during the thirties.

It would, however, take a northern transplant to organize the renegade sport that suddenly was taking shape.

There were all kinds of so-called governing bodies at first, including one with the ominous acronym of SCARS (Stock Car Auto Racing Society) that was, like most of the rest, short-lived and little remembered. The one that survived—the National Association of Stock Car Auto Racing, or NASCAR—was born on December 14, 1947, during a meeting of thirty-five men in a smoke-filled room at the Ebony Bar on the top floor of the Streamline Hotel in Daytona Beach, Florida. Voted president of NASCAR that day was Big Bill France, an imposing man of six feet five inches and some 220 pounds who had drifted south from Washington, D.C., during the fall of 1934, trying to escape not only the cold weather but the economic fallout of the Great Depression.

At the time of his move, France was not a man with the great vision to found and propel what would become a national phenomenon and a billion-dollar industry. He simply was an auto mechanic looking for steadier work. Years later, during an interview with *Sports Illustrated* magazine, France said of his decision to move from Washington to Miami: "At least in Florida, I could work on cars out of the cold and the snow and the rain."

He might have lived to work on cars, but he loved to race them as well. His father was a bank teller who had never understood this passion. As a young teenager, Big Bill frequently risked his father's wrath by sneaking the family car, an old Model T, out to a spacious, banked speedway in Laurel, Maryland. His father often wondered aloud why the tires on the car kept wearing out so quickly, never realizing that it was the result of his son's folly.

Thus, when France moved south in 1934, it wasn't entirely without hope of being involved in some form of auto racing. While still in Washington with his wife Anne and his first-born son William Clifton (or Bill Jr., as he came to be called), Big Bill France saved enough money from operating a small service station near the Potomac to purchase his first real race car. It wasn't much to look at; in fact, it was quite crude. It was an open-wheel, single-seat racer with a modified Model T engine and a body woven of canvas. France used this vehicle to compete in a series of local dirt track races in the Washington area, where he quickly learned that many race promoters were little more than con artists who thrived by cheating drivers and customers alike. He also learned that the most successful drivers always owned the best equipment and spent a great deal of time to maintain it.

When France left for sunny Miami, he didn't have much to show for his racing efforts or anything else. But he knew it was time to make a move. Life wasn't getting any better by staying where he was, so France withdrew his life savings of seventy-five dollars from a Washington bank account and proceeded directly to a hardware/auto repair shop before hitting the road. There he purchased fifty dollars' worth of tools, which he used to make repairs for stranded motorists along his way to Florida, which is how he fed his family and kept moving toward his chosen destination.

Alas, France never quite made it to Miami. He pulled into Daytona Beach, took a job at the local Pontiac-Cadillac dealership—and never stopped thinking about what he had learned on the dirt tracks in and around his native Washington.

He thought about it often over the next fifteen years. He organized and promoted races throughout the South under a variety of would-be governing bodies, including the infamous SCARS group. Other rival groups included one run by Bruton Smith, who would later become a major player himself on the NASCAR scene.

France began to get seriously involved in the promotion business after a group of civic leaders in Daytona Beach announced plans to sponsor a race for stock cars in the winter of 1936. France liked the idea of running stock cars—or cars that were, at least in theory, identical to the ones being driven on the road by the average Joe. Fans could identify with that, he thought. And if they could identify with the idea, they would pay to see it.

The first two races in Daytona were run on a 3.2-mile circuit formed simply by parallel straightaways on the beach and paved Highway A1A that were connnected by slightly banked corners made of sand. It was, like France's first race car, rather crude. But it immediately appealed to other race car drivers, if not at first to the masses. Among the drivers in the very first Daytona race was Wild Bill Cummings, winner of the 1934 Indianapolis 500—open-wheel racing's most prestigious event. France entered too and ended up running fifth in his Ford coupe.

Sometimes France raced in the very events he organized and promoted, a practice he found to be tricky two years later in February of 1938. After the city of Daytona had lost $22,000 on the inaugural race in 1936, the race's founders agreed to step aside and let the local Elks Club have a crack at turning a profit in 1937. The Elks fared little better, which led to France and Charlie Reese, owner of a local restaurant, to step in the following year.

The chamber of commerce had approached France (whose Pure Oil gas station on Main Street had become the unofficial headquarters for local racers) to ask him if he knew anyone who might be interested in putting on the race. France said he was, but he didn't have the money. He did, however, know someone who did—and that was Reese, the man who owned the 1937 Ford Coupe France had been racing himself on weekends.

"I can line up the cars and the drivers. But I don't have the money to put this thing on. Will you back it?" France asked Reese.

"If you do the work, I'll put up the money," was Reese's reply.

True to what would become his form in later years, France made plans not to scale back but to double the efforts. He and Reese announced that they would hold not one, but two races each year on the Daytona circuit. France went to work lining up a number of sponsors who donated all sorts of prizes. He wanted drivers to be rewarded not just for winning the race, but also for the number of laps they led. Guaranteed prizes to lap leaders included a box of fancy Hav-a-Tampa cigars, a case of Pennzoil motor oil, a pair of five-dollar sunglasses from Walgreens, two cases of Pabst Blue Ribbon beer, a bottle of choice rum, a two-dollar fifty-cent credit at a local men's clothing store and a twenty-five dollar credit on any automobile purchased in dealer Dick Rose's used car lot.

The first race drew over five thousand spectators, a large crowd for those days. Driver Smokey Purser took the checkered flag at the finish line—and kept on driving straight up the beach toward the center of town. France, running second, followed him.

Purser maintained his lead long enough to get to Roy Strange's garage in town, where France caught him changing the cylinder heads on his race car. Even then, that was illegal. The car couldn't legitimately be called a stock car if Purser had altered it to give himself an edge.

France wasted no time disqualifying Purser, but he faced a dilemma. Big Bill had finished second himself and should, therefore, have been declared winner of the race. He huddled with Reese.

"There's no way I can knock the first-place man out and declare myself the winner without people thinking there's something fishy going on," France said.

Reese nodded in agreement.

So they declared Lloyd Moody, who had actually run third behind Purser and France, the winner.

Then they took stock of their take at the gate and declared themselves losers two times over. France not only passed on the cash that went to the winning driver, but then realized all his efforts as organizer and promoter of the event had been virtually for naught. He and Reese had agreed to charge fifty cents admission and had sold roughly five thousand tickets. After paying off the winning driver and everyone else, they discovered they had only $220 to split in "profit" between them—hardly enough to account for all the man-hours they had put in trying to make the race a huge success.

"We must be doing something wrong," Reese told France.

No kidding, thought France. But it was easy enough to fix. He and Reese decided to capitalize on the fact that the February race had seemed popular by doubling their efforts—and the ticket prices. Though the next race was to be held only one month later, they decided to increase admission to one dollar. Then they held their breath and went back to work selling tickets.

Much to their amazement and relief, the tickets sold briskly on the morning of the race. Attendance was almost identical to the first race, and this time, when it was over, France and Reese had something in the neighborhood of $2,200 left over to split. They donated about $200 to the Bundles for Britain campaign and divvied up the rest.

"That taught me some lessons I never forgot," France told *Sports Illustrated* many years later.

Another valuable learning experience was a meeting France had with Wilton Garrison, sports editor of the *Charlotte Observer,* shortly after World War II ended. It was then when France resumed his foray into the racing business, following a brief stint at the Daytona Beach Boat Works, where he was a foreman on an engine-installation crew that worked on submarine chasers for the United States Navy. France was trying to drum up publicity for a race at the old Charlotte Fairgrounds and announced to Garrison that it would be for a national championship.

Garrison had heard similar boasts before from other race promoters who claimed to be holding "national championships." It was a frequent trick of the trade of promoters, many of whom would travel from city to city in the Southeast, each time touting the latest race as the one that would crown that year's "national champion." With a number of different organizations governing the sport, and so many shady promoters making dubious claims, it was impossible to determine who really was the best in the Southeast, where almost all the big races were being run, let alone the nation.

"Who's going to be in this race of yours?" Garrison asked France.

France rattled off the names of Buddy Shuman, Skimp Hershey and Roy Hall, figuring Garrison would be pleased to know that many of the local drivers would be competing. Shuman in particular was a popular driver of the day, a local legend of sorts who once had been shot in the neck by revenuers while running moonshine.

Garrison, however, was not impressed.

"How can you call it a national championship with local boys like that running?" he asked. "Maybe you could call it a southern championship, but there's no way it's a national championship race."

Garrison went on to explain to France what he thought France needed to do to legitimize his operation and set it apart from all the others. Create a series of races where the rules are always the same and are consistently enforced. Set up a points standings to determine an overall champion—a real national driving champion.

Garrison went on to suggest that France look for help in accomplishing all this from the American Automobile Association, or AAA, which was at the time considered the top motorsports organization in the United States. France listened and agreed with Garrison's suggestions, but was rejected by the AAA when he approached them for assistance.

According to a *Sports Illustrated* magazine article published about

France years later on June 26, 1978, the reason was simple. "The implication was that such an august body was not interested in a redneck rabble of jalopy drivers," wrote Brock Yates of *SI*.

Nonetheless, France forged ahead. It would be three more years before he founded NASCAR—only after one year trying to run something called "the National Championship circuit" and another running the preposterously named SCARS organization. On February 21, 1948, France incorporated the National Association of Stock Car Auto Racing, with himself as the dominant majority stockholder.

Heeding Garrison's advice, France designed a points system to determine his champion. He also created a fund that placed 7.5 percent of each race purse into an escrow account, which then was to be distributed to the leading drivers in the points standings after all the races had been run each season.

The first driving champion was Red Byron, and he could not have been a better first champion if France had hand-picked Byron himself. Byron was a war hero, an Everyman with whom fans could identify. Driving a 1939 modified Ford, the former tail-gunner's left shoe had to be bolted to his car's clutch because of an old war wound to his leg. Byron made for a good story, and France loved good stories that promoted his races and his blossoming sport.

Byron won the first points championship by edging out the infamous Flock brothers—Tim, Bob and the strangely clad Fonty, who always raced in shorts, black shoes and black socks. The Flocks were talented drivers whose roots were deeply entrenched in the moonshine business. Natives of Fort Payne, Alabama, they entered the trade during the Great Depression with the blessings of their mother Maudi Josie Williams Flock, who figured having her sons run moonshine was the best way to supplement her modest wages from working in a nearby hosiery mill. After all, she had ten children to feed.

Bob and Fonty Flock joined older brother Carl and an uncle who went by the name of Peachtree Williams hauling whiskey from Alabama to the outskirts of Atlanta. Two runs a day from Fort Payne, Alabama, to Dahlonega, Georgia, was worth $200 a week, which was considered a small fortune in those days not only by Maudi, but by all the other townsfolk as well. It fed her children and also fueled their appetite for racing cars on the side.

By the early 1930s (the older brothers had been running moonshine since shortly after their father's death in 1925, when Tim Flock was just one year old), the Flocks were making names for themselves by running in makeshift races of modified cars amongst drivers who made regular moonshine runs to Atlanta. Young Tim Flock, then ten years old, went to watch his older brothers race in a cow pasture just outside Stockbridge, Georgia, in 1934. About 300 spectators were in attendance, literally betting cash on the barrel head to see which cars were the fastest. It was an exciting time.

It was in races like these, which preceded the ones France would organize, that the roots of stock car racing took hold in rural America. That certainly proved to be the case with Tim Flock, who was hooked on the sport from the moment he laid eyes on a crude version of it in that cow pasture in 1934.

Many of the early drivers were fond of buying four new tires from Sears & Roebuck on Saturday morning, the day before they would race. Then they would run them all day Sunday until they were near bald, only to return them to the store on Monday morning with the standard complaint that they had no idea how they got worn out so fast.

Tim Flock not only could drive, but he knew how to help promote the sport in its early days. A few years later, he would even drive with a monkey named Jocko Flocko in his car, a publicity stunt that met a sour fate when Jocko once broke free from his shoulder harness in the middle of a race and suffered a burn that sent him careening crazily about the inside of the car. Tim Flock could not get the monkey off his neck, and suddenly discovered that he could not see where he was driving because of the beast's flailing arms. It was at that point that Flock pulled into the pits, barely taking the time to slow down, pull the monkey off his back and toss it out the window; he wasn't about to lose valuable time and track position. Flock was running third at the time and ended up finishing sixth.

Jocko Flocko never rode with Tim Flock again.

Junior Johnson ran in his first race when he was sixteen years old. He had been running moonshine for his father since he was about thirteen when Enoch Staley, president and cofounder of the North Wilkesboro Speedway, near Ronda and Ingle Hollow, was promoting a preliminary race to "fill in" between qualifying and the main event at his venue in the late 1940s. The catch: Staley didn't decide he needed such a race to keep the restless fans in their seats until about an hour before he wanted to run it. Then he dispatched a number of associates to round up local moonshiners and their cars for the impromptu race.

One of them visited the nearby Johnson household. The first person he saw was L. P. Johnson, Junior's older brother.

"How 'bout you runnin' in this race for ol' Enoch? You might make some extra money," the visitor said.

"Nah. No thanks," replied L.P. "But maybe I'll let my brother drive my car in it."

"Go get him," Staley's associate said.

Junior Johnson was out plowing corn for his father in a nearby field, trudging along behind a mule. He wasn't wearing any shoes.

Years later, Johnson would smile as he related the story to a reporter.

"L.P. yelled from the edge of the cornfield that he wanted me to race his car. So I tied the mule to a fence and went to the house to get my shoes. Then I went to the track with L.P.," Johnson said.

It hadn't taken Staley and his cronies long to assemble enough bootleggers for the race. When Junior Johnson and his brother arrived at the track, there already were another 20 to 25 cars lined up at the start-finish line.

Johnson laced up his shoes and climbed into his brother's car.

Then he put the pedal to the metal and raced well enough to finish second to Gwynn Staley, Enoch's brother, who later would perish in a NASCAR crash on a track in Richmond, Virginia. In Junior's case, though, a racing legend was born.

As good as the stories were in 1948, France still faced the same basic problem that he had been struggling with when he visited Garrison a few years earlier. There still were too many other racing organizations billing themselves as major sanctioning bodies, and they all held their own versions of national championships. The public simply couldn't determine that any one group was all that different from the rest of them.

It was also a major problem that the sport was receiving little attention from sports editors at newspapers around the Southeast. It was so confusing to them that they chose to basically ignore the sport, thinking that the assortment of organizations might confuse their readers as well. Something, or someone, was needed to unify the sport.

This was when France decided to ban modified cars and go with a strictly stock series. It was a simple yet brilliant move. He announced that the first race would be held in Charlotte, and any American with a full-sized American-made car was eligible to compete for a piece of the $5,000 purse. France made it clear that anyone who attempted to modify his car in any way would be summarily disqualified.

This was the beginning of what would become NASCAR's top level of racing, the Grand National series at first, the Winston Cup in later years. Thirteen years after moving south to escape the bitter Washington winters, France was positioned to begin building an automobile racing empire that even he could not envision would grow as powerful as it ultimately would. Big Bill France thought big, but not that big.

It was on June 19, 1949 in Charlotte that the racing series that would come to be known as Winston Cup was born. France was pleased with the results that the 1948 inaugural season had produced, but decided in '49 to outlaw the pre–World War II cars, called "modifieds," that had primarily made up the fields the previous season. His vision: Go with a "strictly stock" series so that folks at home could identify with the drivers and their cars.

Nine brands of automobiles entered the race at the three-quarter-mile dirt track in Charlotte that day—Buick, Cadillac, Chrysler, Ford, Hudson, Kaiser, Lincoln, Mercury and Oldsmobile. Lee Petty drove down with his son Richard from nearby Level Cross, North Carolina, in the 1946 Buick Roadmaster that he planned to drive in the race. A young man with a reputation for partying named Curtis Turner was entered, as was a young woman named Sara Christian and a whole bunch of bootleggers who figured their cars were faster than anyone else's—including all of the Flock brothers.

Glenn Dunnaway of nearby Gastonia showed up at the venue without a ride but full of determination to find one. He roamed the pit area until he ran into a gentleman named Hubert Westmoreland, who was looking for a driver for his 1947 Ford.

Fans came from all over southwestern North Carolina to see the race. Hill Overton Jr., who would go on to become involved in stock car racing for much of the next fifty years as a broadcaster and track announcer, was from Matthews, a Charlotte suburb before the term "suburb" had been invented. He was thirteen years old at the time and had just finished participating in the local competition of the All-American Soapbox Derby.

When he was finished competing in that event, a big deal at the time, all the racers who had taken part were handed T-shirts with the Soapbox Derby logo.

"Wear these T-shirts, guys, and go to this thing. They're having this thing called a 'strictly stock' car race out at Charlotte Speedway," Derby officials told the kids.

The old track was located off Highway 74, near where today Interstate 85 and Little Rock Road intersect. It was, Overton Jr. thought, an odd place for a speedway.

"It was mainly a residential area. There were a lot of complaints about the noise and the dust in the neighborhood," Overton Jr. said.

Hill wanted to go to the race. His father, who would have to drive him across town, didn't.

"But I badgered my dad into taking me," he said. "He didn't want to go, but I finally badgered him into it."

They weren't expecting to run into a huge crowd. But there was such a massive traffic jam, which included more than a few of the cars planning to enter, that the scheduled start of the race was threatened. By the time Overton Jr. and his father arrived, they couldn't get into the place.

"There was an overflow crowd, so we found a weeping willow tree on a high bank over turn three," Overton Jr. said. "There was just a board fence around the track in those days. So we watched the race and ate dirt from up there, and that was my first real NASCAR exposure."

It was enough to hook him for life.

"It was the sound . . . the noise . . . the dirt . . . the roar . . . the furor. It just embedded itself into me and I've been a racing nut ever since those days," Overton Jr. said. "There was a fairgrounds track [in Charlotte] at the old Southern States Fairgrounds. The track was located where the old, pretty well unused Tryon Mall shopping center is today, at North Tryon and Sugar Creek [roads]. I remember the track had a pond or a lake in the infield, and I used to go whenever I could.

"Living in Matthews, there were enough men around there that for whatever reason they kind of adopted me as their racing mascot, I guess. They went on Friday nights up there to the Modified Sportsman races, and I was able to go with them. My mother knew and trusted these men not to get me into trouble. They were real clean-cut guys, but they liked racing. So I would go with them on Friday nights to that track, dating all the way back to about '46."

Overton Jr. was much like many new, young fans back then. It was a budding sport, one about which not much was known. But it was exciting—an assault on the senses even then. One trip to a track and you could be hooked.

Once Hill Overton Jr. saw his first race, there was not much that he would allow to come between him and his desire to be around racing.

"If it had anything to do with racing, I was into it. I wanted to go," Overton Jr. said. "I've always been a pretty persistent type of guy, much to the detriment of my parents. But I've always been a driver, an initiator, a pusher. From an early age, I was always pretty aggressive about things I wanted to do.

"I always listened to the Indianapolis 500 on the radio. My mother was from Alabama, and I'd drive my parents nuts on trips by sitting in the backseat pretending to be broadcasting racing. I was the announcer who'd say, 'Here they go! *Vrrrroommm! Vrrrr-oomm!*' I'd do all that stuff."

What Overton Jr. saw that June afternoon in 1949 at the "new" Charlotte Speedway thrilled him and most of the others in attendance.

"I had seen the dirt races at the half-mile track at the fairgrounds, but the new track we called Charlotte Speedway in those days was three-quarters of a mile. It was a little longer, a little faster. . . . I knew that I would like it," said Overton Jr., who later would work as public address announcer at much bigger, fancier tracks in Darlington, South Carolina, and Rockingham, North Carolina.

"The racers would drive their race car to the track in those days. The thing about the cars then, when they said 'Strictly Stock,' they meant it. What they did do, however, the cars had a door post—the door post where it fitted with the body. And they would take a belt, wrap that belt several times around the post and fasten it with the belt buckle. That was what kept the door from flapping open. They would take duct tape and make an X across the old-style headlights. And they'd go racing.

"Except, even in those days, there was cheating going on from day one."

That much was evident shortly after Glenn Dunnaway beat the rest of the thirty-three-car field to the checkered flag in Hubert Westmoreland's 1947 Ford. During a postrace inspection, it was discovered by Big Bill France that Dunnaway's rear springs had been altered with a wedge—a common practice to add speed in whiskey-running cars. The car had an illegal wooden block inserted to jack up the springs on one side. France, as he had promised to do, summarily disqualified Dunnaway and gave the victory instead to Jim Roper, driver of a Lincoln who had traveled all the way from Kansas after reading about the race in *Smilin' Jack,* a popular comic strip of the times drawn by a racing enthusiast named Zack Mosley.

Dunnaway was disheartened. Westmoreland was furious.

In a display of sportsmanship and generosity that would come to define the sport, Dunnaway's fellow drivers felt sorry for him and passed the hat because they knew he had not known that his car had been altered. He ended up taking away more than he would have received as his cut of the $2,000 first-place check, although his fuming car owner walked away with nothing. It was a contradictory act that would be repeated many times over the years. Drivers and car owners would cheat to gain an advantage one minute, then show compassion and camaraderie the next if one of their competitors needed a hand with a broken car or a relief driver.

Tim Flock finished fifth in that first Strictly Stock race in Charlotte. Curtis Turner thrilled the crowd by flying into the corners sideways, sending dirt spewing every which way. But he ultimately finished back in the pack, no doubt placing too much of a strain on his equipment. Lee Petty got off to an inauspicious start, wrecking the family car halfway through the 150-mile race and temporarily leaving him and his son Richard without a way home after the race.

Lee Petty's 1946 Buick Roadmaster flipped four times before it came to a stop. He had been running second at the time and challenging for the lead when he lost control. Afterward, Lee Petty crawled out of the crumpled car and sat at the edge of the track, trying to regain his senses and figure out how he was going to explain the totaled Roadmaster to his wife Elizabeth.

"He turned it over, tore it all to pieces, so we had to find another way home," Richard Petty recalled with a smile more than half a century later. "I rode with Daddy and them [other family members] to the race in the race car, and we didn't know at first how we were going to get back. I thought my uncle was down there, and we were going to thumb a ride with him.

"But it turned out we didn't have a way home."

Richard Petty eventually thumbed a ride back to Level Cross with another friend of the family who was in attendance. The man who would go on to win more stock car races than anyone else in the history of the sport had to hitch a ride back home from the very first NASCAR-sanctioned Strictly Stock event. All the while, Richard Petty couldn't help thinking about what his daddy had done to the family car.

"They came the next day with a flatbed truck and got the race car. That's how bad it was tore up," Richard Petty said.

Richard and Lee Petty learned an important lesson of their own that day.

Save the car. Do what you can to win a race, but save the car. All too often in those early days, it was the only one a racer owned.

"You can't win the race if you're not in it at the end," Lee told Richard. It would become the family mantra.

Hill Overton Jr. left the track that afternoon with a huge smile on his face. So did Bill France. The former had been entertained and the latter felt like he had done a good job of entertaining.

"It was a noisy, dusty, dirty day," Overton Jr. said. "There was a lot of traffic and a lot of crowds and my dad vowed never to go back.

"Of course, it struck me a little differently and I've been going ever since."

"Bootleggers and a Bunch o' Fools"

Homer Keith Jarrett and his wife Eoline had heard all about stock car racing by the summer of 1951. Homer, known as H.K. to his friends, had even ventured to a few races at small dirt tracks in the area around Newton, North Carolina, near where he and his family maintained a three hundred-acre farm. He made the mistake of taking his son Ned.

It was a mistake, at least at first according to H.K., because it planted a seed in young Ned Jarrett's mind, which quickly and firmly established roots that could not be yanked out, no matter how much H.K. may have tried.

Ned Jarrett was born in Newton on October 12, 1932 and grew up working on the farm that H.K. had purchased from his siblings upon the death of their father, Oliver J. Jarrett. The Jarretts had a thriving farm on their three hundred-acre spread, where they planted sweet potatoes, cotton and corn and also raised and sold cattle, hogs, horses and mules. But they made most of their money from a small yet productive sawmill that also was located on the land.

When Ned Jarrett was just eight years old, his father allowed him to get behind the wheel of a chopped-down school bus that had been converted into a truck and drive it around the farm as he went about performing his various daily chores. When Ned was nine, H.K. let his youngest son drive the family car, an old Reo station wagon to Sunday school—despite the objections of Ned's two older brothers.

"It was not unusual for kids to drive before they were eligible to get their driver's license back then," Ned Jarrett later recalled. "But it was probably a little unusual to drive at that age. I was only nine. I had two brothers who were older than me and, of course, they were pining to get to drive too.

"So my dad had a juggling act to do. My brothers were two and three years older than I was, so they should have had the priority. But that wasn't necessarily the case, because my dad trusted me. He thought I could do a good job."

His faith in Ned was not misplaced. His father eventually rewarded him with increased responsibilities around the farm. When Ned was eleven, H.K. called him aside.

"I'm going to give you an acre of land," the elder Jarrett told his son. "You can plant whatever you want on it and keep any money you earn off it."

Ned Jarrett chose to plant sweet potatoes because they paid more per bushel than cotton or corn. At the time, early sweet potatoes brought $3.25 per bushel, whereas cotton and corn paid, on average, two dollars less per bushel. It seemed a no-brainer, but there was a catch. The sweet potatoes needed to be planted early, yet not so soon that the crop could be wiped out by an early frost. If the potatoes were planted too early and the frost decimated them, the young entrepreneur would get nothing.

Ned Jarrett took the risk and planted the sweet potatoes. It was the kind of calculated risk that later would define Jarrett's career as a race car driver. It paid off over time, and by the time he was fourteen he had earned enough from his personal crops to buy his first car—a 1941 Ford. Now he could begin to pursue what was fast becoming a real love for fine, fast automobiles. At first, that was all. He didn't have the racing bug because there was not yet any local racing bug to catch.

That all started changing about the time Big Bill France was running the first Strictly Stock series car race in Charlotte, not more than forty miles from Newton.

"I didn't really have any thoughts about driving race cars because the sport was not really well known at the time. And certainly in this immediate area [around Newton], there were no tracks," Ned Jarrett said.

But his father had been intrigued enough to take young Ned to some races in nearby Charlotte and North Wilkesboro, and Ned quickly became a fan who wanted to know more about the budding sport.

Then something very exciting happened in 1952. Word leaked out that construction had begun on a speedway just up the road from Newton in Hickory, North Carolina. Ned Jarrett, now nineteen and deeply involved in the family sawmill business, used to go to the local country store on rainy days and listen to the older farmers and "sawmillers" talk about what would come to be known as the Hickory Speedway.

"The farmers and the sawmillers would sit around and say, 'Boy, wait till they get that track built. Then I'll go up there and show 'em how to drive," Jarrett said. "As they got closer to getting it finished, I developed a pretty strong interest in maybe trying to get involved."

His parents did not approve. Sure, it was okay to go to a race now and then and watch as a fan. But H. K. Jarrett was clear with his son about what he thought of those who competed in the events.

"People who race cars are either bootleggers or fools," the elder Jarrett told Ned time and time again.

The father knew his son wasn't the former, and hoped that he would not turn out to be the latter. But young Ned Jarrett just couldn't stay away.

"It was a challenge I wanted to seek," he said.

So in April of 1952, Ned Jarrett finally took the plunge into the world of stock car racing against the wishes of his parents. During one of those days when an unrelenting rain had halted work on the farm and shut down the sawmill, a friendly poker game broke out. By the time the rain stopped, Ned Jarrett had won not only a few dollars but also half interest in a race car that was set to run at the Hickory Motor Speedway. Jarrett decided he wanted to be his own driver, all the time thinking in the back of his mind what his father had told him.

"My father wasn't the only one who thought that way, and he may have been somewhat right," Jarrett said. "Most of the competitors in those early days were considered to be either bootleggers or just a bunch of fools who didn't have any better sense than to risk their necks.

"It was not what my parents wanted me to be associated with back then—and that became a little bit of a challenge for me as well. I wanted to prove to them that it didn't matter who you associated with; that the important thing is that you build mutual respect. That was one of the things always emphasized by my dad—that you should try to build respect for your fellow man. But that was their concern: the image that the sport and the people in it projected at that time."

In his first race at the Hickory Speedway, Jarrett finished tenth in a race that featured nearly thirty vehicles, including ones driven by Junior Johnson, Speedy Thompson and Gywnn Staley, guys who already were making names for themselves in the new sport. Jarrett had caught the racing fever.

"It was not that bad, to finish tenth in my first race, I guess," he said. "It certainly sparked the interest that I needed to keep going. Still, for a couple of years it was just something to do on a Saturday night. I didn't look at it as a career because there was no money in it. It was just something to do on a weekend."

That, as Ned Jarrett and the rest of the world would soon find out, was about to change. His father still wasn't sure of the sport but eventually would be won over as well. Shortly after his first race, Ned agreed to a compromise with his father that would permit him to be a car owner while continuing his office work at the sawmill; Ned promised he would not drive.

Ned refrained from taking the wheel for a while, but he had gotten a taste of driving and wanted to do more. When his driver, John Lentz, became ill at the track one night, Jarrett jumped in the driver's seat and finished second—while borrowing Lentz's name. The next week, he again drove under the assumed name, and it was later reported in the local newspaper that Lentz had won the race. Newton is a small town where news travels fast and secrets are hard to keep. Soon Homer Jarrett received word that it was Ned, not John Lentz, who was driving that car, and he confronted his boy.

"Son," he said, "if you're going to drive and win, you might as well get credit for it. Use the family name."

Not far away from Newton and Hickory, a young man was growing up in Belmont, North Carolina, and was acquiring the same passion that had Ned Jarrett in its grip and would not let go. His name even had a racing air about it: Humpy Wheeler. Born in 1939 as Howard Augustan Wheeler Jr., he became Humpy because his father, a much-respected coach and eventually athletic director at Belmont Abbey College, also was known as Humpy.

Humpy Wheeler Sr. was an outstanding athlete in the 1920s and had played football at the University of Illinois. As a sophomore there, the coach caught him smoking Camel cigarettes and made him run laps around the field before practice as punishment. As he ran, Wheeler Sr.'s teammates poked fun at him, calling him Humpy because of the Camel brand of smokes he had been caught with. The nickname stuck.

As Howard Jr. grew older, he became known as Little Humpy. No matter how often he tried to shake the nickname, it always stuck. Finally, he gave up and accepted his fate. He would be known forever as Humpy Wheeler.

When he was ten, he attended the very first Strictly Stock

NASCAR race in Charlotte, just like Hill Overton Jr. and so many others. But unlike Overton, Wheeler did not come away all that impressed. He liked the older, modified stock cars and did not think the Strictly Stock series had much of a future. But racing in general? That was another story. Wheeler loved it. Even at that young age, he also thought he had an understanding about why so many folks seemed drawn to it.

"This really started in the World War Two days. The South was a pretty different place," Wheeler said. "Belmont was pretty representative of the small towns in the Southeast in those days. It was a textile town. It was a pretty gray existence. There wasn't a lot of color.

"The South was beginning to develop a middle class, which they didn't have at the time."

Like Ned Jarrett's father, Wheeler's father had no use for auto racing. Humpy Sr. preferred the traditional sports and implored his son to try them all, which Little Humpy did with uniform success. He played football and boxed well enough to later do both on the collegiate level at the University of South Carolina. He also learned discipline, following his father around the campus of Belmont Abbey College, which includes to this day a seminary for Roman Catholic Benedictine monks.

"I would line the athletic fields and cut the grass. I was around the Benedictine monks a lot and they had a great influence on me," Wheeler said. "They had a tremendous influence on my life because of how they approach life. They take vows of poverty and chastity and obedience. And part of that obedience is humility. That had an effect on me.

"On the other hand, in Belmont the economic conditions of the day produced a lot of poverty, or at least a lot of people who were struggling to get by at slightly above poverty. In that environment, they didn't have much and there was a tendency to be mean about things. It wasn't much fun to be that way, but a lot of people were. Sports were on a very primitive level at the time. To survive, we had to get pretty tough to make it through that environment."

It didn't take young Humpy long to learn that the crowds at local racetracks were rough, and as a result of their unenviable economic depression, mean and ornery. That didn't, however, stop him from going. At age six, he attended his first motorcycle race. At nine, he saw his first automobile race. Somewhere in between, he got his start as a promoter by setting up bicycle races that included himself and his friends.

Living close to the track, Wheeler would often see race cars drive past on their way to the old Charlotte Motor Speedway. Most drivers didn't have haulers back then, of course; they simply drove their race cars straight to the track, ran the event and then, if the cars would still run, drove them back home. Wheeler would dream of driving the cars himself, and soon he was doing whatever he could to go and watch them race. Children under the age of twelve could get in for free, as long as they were accompanied by a paying adult. Wheeler's father refused to take him, so he would hitchhike the six miles down the road to the track by himself, enlist the help of an unsuspecting adult to pose as his guardian at the track's gate so he could get in and then take in the action.

It was a rush, immediately bringing color to his gray Belmont existence.

"The only other things I could compare it to was going to the fair," Wheeler said. "It was like going to the fair. It was colored, different, neat, fast . . . it was contact. It was all those things.

"And I was a contact person. There was something there about contact with racing that pulled me in."

He was not alone. The young Wheeler noticed something about the makeup of those early racing crowds too. The majority of them all seemed to be from small, outlying towns. The big-city folks and suburban middle-class dwellers didn't come out as much. They had enough color in their lives right where they were; the small-town folks needed to create some excitement, and lived in a rough-and-tumble environment where you had to fight for everything you got. They could appreciate cars banging into each other as they fought for track position and the ultimate triumph, of finishing in front of all the other competitors. It wasn't good, clean fun; it was gritty, dirty fun—the way they liked it.

"Most of the people that got involved in racing when I did were from small towns. I think the small-town atmosphere where you didn't grow up in an all-middle-class environment like you do in the suburban area had a lot to do with how racing developed its blue-collar roots," Wheeler said.

"You would go to a race, and everybody from your small town was there. As racing began to grow, you had the same sort of thing where you deal with groundskeepers and the heads of some companies and everything and everyone in between. That small-town environment has a lot to do with it. It has a lot to do with the success of stock car racing. And it's not in-born in you; it's more a learned thing."

Wheeler learned early on what his place in racing would be. He tried driving some by age fifteen, but quickly realized he wasn't cut out for it.

"If there was anything to hit, I would hit it," he said.

Wheeler's vast contributions to racing would come later as a promoter and track president, serving himself and the sport well. But his early assessment of what was transpiring across the Southeast rang true immediately. He would never forget it, and his perceptive view of the racing world proved to be a valuable asset.

In the early 1950s the Southeast witnessed the dawn of a new sport, which Big Bill France had envisioned coming together under the ever-expanding umbrella of his one sanctioning body. Average folks who didn't have much money to spend on entertainment were beginning to embrace stock car racing, and NASCAR was assuming control of who raced where and when and for how much prize money.

.   .   .

What defines a sport after it grabs a foothold in a nation's subconscious are the personalities that drive it. And in this sport, that meant the drivers. Big Bill France was a strong personality in his own right, but even he realized quickly that the drivers were the stars of his show. He just had to keep them in line.

With some, that would not prove difficult. Junior Johnson remembers the first time France talked to him "and a bunch of other moonshiners." He recalled the group being receptive to France right away. All France wanted to do was bring order to what had been mayhem. No one objected to that.

"I knew Bill France from the very first time he ever showed up, talkin' about racin'," Johnson recalled years later. "He was talkin' to a bunch of bootlegger friends of mine who were older than me. I was young, but I was old enough at the time to remember him talkin' to them about wantin' them to get involved in his racin' organization.

"Back then, each track wanted its own rules. They'd have trouble all the time. In other words, they'd go to a track and run a race—and if someone or another was ruled illegal, the track would decide whether they wanted to throw 'em out or not. France wanted to oversee something that could control all that. He wanted NASCAR to be the sanctioning body that would control what went on. That was his big thing—to get it started, to where it could stay organized.

"I think everybody kindly understood what he was tryin' to do. Most of the drivers and the tracks welcomed that idea. Because a lot of times you would go to a racetrack to run, and the track would put up so much money. But the promoter, if he didn't have a good crowd, he would take off before paying the purse and that kind of stuff. So I think all of the drivers were pretty much in line to like what he was doin.' "

Of course, there were many drivers who liked the general idea of what France was trying to do, but had a habit of doing their own thing whenever they felt like they could get away with it. Even

Johnson admitted to that. He was a notorious cheater, and proud of it. Other drivers embraced France at first but soon came to resent his heavy hand, feeling that he was trying to run the sport like a dictator—which, in fact, he was. The truth was that it was exactly what stock car racing needed at the time.

Among the drivers who immediately captured the attention of Wheeler and others who attended early races was Curtis Turner. In a sport that would over the years welcome its share of outlandish characters on and off the track, perhaps none surpassed Turner. A native of the Shenandoah Mountains near Floyd, Virginia, it seemed Turner was born to race and bred to party. The family business was logging, and Turner used to fondly reminisce about the days when he awoke to the smell of fresh-cut pine. But the lumber business was not all that exciting, and the ruggedly handsome Turner longed for a life more exciting. Much more exciting.

By the time he was twenty years old in 1944, he had helped build the family operation into a highly profitable one. He was, it seemed, on his way to an easy life filled with riches. But Turner had no intention of mellowing and taking any of his money gently with him into old age. He spent cash as fast as he made it, on booze, fast cars and even faster women. When he wasn't running the lumber business, he often hung out with a group of mountain folk he called "a shine clan," and he gladly partook of their moonshine on many occasions. It was while hanging out with his shine clan that Turner began to take an interest in stock car racing. Once he had a taste of the sport, he was hooked. Racing, like all the things that he enjoyed, he embraced with a passion that bordered on bizarre obsession.

He immediately established himself as a driver who operated on the edge, pushing his car to the limits. In one early nonsanctioned event in the Shenandoah Mountains, he took a 1940 Ford and wowed a crowd of onlookers by repeatedly passing slower cars when it looked as if he did not have room to pass. He eventually crashed hard and never finished the race, but glowed afterward when he was swarmed by a number of newfound fans who admired him for his driving style and did not seem bothered by the fact that he had wrecked his car and failed to finish. To Turner, this kind of adulation fed his ample ego and validated his reckless approach to life.

Turner won his first NASCAR-sanctioned event on September 11, 1949 in Langhorne, Pennsylvania, driving a 1949 Oldsmobile. The next year, he captured race victories at Charlotte, Martinsville, Virginia, and Rochester, New York. He won the pole position for the very first Southern 500 at Darlington Raceway in South Carolina, which quickly was establishing itself as the NASCAR circuit's most prestigious—and highest-paying—event.

One time at the old Charlotte Fairgrounds, Turner was assigned the mundane task of driving the race car for a Grand National event that he wasn't slated to compete in because he was running at the time mostly in NASCAR's old Convertible division. Max Muhleman, a local sports columnist for the *Charlotte News* at the time, was standing nearby when Turner took his cue to jump in the pace car and fire it up.

"Hop in, Pop. Get in the backseat and you can see real good," said Turner, who had a habit of calling virtually everyone "Pop."

Muhleman hesitated. He knew firsthand of Turner's wild reputation, having hung out with him on the road many times. Eventually, though, he climbed in. Heck, Muhleman thought, Turner wasn't even in the race. He was just going to take his 1956 Ford convertible around the track a few times, setting the pace for the cars who were racing and then getting out of their way by heading into the relative safety of the pit area.

"Being young and foolish enough, I agreed," Muhleman said years later.

But after climbing into the convertible, Muhleman noticed a familiar look in Turner's mischievous eyes. Right away, it unnerved the journalist, who knew that anything could happen when Turner gave in to his worst impulses.

"Curtis had had a few shooters, as he liked to call them, of

Canadian Club—as was his form. He was just having fun. I don't know if he had just gotten done with one of his timber deals or what, but I remember he had a gray-silver suit on with a white shirt and tie," Muhleman said.

At first everything seemed fine. Muhleman kept turning and looking behind him at Buck Baker and Speedy Thompson, who were driving Chryslers for eccentric owner Carl Kiekhaefer at the time and had qualified one-two in the front row.

"We started going around, and the pace car speed on a dirt track is pretty slow, which is what I had envisioned," Muhleman said. "And I'm looking around at Buck and Speedy, and I'm thinking this is a pretty neat view. Then they came around on the lap where they dropped the green flag along the one turn, and on a half-mile dirt track that's very close quarters."

Turner turned to Muhleman and grinned.

"Hey, Pop, you want to make a lap?" asked Turner, using racer's lingo for taking the car to its top speed.

"Nope, nope. God no, I don't want to make a lap," Muhleman replied. "Let's get the hell off the track like we're supposed to."

"Aw, no. We're going to make a lap," said Turner, laughing.

With that Turner punched it and took the pace car into turn one sideways. There were no seat belts in the car, and Muhleman almost went flying out.

"He just laughed and went on. He floored it and went sliding through the first turn," Muhleman said. "And of course, it's not real smooth. There were a lot of bumps in there. I was desperately trying to find anything I could hold on to. I was trying to grab onto the bottom of the seat and hang on."

The race cars behind were having trouble keeping up. Once the drivers figured out what was going on, they became enraged that Turner was going so fast and would not get off the track and out of their way. Baker and Thompson pulled up as close as they could and started yelling obscenities, flipping Turner the bird.

All the while, Muhleman sat huddled in the backseat, certain that he was seconds away from being thrown from the vehicle.

"I thought I was going to go flying out of the car and get run over by Kiekhaefer's Chryslers," Muhleman said. "I was hanging on for dear life. I could see Buck. He was shaking his fist and all pissed off. He was running up like he was going to hit Curtis. Whenever I had time to squeeze in a look behind me, it never looked good.

"And in the front, here's Curtis laughing and driving like he's in a race. And I don't know if the wheels are going to fold up and fly off or what, or if we're going to get knocked through the fence by Buck, or if I'm going to go flying out of the car and get run over by the rest of the field. It was harrowing, but memorable."

That's how it often was when spending quality time with Turner. Muhleman would travel to races with Curtis and Joe Weatherly, another early driver who became fast friends with Turner because they seemed to have so much in common. In other words, Weatherly loved to have a good time too.

Weatherly was a quick talker who, like Turner, enjoyed fast things off the track as well, partying as hard as he raced. It was after he and Turner had knocked each other around on the track in Darlington, South Carolina, at a running of the Rebel 300 Convertible race that they both took to calling each other and everyone else who crossed their partying paths "Pop." It was during that race when Turner and Weatherly repeatedly slammed into each other down the length of an entire straightaway, tearing up their factory-supplied Fords in front of company executives who did not understand racing and were not amused.

As they banged into each other, distinctive *pops* could be heard around the track.

"I guess we gave each other a few good pops. That was fun, Pop," Weatherly told Turner afterward, oblivious to the glaring Ford executives who didn't like their equipment getting abused at their expense. It didn't even seem to matter to them that Turner won the race and Weatherly finished second.

"Damn right, Pop," grinned Turner. "I can't wait to do that again."

Sometimes they didn't wait until they were in their race cars. On more than one occasion, they raced each other on city streets in rental cars—often wrecking them almost beyond recognition. Then they would attempt to return them to the rental company, feigning innocence and disbelief at the condition of the vehicle. There were a few other times when the cars were wrecked so completely that they simply drove them, hysterical with laughter, into the deep end of the swimming pool at their motel. How they stayed out of jail after all these antics amazed even their closest friends, but both men were charmers who seemingly could talk their way out of trouble almost as easily as they could talk themselves into it.

They didn't always confine their drinking to after-hours, either. Both were known to routinely spike the water jugs they carried with them in their cars, which then would bang against each other, and any other driver for hours on the track. No matter what happened on the track, though, Turner and Weatherly always seemed to walk away laughing about it. They clearly were having the time of their lives as they competed against each other from the mid-1950s through the early 1960s, often carrying the entire show, especially in the short-lived and soon forgotten NASCAR Convertible division.

Turner was on a roll on and off the track. He won the 1956 Southern 500 in the Grand National division that later would become Winston Cup, capturing the $11,750 first-place prize money. That was his only Grand National win that season, but Turner was concentrating on the Convertible division at the time. He started only thirteen Grand National races, but won an incredible twenty-two of forty-three Convertible events he entered that season.

Both men loved to fly airplanes, even though the homespun Weatherly never took the time to learn how to file flight plans, read the instruments or even how to use the radio. He often flew in the wrong direction. Turner used to ride him mercilessly about the time he took off for Dayton, Ohio, and didn't realize he was proceeding along the wrong flight pattern until Weatherly suddenly noticed the Empire State Building in New York City looming in front of him. Another time, Weatherly attempted to fly from Darlington to nearby Charlotte but never made it out of the state of South Carolina. He eventually landed in Spartanburg and asked where he was.

Turner, on the other hand, was considered an expert pilot who had honed his skills while learning the logging business. It often was Turner's job to fly an airplane over wooded areas to assess the quantity and quality of timber below. Ever the practical joker, Turner made a habit of taking businessmen up who were thinking of investing in his logging company and turning one of his two engines off in midflight.

"Gee, I can't figure out what's wrong," he once told one of his frightened passengers, stroking his chin.

Then he handed over the controls to the unsuspecting passenger, who was growing more terrified by the moment.

"Go ahead, you fly it. See what you can do," Turner told him.

The businessmen were so horrified that they never really noticed what was on the ground below. Turner finally fired up the other engine, looked out the window and said, "That's some damn fine timber down there. You really ought to invest in this venture with me."

"Okay, okay, whatever you say. Just get us back on the ground," the businessman stammered in reply.

This sort of ruse was performed more than once by Turner, who knew how to tap other people's money when his ran out—which was often.

One time Turner and Weatherly and a few selected party guests boarded a small private airplane Turner owned. The two racers got to arguing about who was the fastest driver once up in the air.

"Land this thing and I'll prove I'm the fastest!" Weatherly told Turner.

Turner landed the airplane, the two rented the fastest automobiles they could find and they tore off racing down the highway. This time when they returned the cars to the rental agency, they were battered and smoking. The agency's officials were not amused. Word came down that neither Turner nor Weatherly could ever rent a car from the agency again.

"They had an all-points bulletin out: If you see these men, do not rent them anything. Do not talk to them. Do not give them anything—not even a map!" Muhleman said.

Turner would host parties at his Charlotte home and demand that every visitor get as drunk as they possibly could. Sometimes the parties would not only last well into the evening and the next morning, but would rage on for days. Turner would catch a few hours of sleep and then stand on a table to make an announcement.

"All right, folks! Don't nobody leave! There will be a new party starting in ten minutes! It's gonna be even better than the one that just wrapped up!" Turner would shout.

Turner flew himself to events in the small, twin-engine airplane that he owned. He often was suffering from a hangover when he got behind the controls, but that never seemed to faze him. Once while flying over Easley, South Carolina, on a beautiful Sunday morning, Turner became disconsolate because he discovered that he had no booze on board to ease the boredom of the flight ahead. He often liked to have a little nip of the dog that bit him the night before, whether he was racing or flying.

Damn, Turner thought, do I know anybody in Easley who might be able to find me a bottle? He remembered that he did. Despite the relatively early hour, he knew his buddy would have some Canadian Club or V.O. whiskey in stock, so he flew around until he located his friend's house and then proceeded to land the plane on his friend's street. He cut off the engines and rolled to a stop right near the front door, then stumbled out and knocked.

A few drinks later, Turner and his friend remembered that they needed to move the plane before the local cops made their usual Sunday rounds. They rushed outside. Turner grabbed a bottle of liquor and took it with him for the flight ahead, then got in and fired up his bird. Upon takeoff, it happened that a nearby Baptist church was letting out after its Sunday service. Turner, ever the showoff, dipped the plane's wings ever so slightly as if to wave hello to the churchgoers, whose mouths were agape at what they were witnessing before them.

As Turner dipped the wings, the tail of his plane got too close to the power lines and snagged them, ripping them from their poles and sending the congregation below scattering. Turner flew on, unaware of what had happened—no doubt laughing at the top of his lungs in between swigs from his beloved bottle. For once, he wasn't laughing when he landed his plane shortly thereafter at the Charlotte airport. Word had quickly spread of his antics on this occasion, and an offical from the Federal Aviation Administration held out his hand as Turner climbed out of the cockpit.

"Let's have it, Mr. Turner. You're done as a pilot. This will cost you your pilot's license," the official said.

A glum Turner obliged, but promised to fight to get his license to fly back in court later on. Meanwhile, at least he still had racing to provide him with some thrills.

Back at the Jarrett farm, business had taken off by the mid-1950s. They still owned the sawmill, but also owned and operated a lumberyard where they would buy additional lumber off other sawmill operations. Then they would plane the lumber, air dry it and finish it before hauling it up into West Virginia and Ohio, as well as other parts of North Carolina.

Ned Jarrett would count the lumber as it came in and went out. Occasionally he would drive the huge trucks that carried the finished product into West Virginia and Ohio. But he preferred being behind the wheel of something else.

He ran an increasing amount of races in the National Sportsman series (which today is the Busch series) throughout the mid-1950s, and finished second in the points standings in 1956 to Ralph Earnhardt, a legendary champion with a reputation for a no-

nonsense approach to racing. In 1957 and 1958, Jarrett won the Sportsman points championship.

"But still, I was holding down a full-time job throughout all that time," Jarrett said. "I was making my living doing something else."

That isn't what Jarrett wanted to be doing, so he decided to do something about it.

"After I won the championships in '57 and '58, I felt that I had accomplished everything that division had to offer," Jarrett said. "I had always vowed to myself that whatever I did in life, that however far I got up the ladder, I would quit while I was there and not go down the other side—because people had a tendency to remember you for the last thing you did. So I didn't want to hang around and start going down the other side."

Jarrett also thought he was a hot commodity. He was in for a rude awakening on that front.

"I thought car owners would come knocking on my door to go racing in Grand National—since I had won those championships and won a lot of races [in the lower division]. But it didn't work that way," he said. "I had to go knocking on doors to try and find a ride. I floundered around."

As he did so, Jarrett began to appreciate how expensive it could be to compete at the highest level in stock car racing. He was running out of money fast, and was beginning to feel a little like the fool his father had warned he might become by way of getting involved in such a renegade sport. Jarrett kept plowing ahead.

Once, he got a line on a good race car that had previously registered a number of victories with Junior Johnson at the wheel. The owner wanted to sell it, and Jarrett wanted to buy it. There was one small problem. Jarrett didn't have the $2,000 in his checking account to cover its purchase.

Jarrett decided to write the check anyway, waiting until after the bank closed on Friday. That way, he could pick up the car and prepare it to run in a pair of weekend events—a nonpoints race at Myrtle Beach that nonetheless paid a decent purse on Saturday and a Grand National event at the old Charlotte Fairgrounds, also called the Southern States Fairgrounds, on Sunday. The catch: to cover the $2,000 check, Jarrett would have to win both races.

It was an incredible risk, taken by a man who did not consider himself a gambler, despite his success with the sweet potatoes in his youth (and the fact that he had won his first race car in a poker game).

"As I look back on it, I guess it was a pretty big gamble," Jarrett admitted years later. "At the time, in my excitement, I didn't think that much about it. I knew I was buying a race car that was capable of winning. That was the part of the equation that you could forget about. Would it win? Yes. It had been winning races with Junior Johnson at the wheel, so I knew that part of it was good.

"Now, whether I could drive it or not, well, I felt that I could. So we wrote the check, knowing that I had to win the two races over the weekend to cover it."

The first race went well enough, or so it seemed to Jarrett at first. His car was faster than most of the others, and he drove it in his usual reliable way. Other competitors fell by the wayside by pushing their equipment too hard, as often happened. Jarrett was an expert at saving his for the push at the finish.

As usually was the case back then, the steering wheel had been fixed up with foam rubber and then wrapped with black electrician's tape to give the driver a better feel and help prevent cramps as he turned left for the duration of a long race. Unbeknownst to the focused Jarrett, there was a problem. Whoever had wrapped the wheel before the car had been sold to him had rewrapped the steering wheel backward.

"I didn't even know it until I got into the race," Jarrett said. "As I was continually sawing the wheel to the left, I was just tearing meat off the bones on the edge of that tape."

Jarrett won the race, but paid a price.

"I was a total wreck physically," he said. "At the end of the race in Myrtle Beach, they had to put a tourniquet on my right arm to stop the blood flow. It was raw. After we got through the little Victory Lane ceremony, we started back toward Charlotte. There was a hospital just a block off the highway in Conway, South Carolina, so we stopped by there and they cleaned it up and bandaged it up. Then we went on to get back to Charlotte, where we worked on the car all night to get it ready for the next day. But I was in no physical condition to drive a race car."

Yet he had to drive one, or his $2,000 check, written less than forty-eight hours before, would bounce at the bank. He did not hesitate to climb into the car again, although even that proved painful. Even though his hands were heavily bandaged, he did not otherwise protect them with any type of driving gloves. Drivers in those days rarely wore any such thing.

"I don't know if any drivers did. I never did wear gloves, even after that incident," Jarrett said.

The old Charlotte Fairgrounds was a half-mile dirt track built in 1926. Lee Petty had won the inaugural NASCAR event run there in 1954, and again in 1957 and in a previous race in May of 1959. Curtis Turner, Tim Flock, Fireball Roberts, Speedy Thompson and Buck Baker had all won there, and those victories had done much to promote their budding careers as the sport's top talents. So Jarrett knew that a win might mean even more than covering his precious $2,000 check.

He started the race and kept turning left until the pain became unbearable. About halfway through the two hundred-lap event, he was running fourth but could no longer tolerate the pain in his hands. He swung the car into the pits.

Waiting there was none other than Junior Johnson, the epitome of the bootlegger Ned Jarrett's father had warned him about. Jarrett's crew had gone to Johnson and asked if he would be interested in serving as a relief driver. Johnson, whose own car had blown an engine earlier in the race and was done for the day, quickly agreed to drive Jarrett's car the rest of the way.

"I had raced against him for years at places like Hickory and North Wilkesboro," Jarrett said. "I knew him pretty well and I think we had a mutual respect for each other all along. But we were not buddy-buddy by any means. We never were. . . . I don't think any of that figured into the picture of my crew asking him and him accepting to help us out that day. He knew that there was a need there and he liked to drive race cars.

"Plus he knew that was a winning race car because he had won races in it, so he didn't hesitate for a moment to jump in there. And I didn't hesitate to turn it over to him—because I was hurting and I knew he could get the job done."

The bootlegger did. And he saved the sawmiller's rear end.

Jarrett would become friends with Johnson years later, but not before becoming even fiercer rivals on the tracks during their driving primes. But what happened that day, Jarrett never forgot. The record books list him as the winner of that race in Charlotte. He knows better. He knows he could not have won without the help of Johnson, a supposed enemy who stood for everything he was not.

"Even if you were enemies, which we became later on, if you could help another driver out you'd do it," Jarrett said. "That's just the way race car drivers are. So he didn't hesitate to jump into that car. Word had pretty much gotten around about the check, so he didn't charge me anything for driving the race car in that race."

Jarrett's first-place prize money for winning was $800, enough to help him cover the check he had written the previous Friday and pay his doctor's bills.

"We ran five races in that car that year; we won three, finished second in one and third in one," Jarrett said. "So I finally got Junior to take a hundred dollars a little later on for helping me out, but that was it. That was all he would take."

For Ned Jarrett, it also proved the point he had tried to make to his father years before. Bootleggers could be decent folks too.

"Yes, a good percentage of the drivers at the time were bootleggers. They drove cars that hauled whiskey. But my perception of that was that I didn't look at those people as being anything less than I was," Jarrett said. "I had respect for them for what they could do, especially with an automobile.

"They were good people. Their livelihood just came from a different source than where mine came from as I grew up. But everybody had something different that they do. I certainly didn't look down on those people. I knew that they would be hard to beat, and that was the challenge that it presented.

"It was not what they did away from the racetrack that concerned me. It was what they were able to do on the racetrack. Their experience in the moonshining business helped them to become better race car drivers."

Fireball and Daytona

As the sport of stock car racing grew, it began to draw participants—drivers, owners and mechanics—from all walks of life and from different parts of the nation. Soon the former moonshiners blended right in with the rest, which included ex-farmers, ex-cab drivers, former electricians and a number of dreamers who grew up thinking that they wanted to do nothing else. They rarely thought of the danger involved in a sport that was getting faster and more dangerous all the time. The safety standards were not keeping up with the rest of the sport's evolution.

None of them thought about the dark side of racing much. Sure, there could be horrific crashes. There often were. But usually the injured party seemed, somehow, to walk away—or eventually would return to racing after spending some time recovering in a hospital. Ned Jarrett's injured hands were in fact a small price to pay to play the game, and he knew it.

There were other drivers who paid steeper prices.

Tiny Lund was one. Like all folks nicknamed "Tiny," Dewayne Lund actually was a huge man measuring six feet five inches. He weighed more than 250 pounds and was, as one writer of the time put it, "built like a tank." Sometimes he acted like he was driving one. On lap sixty-six of his first NASCAR race in October of 1955 on a 1.5-mile dirt track with high banks in Lehi, Arkansas, Lund crashed and nearly perished on the spot. As his car flipped several times, he was thrown from the vehicle and was struck by the front wheels of another car as he lay on the track. He suffered a broken back and took several months to recover from the injury, but by the 1957 season he was back at it again.

Lund went on to become another of the sport's dynamic personalities. By all accounts he was a gentle, congenial man with a big heart away from the track—and not one to be messed with on it. If someone beat him in a fair race, that was fine. If someone took a cheap shot at him or tried to run him off the road, look out.

He often traded shots on the track with Lee Petty, perhaps the only other driver he openly disliked. Lund had started out sweeping floors and doing general grunt work in the Petty race shop for forty dollars a week. Eventually, he started driving for the elder Petty—and that's when the animosity grew. Lee Petty did not want to pay Tiny the usual 40 percent cut of the purses he won, which was the standard for drivers back then; Petty wanted to continue paying Lund the forty dollars a week he had earned as a laborer back at the shop. It seemed Lund always had to fight and finagle to get his way in racing. In high school, everyone always wanted him to play football because of his strapping build, but he wanted to race. At the age of sixteen on one hot summer evening in Harland, Iowa, where he grew up, Lund entered a motorcycle race with his parents in the grandstands. They were okay with their son competing in that event, but Tiny's father grew uneasy when he had trouble locating his son after the event, and then suddenly noticed the family car circling the track in the main event that featured a stock car race. Tiny was driving, passing everything in sight as he sent his old man's blood pressure soaring.

Lund was colorful, but so was Glenn "Fireball" Roberts. Whereas Lund struggled to win in large part because he found it difficult to secure a decent ride after his early wreck, by 1958

Roberts was developing into what many believed was the sport's first great superstar.

You might say Roberts was born to race. He certainly was born in the right place to fulfill that calling, having entered the world in 1929 in Tavares, Florida, near Daytona Beach—shortly before Big Bill France made the long drive down from the Washington, D.C., and began to turn his grand vision of NASCAR into a reality. As young Glenn Roberts moved into adulthood, the sport was literally growing all around him. He loved watching the races on the sands of Daytona Beach, promoted from 1938 on by France. He earned his nickname, though, not because of any early driving heroics but because he was an outstanding fast-pitch softball pitcher, playing for the Zellwood Mud Hens American Legion team near Tavares.

But by 1947, at age eighteen, Fireball Roberts was ready to make his nickname work for him on the racetracks around the Southeast. He entered his first race on August 5, 1947 at North Wilkesboro Speedway in North Carolina and soon was racing modified cars whenever he could, which often meant he ran seven days a week. His first NASCAR-sanctioned race came, appropriately enough, at Daytona Beach in a modified race in 1948. It was a wreck-filled, 150-lap event in which only twelve cars were able to finish, and Roberts was not behind the wheel of any one of them. On the ninth lap on the 2.2-mile track made of sand and asphalt, Roberts missed the south turn and ended up in the surf of the Atlantic Ocean, his day finished.

It was undoubtedly that day that Roberts decided he liked driving on asphalt better than sand. But at the time, Roberts enjoyed driving whenever he could, wherever he could and in whatever ride he could find. His first NASCAR win at the Grand National level came in August of 1950 at Hillsboro, North Carolina, in only his third start at the sport's highest level of competition. Three weeks later he nearly won again—finishing second at the prestigious and high-paying Southern 500 at Darlington Raceway in South Carolina. The media was falling in love with him, and he with them. His wife Doris later admitted that Roberts put a great emphasis on qualifying well because if he was successful in doing so his name would be mentioned more prominently in newspapers.

"I always thought he was one of the first real superstars the sport had—and he did get a lot of attention," Ned Jarrett said. "He was a neat dresser, a clean-cut-looking individual, very dedicated and focused on what he was doing. And he was a tremendous athlete. He might have been the first one who showed that race car drivers are athletes.

"He was a tremendous race car driver and he didn't shy away from the attention. I don't recall him going out and beating the drums to try and get it, but I don't think he shied away from it. I think it was somewhat of a driving force for him. The more attention he got, the more he wanted to succeed to try to live up to what was expected of him."

Roberts thought it was going to come easily after his fast start in 1950. But it would be six years before he won again on the Grand National level. In fact, he finished in the top five only once in thirty-five starts between 1951 and 1955. Part of the problem was that he did not compete in more than nine races in each of those seasons, as he fought the problems facing many drivers: finding someone (or some company) to back his efforts.

That started changing in 1956. Backed by Ford and owner Pete DePaolo, a former winning driver in the Indianapolis 500, Roberts strung five wins together in a total of thirty-three starts that season and began a habit of running up front. He finished in the top five in seventeen of the starts and in the top ten in a total of twenty-two of them. His race winnings, which had dipped to $199 in 1953 and sunk to an all-time low of $140 when he was able to run only two races in 1955, jumped to $14,742 as he led 1,107 of the 6,891 laps he completed. No driver led more laps. In his previous six seasons, he had been able to complete a total of only 2,500 laps—never more than 825 in a single season—and had led a total of just sixty.

In 1957, Roberts won eight more races and $19,829. He was winning enough to sometimes enter races in his own cars, which he won with on three occasions. The other five victories came in DePaolo-owned, factory-backed Fords.

But 1958 was his best year. He left DePaolo and teamed with Atlanta businessman Frank Strickland, and had one of the best crew chiefs in the business in Paul McDuffie. He won six races in the Grand National division, including the Southern 500 at Darlington, and pulled in a total of $32,219. He also was dominant in the Convertible division.

Racing was beginning to get recognized on a national level, and Fireball's ascension to stardom came at a perfect time. He was poised to capitalize on it, and the sport was eager to capitalize on him. Following the 1958 season, he became the first race car driver ever voted Professional Athlete of the Year by the Florida Sportswriters Association.

"He was just what the sport needed at the time," said Jarrett, who became fast friends with Roberts.

It seemed Fireball was living up to his nickname.

Max Muhleman was a young, impressionable sportswriter at the *Greenville Piedmont,* the afternoon newspaper in Greenville, South Carolina, when he was informed that he would be introduced to stock car racing. This was well before Muhleman took his harrowing ride around the Charlotte Fairgrounds track with Curtis Turner. It was 1956 and Muhleman was fresh out of high school, a freshman student at Furman University who was working at the paper as a way of making some money while he went to college. His sports editor called him into his office.

"Max, I'm assigning you to cover stock car racing," the editor said.

Muhleman's jaw dropped. He knew nothing about the sport.

He loved baseball and basketball and had run track, but stock car racing? He didn't have a clue. He had some ideas about what it was like, though, and those were not favorable.

"Sir, I would rather cover a dog show," Muhleman replied. "I don't know anything about cars. I can hardly even start my own."

"Well, that's your assignment," said the editor, totally unsympathetic.

Muhleman accepted his fate and left the office, muttering to no one in particular.

It's just a gearhead sport. This is going to be awful, he told himself.

His first assignment was a Grand National race at the Spartanburg Fairgrounds. His editor had told him that Tim Flock was the reigning points champion in the relatively new NASCAR organization, and Muhleman had it in his mind that interviewing the 1955 champion might be a good place to start in this strange new world he was about to enter. Flock was supposed to be a good story. He had won seventeen races and his first Grand National title prior to quitting in disgust during the 1954 season after he was stripped of a victory at Daytona by France for what he saw as a minor rules infraction.

For a few months, Flock took a job at an Atlanta gas station. He used to joke that business was so slow at the job that he just about starved to death. His racing career had resumed under strange circumstances when some buddies talked him into traveling with them to Daytona for Speed Week the following February. They were having a few beers on the beach the morning of the qualifying race when Carl Kiekhaefer, an eccentric but very wealthy car owner, pulled up nearby in his sleek, brand-new white Chrysler 300. Flock went over and introduced himself.

"I'm looking for someone to drive an extra car I own in this race. Would you be interested?" Kiekhaefer asked Flock.

Flock couldn't say yes and sober up fast enough. By that afternoon, he was on the beach-and-road course trying to qualify for the race in Kiekhaefer's "extra car." He won the pole with a record qualifying speed of 130.923 miles per hour, and three days later he won the race. He went on to win an amazing eighteen races that season for Kiekhaefer, and he finished in the top five in thirty-two of the thirty-nine starts he made. So it seemed to Muhleman that Flock was the natural choice for his first interview in his new career as a stock car racing writer.

Muhleman arrived at the fairgrounds and started looking around for Flock. Someone pointed him in the direction of Flock's car, but as he moved in that direction he didn't see anyone. Then he noticed a man's legs sticking out from underneath the car.

"Uh, Mr. Flock? Mr. Flock?" Muhleman said quietly, unsure that he wanted to disturb whomever this was napping underneath the car.

But the man pulled himself out and jumped right up at the sound of his name.

"Yeah, yeah, that's me. How ya' doin'?" Flock said.

Flock stuck his hand out and the two began talking. Much to Muhleman's astonishment, he found the man extremely interesting. They talked about Flock's 1955 championship, his upbringing during the days his older brothers and uncle used to run moonshine in Georgia and much, much more. Suddenly, Muhleman found himself getting hooked on racing without yet having seen even a single race.

"I couldn't believe the response I got out of this guy that I saw as a sports figure," Muhleman said. "I was comparing him to other athletes and coaches that I had interviewed in my limited experience as a sportswriter at the time. He ended up inviting me to his house if I ever came down to Atlanta, which I did end up doing.

"There was no such thing as an expense account back in those days, at least not in South Carolina. But I did eventually go to Atlanta and I got to know the whole Flock family. It made me like the sport because I could see how the personalities were, and how willing they were to talk to you. That's what first attracted me to the sport that I thought I was going to hate."

The Flock family history was filled with colorful stories. The Flocks told Muhleman about how they ran moonshine and how, one day, the revenuers had come for Bob Flock when he was in the middle of a race at Atlanta's old Lakewood Speedway, a one-mile dirt track originally built in 1915.

"I never saw any of that moonshine stuff firsthand," Muhleman said. "But they talked about it and laughed about it. They told stories about trying to dodge the feds at Lakewood Speedway. They were coming for Bob that one day, and he was running first or second in this race. They had a pit stop and told the Flocks that the feds were there, and Bob said, 'I'm just going to keep on going after the race.' "

It turned out Bob Flock didn't even wait that long. They had been running on yellow, the caution flag. As soon as officials dropped the green flag to resume the race, Bob Flock literally headed for the door.

"Tim said he went through the fence on the way out," Muhleman said. "It was such a good story that I wondered if it could possibly have been true. But it was told to me as the truth, and you know what? It probably *was* the truth."

Tim Flock also was fond of telling the story of how he had won the 1951 beach race at Daytona. With only a few laps left, he had a three-mile lead on the 4.17-mile course, but his 1950 Lincoln was running low on gas. The engine suddenly started cutting off, so Flock pulled into the pits.

What he saw was his worst nightmare. His pit crew, thinking they had the race in the bag, had already begun celebrating by passing around jugs of moonshine. They were caught completely off guard when Flock arrived in the pits to break up their premature party. There were no radios in those days for drivers to tell pit crews that they were coming in or what they needed when they did come in. Flock's crew couldn't find any more gas in their pit stall to put in his tank.

As they raced up and down pit road trying to find someone who would loan them the gas they needed to finish, driver Marshall Teague, in his 1951 Hudson, passed by on the backstretch and went on to win the race. Flock had to settle for second—and a thousand-dollar check instead of the first-place prize of $1,500.

Racing, at least under the guidance of Bill France's NASCAR, was not yet a decade old, but already it was developing a folklore.

Muhleman loved hearing the tales of these men who put life and limb on the line every time they got behind the wheel for a race. To him, they seemed bigger than life. He soon developed friendships with Curtis Turner, Joe Weatherly and especially Fireball Roberts, with whom he made plans to write a book. Muhleman made his first trip to Daytona in 1956 and came away enthralled by what he had seen on the beach.

"That was my favorite place to watch a race, on the old beach course at Daytona. That was fantastic," Muhleman said. "The idea of a car sliding through a turn and out into the surf and back again was just as fantastic and as picturesque as it sounds.

"Some drivers were better than others, of course. Probably the leading power slider was Curtis Turner. He was just spectacular. It was perfect for him."

Muhleman found that Turner and Weatherly and Roberts and the rest were perfect for him at that time too. With no expense account to work with, Muhleman could afford to go to only a few races. The drivers he had befriended knew that—and like the Flocks, they opened their world to him. Turner and Weatherly would invite him to fly to races in their airplanes. Buck Baker once drove him to a race. When he could, Muhleman would try to reciprocate on the hospitality. Roberts would stay with Muhleman at his small apartment in Charlotte when Fireball came to races there.

One time Muhleman was flying to an event in an airplane piloted by Turner. Weatherly sat in the front passenger's seat, Muhleman was seated behind him. At one point during the flight, Turner caught Muhleman's attention, winked at him and motioned toward Weatherly, who was looking aimlessly out the window.

"Watch this," Turner whispered.

With that, Turner cut the right engine just as the daydreaming Weatherly was gazing at it. Weatherly, an excitable fellow who talked in loud bursts when he got worked up, immediately took notice of the situation.

"God almighty, Pop, the engine just went out! You lost an engine over here!" Weatherly said.

At the time, neither Muhleman nor Weatherly was aware that Turner often pulled this practical joke on gullible passengers when he was trying to sell them timber.

"Damn, Joe, you're right. I can't get the thing going again," Turner said.

Then Turner winked at Muhleman again and cut off the left engine.

"I believe we lost the left engine now, Joe," he said, feigning concern.

Weatherly started going nuts, hollering that he was too young to die.

"You've got to do something, Pop!" he stammered to Turner.

Finally, after Weatherly began screaming and became more hysterical with each passing second, Turner slyly turned both engines back on. Then he started laughing loudly, slapping Weatherly on the back and exchanging knowing glances with Muhleman, who wasn't entirely comfortable with the gag himself. What if, thought Muhleman, the engines don't come back on one time? What will Curtis do then?

"This is about the time when Weatherly was flying by, as he said, an Esso road map, which is how he navigated. If he got lost he would fly low enough to try to read the road signs below; then he would try to figure out where he was on his Esso map," Muhleman said. "Curtis really had poor Joe all worked up that time. Then Curtis would eventually turn the engines back on, and he would laugh and laugh and laugh. I doubt that that's in any flying manual.

"Curtis must have thought I had the same point of view as he did on some of these things, like when I was in the pace car with him in Charlotte. Here we were, and he got it in his head that he was going to scare a guy like Joe Weatherly who made his living racing cars and used to race motorcycles. That's not a guy that you would figure would be easily scared. But in Curtis's way of thinking, he and I are going to scare this guy. That was not the program I signed up for. But that was fairly typical of the times."

Another time, Muhleman was at a race in Columbia, South Carolina. Tom Pistone was looking for a driver for his 1959 Ford Thunderbird, and Turner was looking for a ride. Buddy Davenport was promoting the race at Columbia Speedway, at that time a half-mile dirt track, and wanted Turner to run for someone because Turner was such a crowd pleaser. The factory boys at Ford also wanted Turner to run and offered to kick in some money to help Pistone pay for Turner to drive. These kinds of behind-the-scenes negotiations often were the order of the day at the time.

"Curtis was the guy everyone came to see," Muhleman said. "When he was in the field, it was electric. It was like Tiger [Woods] or something like that today. Or probably more like the early [Dale] Earnhardt, because everyone knew that Curtis would be very impatient about running behind anybody that he could knock out of the way.

"You could make a case for Junior [Johnson] being as talented, but it was hard to not think that Curtis was the best, the most talented run-by-the-seat-of-your-pants driver of the time. That was his coin of trade."

So at first Pistone was excited to have him lined up to race his Thunderbird that day in 1959. But as he began to think more about it, Pistone grew increasingly worried.

"I could see that it dawned on Tom that it's not such a good deal to take a few hundred bucks to have Curtis drive your car—if Curtis isn't going to bring your car back," Muhleman said.

Pistone's concerns increased when he noticed that Turner arrived at the track with a familiar gleam in his eyes, or maybe it was more like a glaze. It was pretty evident right away that Turner had already been dipping into his favorite prerace beverage: Canadian Club whiskey. Pistone approached Turner and promptly began begging him not to do what he had just promised to pay him to do.

"Please, please don't get in the car. I know you've had a few shooters. Please, Curtis, don't drive it. I can't afford to have it ruined," Pistone said.

"Aw, Pop," replied the ever-grinning Turner, "don't worry. Everything is gonna be all right."

Turner had just come from working his timber job and was still wearing a suit and tie. This struck Muhleman as odd.

"Curtis got in the car nonetheless," Muhleman said. "He had his helmet on, but he still had his suit on, as I recall. As amazing as that was, he still had his suit on. So he gets in the car and right away bumps a few people out of the park."

Turner was running up near the front, but Pistone was a nervous wreck. He figured there was no way Turner was going to finish the race at this rate, much less win it. He was proven right, but at least his worst fears weren't realized, as Turner lost his right front wheel and drove the car into the fence. The car was damaged, but not totaled.

Most drivers would abandon a disabled car when the wrecker came out to remove it from the track. Turner did not on this occasion. He stayed in the car and rode with it all the way to the pits, where he climbed out and proudly presented himself, suit and all, to Pistone.

"Well, there it is, Tom," said Turner, gesturing to the crumpled Thunderbird. "I told you I'd bring it back."

The shaken Pistone was incredulous.

"Tom was probably relieved that it wasn't wrecked any worse than it was," Muhleman said.

Turner's fun for the night was just getting started. After the race, he asked Muhleman to come along for dinner and a few drinks, as well as what proved to be an eventful ride to the motel in Turner's rental car. Joe Weatherly was to follow them in another rental car. They were driving separately because both had young women with them; Turner with his date for the night and Weatherly with his steady girlfriend, whom the five-foot-eight Weatherly had nicknamed "Short Track" because she was even shorter than he was.

"They're driving in one car and Curtis is driving in another," Muhleman said. "And all of a sudden, they start banging into the sides of each other like they're in a race."

Short Track was startled. Weatherly tried to back off for her benefit, but Turner was relentless. He kept trying to bash into the side of Weatherly's rental car.

"Joe didn't want any part of it," Muhleman said. "He would try to brake and get out of his way, and finally Curtis decided he wasn't any fun."

But Turner was going to have his fun, and it didn't much matter at whose expense.

"So we started slaloming the telephone poles on a Columbia street," Muhleman said. "We would drive up over the curb and then back down again, over and over. This was like after midnight or one o'clock in the morning . . . the same night Curtis drove for Pistone. Columbia wasn't that big a city at the time."

Finally, they arrived at the motel.

"I don't have a room here. Where am I going to stay?" Muhleman asked.

"Aw, don't worry about it, Pop. We'll find you a room," Turner replied.

But when they stopped at the motel office, the lights were on but nobody was home. Repeated calls out to the manager went unanswered. Turner, Muhleman and Turner's date for the evening went back outside.

"Why don't we drive the car into the pool?" suggested the young woman.

That was all Turner had to hear. He climbed into the rental and gunned it, but the vehicle got stuck trying to climb a hill that led to the swimming pool. Turner finally decided to abandon the car and the idea.

"Curtis, why don't we go back and see if the manager is back yet?" Muhleman suggested.

Turner laughed.

"Aw, no, Pop. Don't worry about it. I'm sure they got a room somewhere for us," he said.

With that, Turner started going from room to room banging on doors to try and find one that was open. After several tries, he found one that was—and a stunned Muhleman watched as Turner stormed in.

"This one'll do, Pop," he said.

Next thing Muhleman knew, Turner was firing somebody else's clothes out the door.

"There was somebody's clothes in there, and he just threw their clothes out and declared that room his," Muhleman said. "I went back to the office and waited for a manager and got my own room. That was a small slice of what it was like to be with Curtis back then."

It was remarkable that Turner and Weatherly never got arrested. Or at least that they never got into serious trouble. But times were different from what they would become later on, in an increasingly politically correct society that wouldn't necessarily jibe with the early NASCAR folks, as Muhleman recalls.

"That is amazing," he said. "I think, first of all, that most of the police officers [in the Southeast] knew them and kind of liked them. But the law then wasn't what the law is today. It wasn't as tight. But I still don't know the answer to why didn't they get arrested, and they probably did a few times along the way. I just don't know about it."

That is because Turner had a knack for talking himself and his buddies out of trouble. He soon would find out that he also could talk himself into it.

. . .

Big Bill France knew that he was onto something by 1953. But how could he get the sport to grow? One of his first thoughts was to build bigger tracks. Not just bigger in terms of seating capacity, but bigger in every conceivable aspect. Higher banks. Longer straightaways. Bigger, bigger, bigger. And the new tracks needed to be built on asphalt surfaces, not dirt.

France knew what the end result would be, should he be able to accomplish his goal: the cars would go faster, much faster. Some wondered aloud if bigger would be better. They wondered if the type of bigger, faster track with higher banks that France envisioned would be safe.

It was sometime in 1953 that France decided to build a "super-speedway" in Daytona Beach, the likes of which the world of stock car racing had never seen. He had noticed that, while the crowds for the Daytona Beach races had increased each year, the races weren't generating much excitement nationally, and it was becoming increasingly difficult to control the crowds of people who wanted to watch. In the first few years after France had turned the Daytona Beach races into something people felt they had to watch, manufacturers from automotive-related industries from throughout the country had dispatched countless numbers of engineers, mechanics, admen and public relations spin doctors to determine what it might mean for the future of their companies. By the mid- to late-1950s, their numbers had been dwindling—and that meant less publicity for a sport that wanted and needed it to grow.

France also was tired of sweating out the unpredictable weather for the beach races. He knew he needed to build a new venue that not only was bigger, but more reliable and less dependent on forces even he could not control.

Control was very important to France, and he had gained an increasing amount of it in NASCAR in a very short time. It helped that he had the precedent of a federal court case working in his favor. Hubert Westmoreland, the owner of the 1947 Ford that appeared to have won the very first Strictly Stock series race back at the old Charlotte Fairgrounds in 1949, had sued NASCAR over the disqualification of his car after Glenn Dunnaway had driven it to apparent victory. Westmoreland claimed in his suit that the governing body had no right to disqualify a car it had accepted for entry. Had he won, France's stranglehold on the sport might have been broken before it ever was really in his grip. But a federal court ruled in favor of France and his new organization, and NASCAR firmly established a right to enforce its own rules as it saw fit. More often than not, that meant as Big Bill France saw fit.

It took France nearly five years to patch together enough pledges to secure a $1.9 million construction budget for his dream track in Daytona. He founded a company called Bill France Racing, Inc., to oversee the efforts. Actual construction began in January of 1958.

Even after construction began, France needed to keep hustling to make sure of the track's completion. He looked for opportunities to secure additional funds whenever he could. Once he was attending an air show at Elgin Air Force Base in Florida, and he happened to meet Clint Murchison Jr., the son of a gas and oil magnate from Texas. The young Murchison mentioned that he needed to make a quick trip to Miami, but that he didn't have a way to get there.

"Well, Clint, I happen to have a private plane here at my disposal. Would you like to use it?" France said.

France went on to suggest that perhaps the wealthy Murchisons would be interested in investing a little money in his Daytona project. He could, he said, use a low-interest loan in the neighborhood of $500,000—which in those days was a rather staggering sum.

Murchison Jr. agreed to send someone out from his family's construction business to look into the matter. Shortly thereafter, upon the recommendation of the younger Murchison, France had his loan secured and was one step closer to completion of his dream, which he planned to call Daytona International Speedway.

The track was finished early in 1959 and hosted its first series of races in February of that year. True to his form, France had events set up for virtually the entire month, weaning fans off the beach races by staging some events at the old venue, but having them lead up to the grand finale: a five hundred-mile race for the biggest purse in stock car racing history, $60,160.

On the eve of the race, France told *Sports Illustrated* magazine that he was optimistic about his new track's future.

"Over on the beach, the good Lord always looked after us," he told *SI* reporter Kenneth Rudeen. "When things looked bad and we needed an east wind to send those big waves to smooth out the sand, we always got one just in time. If we keep getting the breaks, this track will have to be equal to any."

Others weren't so sure. Max Muhleman, who was close to several of the drivers and had moved on from the *Greenville Piedmont* to the *Charlotte News,* wrote in 1959 that France was ruling the sport with too much of an iron hand. It was beginning to infuriate many of the top drivers, including Fireball Roberts—the sport's most marketable star. Furthermore, they all had safety concerns about running at high speeds on the new Daytona track.

Was France selling speed at a price that might cost them their lives? They weren't yet sure.

"I wrote that now there were two dictators in Daytona Beach—Fulgencio Batista and Bill France," Muhleman said. "Batista had just left Cuba, where he had been a dictator before Fidel Castro came along. That was a time when a lot of drivers were beginning to grumble. Fireball was sort of the inspiration for that column. He was always complaining to me that it was hard for the drivers . . . about the way the rules were dictatorially levied, and some of the drivers were disagreeing with it. I was taking the drivers' point of view on it, and wrote about it."

France was not amused.

"While I admired the heck out of Bill France, it was one of those lines that comes to you and you decide it's too good to pass up," Muhleman said years later. "It did rankle him to the point that he flew up from Daytona Beach and met with my editor, I presume, to get him to fire me or to threaten a lawsuit or whatever. But I had a crusty old editor named Brady Griffith who was a classic newspaper guy and he explained the rights of newspapers and of a columnist who could voice his opinion."

Over time, Muhleman would patch up his relationship with Big Bill France. But what he wrote about France was pretty much true. He *was* a dictator—and it was, in fact, exactly what the sport needed at the time.

"That became clear later on," Muhleman said. "There really was no one I admired more than Big Bill. And we became friends over time. But I was a real young, dumb kid at the time, or at least real inexperienced. I didn't appreciate what he was doing until much later on.

"If nothing else, there were so few people writing about NASCAR at the time that it probably did some good to let Bill know that if you grow a sport in the public eye, at some point you have a media accountability too. The media wasn't always right and I certainly wasn't always right. But still, that was probably a helpful thing. It said to him, 'Be careful what you do, because what you do may be called into question—right or wrong.' "

And right or wrong, France's motives for building Daytona International Speedway were being questioned in 1959. Muhleman had mixed feelings the very first time he visited the place.

"My first thought was, These guys will never survive this track," Muhleman said.

He wasn't alone. Roberts privately confessed his concern, as did many other drivers. It was a spectacular-looking facility, without a doubt. There was parking outside for 35,000 cars. Grandstands were in place to seat 18,800, with portable bleachers available to accommodate 6,500 more. The enormous infield could handle up to 75,000 spectators, should the event take off as France envisioned.

The track itself was two and a half miles, built of a combination of concrete and asphalt that France liked to call "asphaltic concrete." The lap distance was precisely the same as the one run by Indy cars at the Indianapolis Motor Speedway for the famed Indianapolis 500, which France hoped his event would some day rival in popularity. Again, his critics thought this was a pipe dream.

The shape of the Daytona course, though, differed from Indy or anyplace else. It was a tri-oval, conceived by France to allow for an unobstructed view of the track from the grandstands. The track was banked at a stunning thirty-one degrees in its top big turns, and at eighteen degrees in the apex of the swift dogleg that would run past the grandstands. Asked why the degree of the bank was set at thirty-one degrees, France replied simply, "Because they couldn't lay the asphalt any steeper." There was no place else like it in the entire world of racing.

This was progress. But many didn't like the looks of it.

"I lamented the loss of the beach course at Daytona. A lot of people did," Muhleman said. "But at the same time, it was clear that there were so few amenities at the beach. It was just basic high school football bleacher stands—where there were any. And it was very hard to police. It was amazing that there were no spectator injuries in the years they ran there. How they secured the course was an unbelievable feat, just to keep people from wandering in wherever they wanted to.

"Once you saw a car go around the new track in Daytona, the impact was something."

Muhleman had been to Darlington, which previously had been the crown jewel track of the stock car racing industry. It was paved and had the high banks, which made it a legitimate superspeedway in its own right. But it was an egg-shaped oval, measuring only 1.366 miles around. Daytona was nearly twice its size.

"I remember going inside the first time and trying to find the backstretch," Muhleman said. "My eyes didn't know where to look. You couldn't see the far end of the straightaway. You had never seen a bank that high before. Darlington had banked turns, but nothing like that. It was an awesome thing. When you saw a car go on it, it was incredible."

It was also frightening, to competitors and spectators alike. Even to someone like Fireball Roberts, who was used to running hard and fast.

"That was still in the era when guys would blow tires," Muhleman said. "That was a strange part of racing there then. Everyone would be going along and then you would just hear this *boom*. And you knew immediately what it was. Somebody had blown the side out of a tire. And they would make these cannonlike reports. You would hear one of those and everybody's head would whirl around to see who it was, because you knew somebody was headed into the fence. And the harder they ran, the harder they hit. Fireball was a very hard runner and blew quite a few out. It was always happening.

"The tire technology got better and better as they went along, but in those early Daytona Superspeedway days, going fast at the risk of blowing tires took a special kind of courage. It took some real guts."

Driver Jimmy Thompson was more succinct when asked for his assessment of the new facility just prior to its opening.

"There have been other tracks that separated the men from the boys," Thompson said. "This is the track that will separate the brave from the weak after the boys are gone."

The first Daytona 500 was run on the afternoon of February 22, 1959. True to NASCAR form, it was embroiled in controversy, from the start of the race until nearly three days after its completion. The drivers were concerned because none of them in the sixty-four-car field, which included Junior Johnson, Curtis Turner, Joe Weatherly, Fireball Roberts and Lee Petty, had ever exceeded 140 miles per hour in a race. In this one, they knew they would have to. It wouldn't be long before they figured out how to go even faster thanks to the wonders of aerodynamic drafting.

With fifteen laps remaining, it came down to a bumper-to-bumper duel between Petty and Johnny Beauchamp. They exchanged the lead five times over the next fourteen laps before Petty moved in front just before taking the white flag that signified one lap to go. As they came around the track a final time, they encountered the ornery Weatherly, who would not get out of their way even though he was two laps down and had no chance of winning the race. The three cars tore around turn four and charged into the track's unique tri-oval with Weatherly's No. 48 Chevrolet slightly in front of Petty's No. 42 Oldsmobile and Beauchamp's No. 73 Thunderbird.

As they barreled toward the finish, Beauchamp slipped to the inside and attempted what would later come to be known as a classic slingshot pass. The three cars crossed the finish line almost simultaneously—and confusion reigned immediately after the checkered flag was thrown at Daytona International Speedway for the first time.

Johnny Bruner, the official starter, declared Beauchamp the winner. Big Bill France agreed with him. But in a poll of twelve newsmen who had been watching, Petty was the unanimous choice as the victor.

As Beauchamp made his way to Victory Lane, Petty was becoming increasingly angry that he had not been awarded the win. A smiling Beauchamp was photographed with one arm thrown around a three-foot-high trophy and his other around a Daytona beauty queen, unaware that Petty already was campaigning furiously to have France change his mind and rule him the winner instead.

It was reminiscent of the first Daytona beach race France had promoted, when he had followed apparent victor Smokey Purser into town and caught him tinkering with his car in a local garage—which led to Purser's disqualification. Or of the very first Strictly Stock series race in Charlotte, when France had disqualified the winning car and declared Jim Roper the winning driver instead of Glenn Dunnaway, infuriating the owner of Dunnaway's car.

Only this time, France did not immediately change his mind. Petty stuck around Daytona Beach for three days after the race, pleading his case to anyone who would listen. France finally did.

119

He called Petty on the phone sixty-one hours after completion of the race and declared Petty the winner. His average speed: an amazing 135.521 miles per hour.

Pete DePaolo, the car owner who earlier had registered a number of Grand National victories with Fireball Roberts as his driver and was a former winner of the Indianapolis 500 himself, hinted that France had wanted controversy all along and had milked it for every ounce of publicity he could get for the race at his new track.

"Let's face it," DePaolo told reporters. "Hollywood would have rejected a race script like this as too unbelievable."

Now it was Petty's turn to be ecstatic, and Beauchamp's turn to be furious.

But Lee Petty made a confession about running that historic race at Daytona. Talking later of the new facility, he said: "There wasn't a man there who wasn't scared to death of it."

Two years later, Petty spun out at Daytona and sailed right out of the new venue—soaring 150 feet into the air over the guardrail on turn four before landing in the parking lot. He suffered a crushed chest cavity, a broken collarbone and a broken leg. He would race only six more times after that horrible accident and never won again, telling son Richard at one point: "I feel like I'm working now. It's not fun anymore."

The superspeedway had taken the fun out of it for Lee Petty and many others. They feared for their lives. From 1949 through 1960, Lee Petty won fifty-four races—more than any other driver when he retired. He had worked on his own cars and driven them, but he never forgot how foolish he had felt when he wrecked the family car in the very first Strictly Stock series race in Charlotte, and the lesson learned there he put to use for the rest of his racing career: Save your equipment for the right time. You cannot win if you're not around at the finish.

As for retirement, though, Lee Petty knew when to get out. After his terrifying wreck on the superspeedway at Daytona that he never got used to in 1962, he knew it was his time.

Survival of the Fittest

By 1960, Humpy Wheeler was beginning to learn the intricacies of running a racetrack. While completing his college education at the University of South Carolina (where he played football and boxed before a back injury prematurely ended his athletic career), he spent his summers working at Darlington Raceway. When he graduated with a degree in journalism in 1961, he went to work in the promotions department of WBTV in Charlotte briefly, but soon found he was bored.

"There wasn't enough to do. So I went to work at this fabulous little speedway in Gastonia called the Robinwood Speedway," Wheeler said.

Marvin Panch, a formidable yet mild-mannered NASCAR driver and family man who was the opposite of the likes of Turner, Weatherly and the other party animals, had bought the struggling speedway and was trying to turn the place around, but it was an uphill battle. Part of the problem was discovering what kind of racing the fans liked the best. It was at these little dirt tracks where the fans for the bigger events were weaned on racing. They were all over the Carolinas, Virginia, Georgia and Florida in the 1950s and 1960s.

Wheeler got creative with the track's marketing, and that was a start. Among the drivers he promoted was one called Jungle Boy Lane, billed as "a wild man" from right there in Gastonia. He was a local and Wheeler wanted to play him up, to get the fans to take to him.

But he knew the truth about Jungle Boy. Wheeler knew that Jungle Boy wasn't wild so much as he was weird.

"Actually, Jungle Boy wasn't wild at all," Wheeler said. "He got the nickname when we were kids growing up together around Belmont and Cramerton. He became 'Jungle Boy' because he loved to go to Tarzan movies on Saturday afternoon, and then he would go home and put on shorts and run around in the neighborhood woods making that Tarzan yell and acting like he was swinging on vines."

Wheeler knew that he had to give fans the type of racing they liked best; the kind they could identify with. He also had to make sure it was affordable enough that he would get a fair amount of local Jungle Boy–types to fill his race cards, which seemed a sure way to bring in the local fans.

"Robinwood Speedway was originally a midget race course," Wheeler said. "A lot of people don't realize it, but in the aftermath of World War Two there was a fight between the stock promoters and the midget promoters. Open-wheel racing at that time was predominantly short-track racing with heavy interest in the Midwest and New York. So this track was built as a midget track with a high bank. It was very fast."

The midgets lost the battle with the stock cars because racing stock cars was more affordable and arguably more entertaining. That meant more people could do it, and more would watch it. But it took some time for the folks who previously had run Robinwood Speedway to figure that out.

"They had been racing some pretty expensive cars on there and it didn't work out," Wheeler said.

Wheeler preferred the modified stock cars and struck up a relationship with Ralph Earnhardt, king of the modified Sportsman division of NASCAR whose son Dale was born in 1951 just as the father was beginning to take racing seriously. Earnhardt's modified stock cars cost him roughly $800 and were built with various pieces Earnhardt would find at local junkyards.

Earnhardt would call Wheeler over to explain how he built his cars.

"See this '39 Ford?" Earnhardt asked. "It's got a teardrop hood on it. You put a Lincoln radiator in it and the hood will fit right over it. Then you put something between the radiator and the hood like asbestos and then you hold this by the front end with something like rope."

In other words, it wasn't fancy.

"If you wreck one, you don't have to think much about it," Earnhardt told Wheeler. "You buy the body for another one for fifty dollars down at the junkyard. And you can find the rest of what you need at the junkyard too."

Midgets cost about $3,000 to build and were more expensive than stock cars to maintain. They ran engines that couldn't be found in a junkyard and it proved to be a more dangerous form of racing than the stock version. Essentially, the stock cars were more durable and were safer too. It's no wonder that over time the midgets began disappearing from the short tracks in the South, while the stock cars continued to gain a stronger foothold.

"There was so much metal in those old stock cars that you almost didn't need roll bars because they were so strong," Wheeler said. "That was the economics of it."

That may have been the economics behind deciding what style to feature at a smaller dirt track, but Wheeler had much to learn about the sociology of racing. The fans were demanding and tough. One time a fan attacked the public address announcer, hitting the PA man in the head with a wrench. Another time a driver pointed a gun at Wheeler after a disagreement on a ruling in a race.

The driver not only pointed the weapon, but fired. And missed. Wheeler never was sure if the driver missed on purpose.

"The man is dead now and I always wanted to ask him that

question," Wheeler said. "But these places were rough. Number one, most of these drivers came from small southern towns. They were in the lower middle class. They were just above poverty. They were tough people to start off with."

It was a good thing Wheeler was tough too, as his collegiate boxing record of 40-2 attests. There were many times when he had to use his fists—or at least the threat of them—to settle disputes at tracks.

"There has always been this thing about a racetrack, where you can take somebody that has to be to work at six o'clock in the morning and gets off at two o'clock in the afternoon and everything is pretty structured for them. Now he gets to the racetrack with a race car, and he's his only boss. Nobody is going to tell him what to do. That's when all hell broke loose, when one of those guys didn't get his way," Wheeler said.

"That's also why NASCAR thrived. You had to run it with an iron hand because you had to lay down the law. If you didn't, those drivers would just take it over."

There were times when Wheeler witnessed that firsthand. One time at Robinwood, he had a handful of drivers block the entrance to the racetrack so fans couldn't get in. The drivers were angry because Wheeler had declared their vehicles illegal.

"They were outrunning everybody and ruining the entertainment part of it," Wheeler said. "So one night I noticed no cars were coming into the parking lot, and a sheriff's deputy came and told me what the drivers I had outlawed were doing."

Wheeler confronted the drivers and told them what he had planned.

"See that water truck over there?" he said, pointing to a huge truck that sat nearby and was used to hose down the track and keep dust to a minimum. "If you guys don't move those cars, I'm going to get in that water truck right there and drive it right through your little roadblock and destroy those cars."

Years later, Wheeler thought about that incident.

"Those are the kinds of things that went on at the smaller

tracks," he said. "This didn't happen all of the time, but you always in the back of your mind had the possibility of something happening. What you didn't want was the people sitting up in the grandstand getting involved in a riot. That's where the wheel fence probably saved this whole sport. In Europe at the soccer stadiums they had fences to keep the spectators off the field. That wheel fence served a double purpose for us back in those days. It kept the fans safe and it also kept them from going onto the track and causing trouble."

These smaller tracks represented the fan base for the bigger tracks that were being built. What was learned at that level could not be ignored by promoters such as Wheeler, and for the most part they weren't. But Wheeler, like everyone else in stock car racing's golden age, already was yearning for a role in something more . . . something bigger.

Curtis Turner felt much the same way. He thought he could see the future of the sport as Daytona International Speedway neared completion, and wanted to secure a piece of that future for himself in Charlotte. Bruton Smith, the longtime race promoter who had ruled his events with an iron hand similar to the bullheaded style employed by France, had a similar vision at the same time.

So on the same day in Charlotte in 1958, Turner and Smith made separate announcements of their unrelated plans to build a superspeedway in Charlotte—at, of course, different sites. The catch: Neither had the money to build the elaborate tracks they were planning. Much like France when he was setting about building Daytona, they needed to raise funding and they needed to raise a whole lot of it rather quickly.

It didn't take long for the two men to realize that they could not go it alone, fighting each other for resources along the way. If they didn't team up, there would be no superspeedway built at all in Charlotte. They would snuff each other out before either broke ground. So they decided to join forces.

"Obviously they saw the handwriting on the wall and got together to build a track," Wheeler said. "They were selling stock out of the trunks of their cars for a dollar a share to try and raise the money they needed to begin construction. It was a tough way to go."

Gradually, though, the pair began to raise enough money and secure enough loans to begin construction on the 1.5-mile asphalt oval track with twenty-four-degree banked turns that weren't quite as steep as those at Daytona, but nonetheless were quite impressive. As construction began, however, problems mounted and cost overruns soared. Unusually poor weather turned the site into a sea of red mud, courtesy of the clay-based soil and repeated, relentless rainstorms. The more they dug, the more they also ran into bedrock—which they had totally underestimated.

There were times when workers, who sometimes were slow to get paid, refused to perform their jobs. Turner or Smith occasionally would have to go out and prod them along. With only hours to go before the first scheduled practice sessions, one small strip along the homestretch was all that remained to be paved—but contractor W. Owen Flowe halted the work and demanded outstanding payments. Flowe ordered the operators of more than thirty bulldozers and other heavy earth-moving machinery to park their equipment on the short strip of unpaved homestretch and remain at the controls, but with explicit orders not to move any of the equipment.

Turner was furious, and again a little desperate. He sought the assistance of a local sheriff and attorney, both of whom declared that the dispute was on private property and that, if invaded, Turner had the right to protect it. Still, Flowe and his workers refused to move. They did so only when marched away at gunpoint by local law-enforcement officials.

"The sight of shotguns and a revolver had an instantaneous effect," according to Dr. D. L. Morris, who later wrote an account of Turner's life entitled *Timber on the Moon,* which was published in paperback in 1966.

Curtis's brother Darnell and friend Acey Janey then shorted

the wires on a heavy Caterpillar tractor that, once started, was driven by race car driver Bob Wellborn and used to shove the rest of the heavy equipment off the area that needed to be paved. That night, lights were set up and armed guards stood by—and the next morning the last bit of the track finally was paved and completed.

When the forty thousand-seat facility finally opened on June 19, 1960, it was overbudget and debuted nearly a month later than anticipated. The first World 600—NASCAR's first six-hundred-mile race on a closed course—had originally been set for May 29 but had to be postponed because the track was not ready. The fact is that it still wasn't ready on June 19, but the race was held anyway.

Each time cars took to the track, it failed to hold up. The fresh asphalt crumbled, large chunks of it flying every which way. This was especially true (and most dangerous) in the twenty-four-degree turns. The more Turner and Smith tried to fix the problems, the worse they seemed to get. As the holes were patched it created what racing writer Bob Myers of the *Charlotte News* called "a bumpy asphalt quilt."

The night before the race, eight hundred tons of asphalt were removed and replaced in the track's four corners. The new asphalt was covered by two thousand gallons of liquid rubber sealer, or "bear grease." The worries of the drivers grew with each passing moment. Daytona, they had feared, might be unsafe because it was too fast. Charlotte, they fretted, definitely was going to be unsafe because they would be going almost as fast as they had at Daytona but it looked as if they would be doing so while also avoiding chunks of flying asphalt.

Fireball Roberts took the pole with a top qualifying lap speed of 134.904 miles per hour. No one else in the sixty-car field came within four miles per hour of matching him, but even Roberts refused to sing the track's praises prior to the first World 600.

"I don't believe anybody could finish this race in a tank," he told Myers.

Ned Jarrett, in his first season of racing on the Grand National level full-time, said that he felt bumps that he had never felt before in all his years of driving.

"The race is going to be a real test of every single piece of equipment on the car," he said.

Crew chiefs and mechanics were so worried about loose rocks and broken chunks of asphalt crashing into the cars that they mounted shields on hoods to protect windshields. Fender flaps were attached behind rear wheels as an additional precaution, and wire screens covered grilles to protect radiators and engines from potential disaster. One flying piece of asphalt could disable a car or send it spinning out of control, which could then trigger a chain reaction of wrecks that might take any number of cars out of the race at any given moment.

Noting all the attempts at innovative, spur-of-the-moment safety improvements, Myers wrote that "the front of the cars resembled a steam locomotive's cowcatcher."

Lee Petty was in the field at the robust age of forty-five, and so was his son Richard, an emerging star at age twenty-two who was in his first full season of driving on the Grand National level. Driver Bobby Johns joined them on a three-car team backed by Plymouth. Jack Smith, the second-fastest qualifier, was entered in a Pontiac along with top driver Cotton Owens. Driving Chevrolets were Buck Baker, Tom Pistone, Rex White and Junior Johnson, while Ford was backing Turner, the third-fastest qualifier, his buddy Joe Weatherly, Tiny Lund and another talented friend in Banjo Matthews.

Petty joked with reporters that he needed to win to get back the $8,000 he spent on his three Plymouths that were entered. What kept all the drivers interested despite the obviously poor condition of the asphalt on the track was a NASCAR-record purse of $106,775, with $27,100 slated to go to the race winner.

Myers was there and later wrote of the event: "There was no waiting for the drama to begin. Cars spun off the track like tops in clouds of smoke, dirt and dust, especially on the frontstretch dogleg. There were multicar wrecks and at least one caught fire.

William France Sr., NASCAR founder and ironfisted dictator, ruthlessly guided his circuit to great heights. With Big Bill, there was only one way of doing things—his.

1

Once a moonshine-runnin' outlaw, the legendary Junior Johnson (here as a car owner) forever changed NASCAR by brokering a sponsorship deal with R.J. Reynolds

2

3   Tim Flock, one of NASCAR's earliest stars, celebrates a victory with members of his family. Big Bill France would eventually ban Flock for life for agreeing to join the aborted union.

4

Patriarch of stock car racing's first family, Lee Petty's dominance extended all the way down to, literally, the nuts and bolts.

Unlike many of his hard-runnin' fellow drivers, Ned Jarrett was steady and composed both on and off the track.

6

7

Two wild and crazy guys: Champion drivers and notorious party animals who lived as wide open as they raced, Curtis Turner (in car) and
Joe Weatherly pursued good times as hard as they did checkered flags.

8

Two generations of superstars come together as Joe Weatherly and a
twenty-four-year-old Richard Petty kick back in May 1961.

9

Glenn "Fireball" Roberts's Holman-Moody Ford gets a tire change during a race in 1963.

Ominous plumes of black smoke hover above Charlotte Motor Speedway in May of 1964, after a violent collision involving Fireball Roberts, Junior Johnson and Ned Jarrett. Roberts, whose allergies kept him from wearing flame-retardant suits, was severely burned and succumbed to pneumonia thirty-seven days after the crash.

10

11

Wendell Scott, the first African-American racer, found himself sabotaged by other drivers and largely ignored by sponsors, but persevered despite the virulent racism of southern society. More than three decades after Scott's departure from the circuit, NASCAR still struggles with race relations.

With seven points championships and over two hundred wins (including an astonishing streak of ten in a row in 1967), Richard Petty is now and forever the King.

Dale Inman, Richard Petty's longtime crew chief.

NASCAR glamour: David Pearson is ready for his close-up as he poses for a picture with (from left) car owner Leonard Wood, Virginia Senator John Warner and Hollywood diva Elizabeth Taylor.

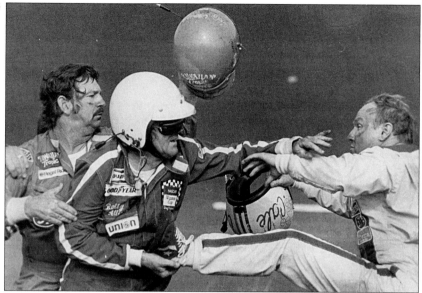

At the 1979 Daytona 500, Bobby Allison, Donnie Allison and Cale Yarborough whaled on each other in the infield as Richard Petty took home the checkered flag. Bobby is seen here thwarting Cale's best Bruce Lee imitation, while Donnie prepares to whack Yarborough with his helmet.

Bill Elliott, "Awesome Bill from Dawsonville," came from humble moonshine country roots to become a fan favorite.

Darrell "Jaws" Waltrip, doing what he does best.

Quiet before the storm: "the Intimidator," Dale Earnhardt, stands calmly by before unleashing hell in his No. 3 Chevy.

"Wonder Boy" Jeff Gordon and former crew chief Ray Evernham combined forces to dominate NASCAR in the mid-nineties. Evernham is credited not only with propelling Gordon to victory but also with revolutionizing the way pit crews operate. Gordon here is celebrating his win at the 1999 Daytona 500.

21

Gettin' out while the gettin's good, Bobby Labonte (pictured here while still driving on the Busch series) escapes from his burning car.

22

It's safety first as NASCAR veteran Dick Trickle sucks down a smoke during a Happy Hour pit stop at Bristol.

The stars and bars are always in sight at a NASCAR event. One of the circuit's dilemmas in the twenty-first century is how to widen its appeal without driving away its most loyal fan base.

Perched high above Charlotte (now Lowe's) Motor Speedway, longtime promoter Humpy Wheeler has been a part of NASCAR since the earliest days of the circuit.

24

2000 Winston Cup Points Champion Bobby Labonte and his son Tyler celebrate along with team owner and former Super Bowl–winning coach Joe Gibbs.

25

Kyle and Adam Petty during Adam's rookie year. Tragically, Adam was killed in 2000 in an accident at New Hampshire International Speedway, only weeks after his great-grandfather Lee passed away.

NASCAR's darkest hour: Ken Schrader (36) plows into Dale Earnhardt seconds after the Intimidator slammed into the wall during the final lap of the 2001 Daytona 500. Earnhardt, the circuit's greatest star, was killed instantaneously.

Michael Waltrip sits stunned in Victory Lane at Daytona after hearing that Earnhardt had been critically injured. Only seconds earlier he had been celebrating his first Winston Cup win in 463 starts.

28

A fan crouches at the makeshift memorial to Dale Earnhardt in the Daytona infield. Visible at the top is the wall at turn four, still scarred from the crash.

Dale Earnhardt Jr., who took NASCAR by storm as a rookie in 2000, now must struggle with the loss of his father while still racing on the Winston Cup circuit.

Joe Weatherly blew a tire on his Ford and crashed into the guard-rail. After leading 114 laps, Fireball Roberts threw a wheel and hit the wall shortly before the race's halfway point. Tom Pistone broke an axle; Junior Johnson ripped into a fence on the back-stretch. The asphalt broke apart and holes developed, causing broken axles, wheels, bearings and differentials and blown tires. Adversity played no favorites, claiming the high and mighty and the lowly."

As the big names fell by the wayside, a driver by the name of Joe Lee Johnson from Chattanooga, Tennessee, moved toward the front. At lap 250, he was running fourth. By lap 300, with one hundred laps to go, he was second. But he was five laps down to the leader, Jack Smith, who looked unbeatable.

Everyone knew, however, that anything could happen. And anything did. After he had led a total of 198 laps, Smith was un-done by a chunk of flying asphalt that ruptured the car's metal gas tank. This was in the days before the fuel cell had been developed. Members of Smith's pit crew tried to salvage the day by stuffing rags into the hole, but nothing could stop the gas flow. He was fin-ished for the day.

"It was a freak," Smith later told reporters. "In stock car racing, you never know what's going to happen, but sometimes it makes a fellow want to throw up his hands and quit."

Smith's demise was Johnson's good fortune. He inherited the lead with forty-eight laps to go and went on to win for only the second time in what would be a brief driving career. He would never win again.

Following the race, controversy bubbled up again when NASCAR, acting a day later, announced that Lee and Richard Petty had been disqualified along with four other drivers for mak-ing improper entrances into the pits. During the race, both Pettys had spun out on the frontstretch and proceeded directly to their pits without using the entrance to pit road. Drivers had been warned against making this mistake in the driver's meeting before the race, but no penalties had been mentioned.

Lee Petty was outraged when the penalties were announced, which cost him and his son more than $6,000 in prize money and all of their points in the season-long driving championship. He threatened to quit NASCAR altogether and withdraw his popular three-car team. Max Muhleman wrote another column, an open letter to Bill France Sr., pleading with the head of NASCAR to at least restore the points to the Pettys, who had entered the race running one-two (son over father by eighty-six points) in the championship standings. But Big Bill France upheld the ruling.

Rex White, who had finished sixth, moved into the points lead for the season and stayed there the rest of the way. Richard Petty, who ended up finishing second, felt as if the World 600 ruling robbed him of what would have been his first points championship.

Turner, meanwhile, had encountered bigger problems. Many of the stockholders who had invested in his Charlotte venture one dollar at a time were less than pleased with the track's failure to hold up during its inaugural event, which drew about 36,000 fans. When a much smaller crowd showed up for the subsequent fall race there, they started demanding to see a return on their investments.

All Turner could show them was a trail of red ink. He and Smith were out of money again and growing increasingly desperate. They couldn't pay their bills, which included numerous large loans.

Many felt that Turner's desperation boiled over onto the track, leading the daredevil to do things even he had previously not done. After losing the 1961 Rebel 300 at Darlington to Fred Lorenzen, a brash and handsome newcomer who happened to be his teammate, Turner plowed into Lorenzen's car in an act of frustration. Lorenzen had beaten Turner at his own game, shoving him out of the way on the final lap to go on to win the race—indicating that maybe times were beginning to change.

Turner not only figured he was going to win that race, but he was counting on the first-place prize money of $8,420, which went instead to Lorenzen. Turner had to settle for second place and $4,600.

Losing the winning share of that race purse limited the amount of bargaining power Turner had for securing more loans. Without more borrowed money, his beloved new track—less than two years old—was in grave danger of being closed. Turner was desperate. He went to see William R. Rabin, the accountant hired to maintain the books for Charlotte Motor Speedway.

"You do have an option," Rabin told Turner.

Rabin went on to explain that he had connections with some very powerful people who might be willing to loan Turner the money he needed. He was talking about the Teamsters union, headed by Jimmy Hoffa. The Teamsters would, however, want something in return.

The Teamsters at the time were attempting to unionize professional athletes, and race car drivers were no exception. They were willing to loan Turner whatever he needed, as long as he delivered what they wanted: they wanted him to unionize the NASCAR drivers.

Turner agreed. It was an act of desperation doomed to failure.

Most of the drivers, many of them uneducated, had little or no interest in forming a union. They did not seem to understand that to battle Big Bill France and his tyrannical ways, forming a union appeared to be in their best interests. The popular Turner overestimated his ability to talk the fellow drivers into following his lead. He promised Hoffa something he ultimately could not deliver—and to make matters worse, France got wind of his failed plan.

In June of 1961, Turner was fired as president of Charlotte Motor Speedway. His fate was decided at a board of directors meeting to which he had not been invited. Now he couldn't manage the facility he had come to love.

France had once teamed with Turner to drive in the Mexican Road Race, an international event covering 2,176 miles of rugged terrain. France had embraced Turner as one of the sport's earliest and most dynamic stars, and the two had considered each other friends. But Big Bill France would not tolerate an insurrection amongst his drivers, much like he would not tolerate drivers who ignored any of his dictatorial rules. He was pleased that Turner's initial attempt to organize the drivers, which was initially done somewhat informally and behind the scenes as Turner simply tried to feel out the drivers on the issue, had been met with general disapproval.

It was yet another victory for France, who continued to feel the need to stamp out anyone and anything that went against his decree.

"It was tough, particularly on what they used to call the outlaw circuit," Humpy Wheeler said. "There was NASCAR and the NASCAR-sanctioned speedways. They would pay NASCAR the sanction fee and then they started their association. NASCAR had a strict policy back in those days. If you ran a NASCAR track and then went to a non-NASCAR track and raced, then you couldn't come back without a penalty. Usually you couldn't race for a while. So what a lot of guys did is change their names to run at the non-NASCAR tracks, which came to be known as the outlaw tracks. They ran hundreds of races in the Carolinas during the embryonic times."

Turner could not change his name, nor could he run and hide from France's wrath. He was too well known. But he was not going to give up without a fight. He decided to approach the Teamsters again in an effort to get himself reinstalled as the president of Charlotte Motor Speedway. The union was still very much in favor of helping Turner out, but it stood firm on what it wanted in return. Turner promised to try to unionize the drivers again.

A meeting was held in Chicago. Fireball Roberts was among those who agreed to attend this time, along with Turner and Flock and a number of other NASCAR drivers, plus other representatives from various automobile racing organizations, including

USAC (the United States Automobile Club) and IMCA (the International Motor Contest Association). The Teamsters laid out their plans for the "Federation of Professional Athletes," explaining how they would use collective bargaining strength to ensure better working conditions. Targeted benefits for members included better purses, pension plans, adequate insurance coverage, a scholarship fund for children of deceased members and "upgraded facilities for drivers at the speedways—including shower areas and lounge facilities."

This time, Turner did not try to organize NASCAR's drivers behind the scenes. He was very open about it, making public statements that included the drivers' demands. He did not reveal his hidden motive, that he was doing so only in order to secure a loan that would enable him to make a power play and return to power at Charlotte Motor Speedway.

France's reaction to the public meeting was swift and left no room for misinterpretation.

"No known Teamster member can compete in a NASCAR race, and I'll use a pistol to enforce it," he said.

He met with the drivers and told them in no uncertain terms how he felt.

"Before I have this union stuffed down my throat, I will plow up my track at Daytona," he said.

Fireball Roberts withdrew from the union alliance immediately, followed by virtually everyone else. The only driver who stood by Turner was Tim Flock. France banned both for life.

Now Turner could neither manage the Charlotte facility nor drive in any NASCAR events. His lifelong party within the tight-knit racing community appeared to be at a sad and unfortunate end.

France, on the other hand, thought he had accomplished precisely what he wanted and what he believed was necessary to maintain order within his organization. He even mentioned that stock car racing "was one of the few sports which has never had a scandal."

In truth, stock car racing was scandalous in its very nature. That was a large part of its appeal.

The fact that there were no real widely reported public scandals (in the end, even the Turner attempt to unionize the drivers and his subsequent suspension did not rate as the big news it would have been in later years) was more than anything else a testament to France's ability to totally control NASCAR. It was not a politically correct sport, nor was it a politically correct time. There were concerns among other drivers, for instance, about party animals such as Turner and Joe Weatherly actually consuming alcohol *as they drove in races.* Drivers even met one time to threaten boycotting an event if Turner, who obviously was suffering from one of his severe hangovers, wasn't prevented from driving. But rarely did anything seem to come of it, at least not while Turner was at his best and remained a top drawing card.

Like many other professional athletes of the time, many drivers also had a dirty little secret. Humpy Wheeler noticed it right away. But little or nothing was said about it at the time.

"Actually, let me tell you, back in the late fifties and early sixties, there was a lot of drug use in racing," Wheeler said. "It was sometimes prescribed by physicians. Amphetamines were all over pro sports in those days, because a lot of doctors—serious doctors—thought they enhanced the ability to see and do things. Of course, over time that was proved wrong. But back then, that's what a lot of doctors thought."

Imagine the thought of Curtis Turner or Joe Weatherly or any other driver on a mixture of amphetamines and alcohol, plowing ahead at increasing speeds of more than 150 miles per hour. Yet in the early 1960s, these guys not only escaped condemnation, they were embraced as colorful personalities in the sport that celebrated the common man, flaws and all. France, though he suspended Turner because of insubordination, also sensed that it was time to begin doing some cleaning up. As NASCAR plowed ahead into the decade of the 1960s, France thought he knew where to start. To continue its growth, the sport needed the same thing

Turner had sought to complete his dream track in Charlotte: more money. That meant increased corporate involvement.

Long before the Teamsters sought to organize the drivers, the big automobile companies looked to form an alliance of some sort with Big Bill France's budding organization. Chevrolet was the early brand leader, winning more races than the others and bragging about their car's on-track success in full-page newspaper advertisements that caught the attention of fans and boosted sales. General Motors executives understood very early on that one of the keys to making a good car for the public was to take what was learned on a racetrack and then incorporate it into their car designs. If the car won at the track, this in turn generated positive publicity for the vehicle that later would roll off the assembly line and be made available to consumers.

In the mid-1950s, Ford Motor Company executive Bill Benton invited driver Buddy Shuman to Detroit to talk with design engineers about what it would take to produce a winning race car on the track. Shuman talked openly, and his comments weren't greeted with much enthusiasm. He was, in fact, talking about making design commitments before they would be tested on the track—and not the other way around as General Motors had been doing. Ford would take years to realize their mistake.

Benton talked his engineers into building two Fords for the 1955 Southern 500 at Darlington. Curtis Turner and Joe Weatherly drove them, but failed to finish the race, much to Ford's embarrassment. Herb Thomas, a highly successful Chevrolet driver, won his third Southern 500 and added to Ford's frustration.

Shuman eventually was hired by Ford to manage East Coast racing operations, and he hired John Holman, a truck driver whom he thought possessed great organizational skills, as his assistant. Shortly after Shuman died tragically in a hotel fire in Hickory, North Carolina, while there for a race in 1955, Holman was promoted to take his place. Holman was at Lehi, Arkansas, for a race in June of 1956 when Ralph Moody drove a Ford to what appeared to be a second-place finish behind driver Jim Paschal's Mercury. Holman protested the finish, arguing that Moody had completed one more lap than Paschal and therefore deserved the victory.

After much persuasion from Holman and repeated checks of the handwritten scorecards that recorded the number of laps each racer completed individually, Moody was declared the winner, and a friendship formed between the two. It was a union that would last for nearly twenty years and put a stamp on the sport, because in June of 1957, the Automobile Manufacturers Association banned participation in auto racing, citing out-of-control expenses. It was a stunning development, and it led to the formation of Holman-Moody. They would build the race cars that the motor car companies would not.

"The big motor companies were all involved in the mid-1950s—in 1956 and 1957 in particular," driver Ned Jarrett said. "They had factory teams. Ford probably had eight or ten cars, and Chevrolet probably had that many cars too.

"The word goes that at some cocktail party for the American Automobile Association, they all got together and said, 'Hey, we're out here spending a lot of money and just beating our heads against the wall. If you quit, I'll quit.' So they made an agreement to quit."

John Holman wasted no time in pouncing on what he perceived as a rare opportunity. He went to Jacques Passino, who had been head of Ford's racing operation, and offered to buy all the remaining racing equipment the company had in stock. For $12,000, Holman-Moody purchased an enormous amount of race cars and equipment. Over the next several years, their operation grew increasingly as they made a tidy little profit off selling the stockpile they had accumulated, plus the manufacturing of new racing chassis for anyone who wanted them and could afford to pay for them.

Working out of Charlotte, near where Charlotte-Douglas International Airport is located today, Holman-Moody's operation eventually employed 325 workers and produced countless race cars in assembly-line fashion. They sold for about $5,000 apiece.

Holman organized everything in the operation; Moody, his driving days now behind him, took care of chassis preparation. They streamlined and standardized parts so that they could be used on any car. Holman was a tough individual who said whatever was on his mind and often clashed with anyone who opposed him, including Moody.

But their alliance soon proved fruitful not only away from the track but also on it. They fielded teams that won a number of races and included drivers such as Turner, Weatherly, Lorenzen and Fireball Roberts, not to mention stars that would come later such as Bobby Allison, Cale Yarborough, Benny Parsons, Jimmy Clark and Mario Andretti.

What Holman and Moody really did was hold together the sport during the years when the big automobile companies bailed out on it. The ban did not last long. After all, this was stock car racing—and they sold stock cars. It was a natural if often expensive and uneasy alliance. Less than two years after announcing the ban, the automotive companies were looking for ways to get back in.

For guys like Ned Jarrett, that was good news.

"I was frustrated at the end of 1960," he said. "Even though we had won five races and finished fifth in the points standings, I didn't have any sponsorships. There was no way to make money out of it and no way to make a living at it. Fortunately, Chevrolet was looking to come back into the sport. They were already involved with Rex White, and they were looking for another young driver to become associated with. Rex recommended me.

"So I was able to get some help through them. Of course, they did it under the table through Jim Rathman down in Melbourne, Florida. He had a Chevrolet dealership down there and used to drive Indy-style cars. In fact, he won the Indianapolis 500 in 1950. Anyway, they gave me some help that I needed. I had a wealthy couple that was listed as the owners of the car, and that relieved me of the financial responsibilites that were involved. Between what Chevrolet was doing and little sponsorship deals that we picked up along the way, we were able to run."

The wealthy couple, in fact, spent very little of their own money. Chevrolet footed the bill for the rest. That didn't mean Jarrett was forever going to be loyal to Chevys.

"Chevrolet started easing back into racing behind the scenes in 1959, and Ford announced in September of 1962 that they were coming back and that they would do it out in the open," he said. "Ford said they were going to support four teams, and they asked me if I would be interested in being one of those teams. I said yes."

France was pleased to have the motor companies come crawling back to his sport. In their absence, the emergence of Holman-Moody had only made it stronger. Now it looked like it could survive anything.

"My God! Help Me! I'm on Fire!"

One little-known fact about the first Daytona 500 was that NASCAR permitted convertibles to run along with the traditional "hardtop" stock cars, because Big Bill France thought it would make for a more entertaining show to have the ragtops mix it up with the hardtops, even though the aerodynamics ensured that there was no way the convertibles would be able to keep up. Drivers were so skeptical that France enticed them to run in convertibles by offering a thousand-dollar bonus to anyone who agreed to cut the tops off their cars.

Marvin Panch was one who agreed to do it. A quiet family man who received little publicity because the writers always seemed more enamored with the party animals like Curtis Turner and Joe Weatherly or the former moonshine runners like Junior Johnson, Panch was nonetheless a competent driver who would in a fifteen-year career (from 1951 through 1966) win a total of seventeen races at the Grand National level—the same number of races won by the legendary Turner (although he was robbed of some of his most productive years by France's "lifetime" suspension in 1961).

Like many drivers of that day, Panch could use any bit of extra money he could pick up. There wasn't much sponsorship money available. By 1960 Junior Johnson had Holly Farms, Fireball

Roberts had Pontiac and Lee Petty was aligned with Oldsmobile and Plymouth; Ned Jarrett and a handful of other drivers had under-the-table deals with Chevrolet or Ford, and that was about it.

Along with Roberts, Panch was one of the first to understand the value of drafting at Daytona and the bigger tracks that followed. He and Roberts often would team up together to draft on those tracks, where two or more slower cars working together could easily outgun a faster single car that chose not to draft and go it alone. Of course, in the first Daytona 500, Panch learned the hard way that running in a convertible took away any aerodynamic advantage he might have had. Getting lapped repeatedly by the hardtop cars about every ten laps, it was all Panch could do to finish seventeenth. The first fifteen finishers were hardtops.

Recognizing his mistake, France never allowed convertibles to run with the hardtops again at his prized racetrack. Soon, in fact, the Convertible division that had featured so many great duels between Turner and Weatherly faded away altogether.

Panch wasn't the typically flashy convertible operator anyway. He didn't like to make a fuss over anything and rarely complained about his struggle making a living on the racing circuit, although it often was difficult. If anyone might have benefited from a drivers' union at the time, it might have been a guy like Panch, but he didn't give it a thought. He was cutting grass at his home near Daytona Beach in 1961 when Turner was trying to organize the drivers, and Big Bill France pulled up in the driveway.

"You gonna sign up with Curtis?" France wanted to know.

"Nope. I hadn't planned to," Panch replied.

"That's all I wanted to know. I appreciate that," France said.

By 1963, things were looking up for Panch. The big motor companies were beginning to pump more money into the sport again, and he was driving for the respected Wood brothers team from Buffalo Ridge, Virginia, formed in 1950 when Glen Wood, Leonard Wood's older brother by nine years, pooled his resources with five other men and bought his first race car. Soon thereafter, three of the original partners bailed out, leaving only Glen Wood and local sawmill owner Chris Williams, an intense racing enthusiast, in the ownership group.

Glen Wood soon became the driver of the car. It was not something he originally had intended to do, but he saw a fellow Virginia native doing pretty well one afternoon at Morris Speedway near his hometown, and thought he could do just as well. So he took his own car (not a race car) onto the track and did a pretty good job of keeping up with the other guy. The other racer was none other than Curtis Turner.

By 1960 the Wood brothers were well-respected in the racing business and were making a pretty good living at it. But that hadn't always been the case.

One time when Leonard was still a teenager, he and Glen were towing their 1950 Ford back to Buffalo Ridge after a race. Glen had wrecked badly during the event and the vehicle had sustained heavy damage, including a bent rear-end housing. On the ride home, the race car's rear axle broke and the gas-filler neck hit the highway pavement—causing the car to burst into flames immediately, right in the middle of the highway. Feeling helpless, Glen and Leonard Wood could do nothing but stand aside and watch it burn.

By 1955, though, enough good fortune had allowed Glen Wood to buy out Williams and become sole owner of the team. Actually, he had no intention of becoming sole owner, calling his outfit Wood Brothers Racing and eventually involving siblings Clay, Delano and Ray Lee in addition to Leonard, who was employed by the team from the start and went on to establish himself as one of NASCAR's finest mechanics.

The Wood brothers' real claim to fame in racing came in the pits, where they were the first to recognize that precise pit stops could pave the way to Victory Lane. Time after time, they proved they were the best in the business, even when everyone else started trying harder to keep up. Even in the early 1960s, they could change four tires and put twenty-two gallons of fuel in a car in just over twenty seconds, an amazing feat for the time. They were so good that in 1965 Ford Motor Company asked them to provide the pit crew for Jimmy Clark in the Indianapolis 500, where they astounded the racing community by doing seventeen-second pit stops for the Indy-style open-wheel racer. Clark won the race going away and gave much of the credit for it to the Wood brothers' performance in the pits.

Despite winning three Grand National races in 1960 and one more in 1963, Glen Wood soon was content to let someone else drive the Wood brothers' cars.

Panch became a driver for the team under unusual circumstances in 1962. His fortunes had changed since 1960, when he struggled to find a ride for just eleven races. In 1961, he drove part-time for genius mechanic and car owner Smokey Yunick, whose primary driver was Fireball Roberts. Panch didn't even mind that he had to drive Roberts's old car, a 1960 model, when Roberts went to a 1961 Pontiac. The car proved good enough for Panch to finish second to Weatherly in a preliminary event run before the Daytona 500, after which Panch shocked everyone by winning the main event two days later. Yunick had told Panch to run a half lap behind Fireball in case Roberts got involved in an accident or something else went wrong.

"That way you won't get taken out of the race at the same time," Yunick told Panch.

With fourteen laps left in the race, Roberts blew an engine. Panch was running second and Yunick finally gave him the green light to run for the checkered flag. Panch won going away and took $21,050 in race winnings—of which he was entitled to 40 percent.

Panch was thrilled. He was basically broke at the time and could use the money to provide for his family, which included two small children. Yunick called him over.

"Take fifty percent of the winnings," Yunick told him. "Anyone good enough to win this race has earned it."

Panch thanked him, took the money and bought a home in Daytona Beach that he would live in for the next forty years.

Henry "Smokey" Yunick was a master mechanic who favored salty language and was considered a genius around the garage, despite the fact that he never completed high school. He left school after the tenth grade to take a job for five dollars a week in an automobile repair shop near Philadelphia, where his family had moved shortly after his birth sometime in 1923 in Maryville, Tennessee. His exact birthdate was not known because no documentation of it could be found. He had discovered his gift for doing mechanical wonders when he was twelve years old and the horse he used to power a hand-driven plow died. After assisting with the burial of the beast, he went to work building a motor-driven tractor out of junk parts so he would never have to rely on the whims of an animal again.

Yunick earned his nickname in 1939 when he drove a motorcycle in a race at a local half-mile dirt track. The motorcycle performed well again and again in the weekly races, although it smoked heavily each time it took to the track. Thus, friends took to calling Yunick "Smokey."

He had landed in Daytona Beach after serving in World War II as a B-17 fighter pilot with the 97th Bomb Group. While flying over Florida during a training exercise, he told his fellow flyers that he liked the landscape below and that's where he wanted to live. He moved there in 1946 and soon opened up a place that he proudly called "Smokey's—the Best Damn Garage in Town." Not long afterward, he became involved with NASCAR.

But much to Panch's dismay, Yunick was only a part-time owner. Usually Yunick worked on cars fielded by other teams, and therefore he could not provide Panch with a full-time ride in 1962. That eventually led to Panch driving for the Wood brothers.

At the 1962 Daytona 500, Panch was driving for owner Bob Osiecki in a Dodge but the car wasn't very good and he fell out of the race early. Speedy Thompson was driving for the Wood brothers, who favored Fords. Thompson kept complaining about the car, saying it vibrated. He stopped in the pits and the Wood brothers changed the tires and did every other procedure they could think of, but Thompson kept complaining. Finally, Glen Wood decided he had heard enough.

The next time Thompson came in, Wood told him to get out of the driver's seat. Panch was standing nearby.

"Jump in that car and drive it for us, will ya?" Glen Wood said to Panch.

Thus began a relationship that would last for eighty-one races. When he returned to Daytona International Speedway for the 500 in 1963, Panch was driving for the Woods and had already qualified the car for the race when he again encountered an opportunity to make a little extra money for his family. A company that ran Maseratis at LeMans wanted to experiment with a Grand National engine in a Maserati and was looking for a test driver. Panch volunteered.

At first the Maserati didn't feel right, and Panch took it easy. But in the back of his mind he also knew that Bill France was offering a $10,000 bonus for the first driver to post a speed of more than 180 miles per hour, and he knew this might be a good time to try and do it. He spoke with Leonard Wood and they made some adjustments to the car, after which Panch went for it.

Heading into the third turn, the car soared airborne; it did not have spoilers to prevent such a calamity. It landed hard on its side, rolled over onto its top and slid upside down all the way to the tunnel leading to and from the track, bursting into flames along the way. Panch kicked to get out, but the doors on the Maserati closed at the top and were jammed. The fire quickly spread.

Firemen were on the scene, but could not contain the blaze. Panch continued to kick furiously to get out, and for the first time he thought maybe he wouldn't make it. He wondered what was going to happen to his wife Betty and their children.

About that time, fellow driver Tiny Lund and four others arrived on the scene. They had been walking through the tunnel when they saw the crash, and had come running, jumping over a fence, to see if they could help. Lund, a powerful man, helped lift the car just enough for Panch to kick open the door. As he attempted to scramble out, though, the gas tank blew. Lund and the others had to drop the car.

The flames grew more intense with each passing second. Lund and Steve Petrasek, an engineer from Firestone, ran into them with total disregard for their own safety. Lund grabbed Panch by one of his legs and jerked him out of and away from the car. Petrasek went temporarily blind as a result of his heroic effort.

The Wood brothers were left without a driver for their car. Lund had been looking for a ride—and if ever someone had earned a ride, it was Lund for what he did that day. The Wood brothers agreed that he should drive the car.

Lund not only drove it, but won the race in remarkable fashion. He outdrove Fred Lorenzen, the sport's newest star who was driving a Holman-Moody Ford, to win in what had been Panch's ride. It was the biggest win in stock car racing that Lund would ever have, and it could not have come under more dramatic circumstances.

"That is one of the all-time great stories in our sport, how Tiny stepped in and drove for Marvin Panch and won the 1963 Daytona 500 after basically helping save Marvin's life. It really was remarkable," said Ned Jarrett, who ran third in that race and was the only other driver besides Lund and Lorenzen to complete all two hundred laps.

It also once again underscored how dangerous racing could be. Marvin Panch was lucky to be alive.

Bill France's empire was beginning to show some more cracks about the same time. He was rethinking his "lifetime" ban of Curtis Turner and Tim Flock, two of the more popular drivers at the time when he drove them out of the business. For Flock, who was considering retirement anyway, it had not been that big a deal. But it was killing Turner, who still wanted to race.

The way to get to France was through the gate. In other words, if ticket sales and publicity for his NASCAR circuit lagged, then he would consider making some changes.

He wasn't yet ready to reinstate Turner in 1964, but some events that would take place encouraged him to change his mind.

Humpy Wheeler had by that time taken a job with Firestone Tire and Rubber Company as director of racing. He was only twenty-five. He was tired of dealing with all the hassles of running a small track and promoting races at other little speedways in the Southeast.

"I made a fair amount of money promoting races, but I didn't get to keep any of it," Wheeler said. "Lawsuits are what brought me down. I was always getting sued for something. I thought I was smarter than I was, I guess. But the fact of the matter was after working awful hard for several years after getting out of college, I didn't have any money. I felt like I was twenty-five going on sixty and sixteen at the same time.

"At twenty-five, the Firestone job was a dream job for me. I had been around the dirt tracks and I really didn't know what was going on. I mean, I knew I had to get some experience. Firestone at the time had the longest run in auto racing in the world. So that was great for me. I got a chance to see a lot of things. The time I was at Firestone was probably the funniest period in the history of motorsports. I saw so many drivers do so many crazy things. I got involved in every kind of racing there was, including Formula One. The Indy cars I was really involved in. At that time stock car racing was just getting going."

Wheeler had certain drivers test tires for him. He got to know others by driving to races with them. They often would take Wheeler's car and implore him to drive, but then would constantly harass him about driving too slow. Usually he was driving around 100 miles per hour on the public interstate highways, which made their complaints difficult to digest.

"We'd drive down to Daytona and we'd drive at night," he said. "We made some pretty fantastic trips down to Daytona. I think the record run [from Charlotte] was five hours and ten minutes. It was pretty fast.

"We would go as fast as the car would run. You could run one hundred thirty or one hundred forty miles per hour through some stretches of Georgia. We always had access to some pretty powerful cars. We made sure the tires were good on it, and we usually kept it to one hundred miles per hour. But driving with race drivers was a pain in the butt because they're the worst backseat drivers. They would always see things, little details, that you wouldn't even notice."

And they would always want to go faster. One of the drivers Wheeler had test his tires was Ralph Earnhardt. He recalled one conversation the two had, during which Ralph Earnhardt talked about the time he first got involved in racing. Martha Earnhardt, Ralph's wife, had been very concerned that he was merely throwing away the family's meager life savings at the time.

"She really didn't want that going down the drain," Ralph Earnhardt told Wheeler. "I promised her that I would never do that. I promised her that she would never be wanting for anything we needed."

Wheeler thought about that statement for a long time.

"That was a hell of a thing to say back then. Those are the days when they paid one hundred fifty or two hundred dollars to the winner at the dirt tracks. Those were the kinds of races he ran in," Wheeler said.

But Wheeler found himself drawn to this man, who seemed to possess more commonsense racing ability than most others he had encountered during his years in the business. Earnhardt had a common-man quality to him that other working-class folks seemed to identify with, much like his son Dale would exhibit later with his own fans. Unlike Dale, who would go on to earn fame and fortune at stock car racing's highest level, which his father could not possibly have imagined, Ralph tried his hand briefly at the NASCAR Grand National level, running part-time for a total of fifty-one starts from 1956 through 1964. But he rather quickly decided that it was not for him.

He never won at what later would be called the Winston Cup level, finishing second twice—including in his very first race, for which he also won the pole in qualifying. He never felt comfortable, though, and didn't like all the attention the bigger series attracted. Even though he continued to race a handful of Grand National events through '64, he basically returned to his roots and kept racing the short dirt tracks at Monroe, Concord and Hickory in North Carolina and at places like Columbia and Greenville-Pickens in South Carolina throughout the late 1950s and early sixties. Records aren't exact, but Ralph Earnhardt won more than 250 races at these and other venues just like them. It was where he was in his element, where racing was pure and simple.

"Ralph was taciturn. He didn't have much facial expression, and he did not talk to anybody much," Wheeler said. "And when he showed up to race, his typical deal was that he would show up at the track and he might be the only person with his car. I saw him many a Thursday night in Columbia, South Carolina, where he would show up in that number eight and he never got a wrench out on that car. He was always maximumly prepared with his cars.

"If it was a one hundred-lap race and he won it, he usually did it in the following manner: he would run second or third half the race, then he'd run up to second the last half of the race and then with three or four laps to go, he'd pass the guy and win the race.

"He didn't jump out there in front and stay out there. He knew how the game was played, and he knew not to run away with things—because that was when the heat comes down [and you would often get disqualified for something that may or may not be illegal with your car]. Ralph was my chief dirt-track, southern, weekly test-driver when I was at Firestone."

Their conversations weren't typically long ones.

"I used to call Ralph up and say, 'How'd the tires do?' And if they were really great he'd say, 'Not bad.' If they were awful, he would try to be polite and say something like, 'You might want to look into that a little bit more,' " Wheeler said.

"You had to speak his language or you couldn't figure out what he was talking about. It's just the way he was. He was very quiet, he loved his family and he kept them up as much as he could."

While Ralph Earnhardt was tearing up the dirt tracks, Fireball Roberts, Joe Weatherly and the rest of the Grand National NASCAR drivers were trying to compensate for the star power absent since the banishment of Turner and Tim Flock. There were times when they measured up; other times they did not.

Roberts and Weatherly were getting older, but they refused to slow down. Weatherly, in fact, was just beginning to hit his stride as a driver. He won the points championships in both 1962 and 1963—with his efforts in 1962 ranking among the finest in the history of the sport. With no Turner to contend with on or off the track, maybe he got more sleep than usual; whatever the reason, he won nine races (same as 1961) but also finished second in twelve others and third in ten more. This was back in the day when the schedule included as many races as could possibly be run, and Weatherly tried to run in them all in '62 and '63. He made fifty-two starts in 1962, and fifty-three more in 1963, when he successfully defended his championship despite winning just three races.

Roberts, by contrast, was picking and choosing where he wanted to run by 1962. He made a total of just thirty-nine starts over the two years combined, winning seven times and finishing second on five other occasions.

Muhleman and Roberts had become fast friends who were developing a close relationship, and were talking about writing a book about Roberts's life. Fireball was beginning to think of life beyond racing, or at least life beyond driving. There were days when he didn't seem to possess the same fire he once had.

Their friendship began one day at Darlington after Roberts had once again qualified on the pole. At first Muhleman, then with the *Charlotte News,* was in a group of reporters talking with Roberts under a pagoda that stood in the infield. One by one, though, the other reporters began to drift away, leaving only Muhleman with the driver.

"We had known each other a little bit, and we started kidding each other," Muhleman said. "Somehow it got around to the fact that I had run a good bit of track in high school."

"Is that right?" Roberts had asked.

"Yep. You don't run the track like a real man. You ought to try running it on foot," Muhleman joked.

"Oh yeah? I bet I could get around it in ten minutes, maybe twelve. Just how fast do you think you could run it?" Roberts asked.

Darlington measured 1.366 miles around. Muhleman thought about it for a minute.

"I bet I could beat you," the reporter finally replied.

"Let's bet a steak dinner on it," Roberts said.

Muhelman started to climb down from the pagoda.

"You're on. Let's go," he said.

Roberts laughed heartily.

"Wait a minute, wait a minute. Anybody who would actually try that deserves a steak dinner."

So Roberts took Muhleman out to dinner and the two talked long into the night. They seemed to have much in common.

"He was just a great guy to talk to," Muhleman said. "He was very, well, you almost want to say intellectual. He was really interested in politics, culture, art, wars, books . . . whatever you wanted to talk about. You know, I hadn't seen a lot of that in racing. Not that a lot of other guys weren't that way to some degree, but those weren't conversational topics with most stock car drivers in the late 1950s and early sixties. Part of it was just chemistry. We just hit it off."

They eventually agreed to write a book together about Fireball's career as a racer. They worked on it whenever Roberts came for a race in Charlotte, when he usually would stay at Muhleman's apartment.

Weatherly was not exactly the intellectual type. Remember, this was the guy who used to stay with Turner at a place called the Party Pad just across the street from Robinson's Bar in Daytona Beach. There he and Turner would keep score of how many women they bedded, which they called "chopping kindling." Weatherly was notorious for throwing back mixed drinks out of a huge vase that actually was the bottom of a lamp, and once was spotted at a Party Pad bash firing drinks into guests' glasses from a souped-up fire extinguisher. But Muhleman enjoyed being around Weatherly as well. He was a fun-loving guy who seemed to have a big heart.

Early in the 1964 season, on January 19, Weatherly was making just his fifth start of the year as he began an attempt to become the first driver to win back-to-back-to-back points championships. He was optimistic about his chances that day in the Motor Trend 500 at Riverside, California.

"Don't forget to put your shoulder harness on," crew members reminded him as Weatherly climbed into his car just before the race.

But Weatherly simply nodded and said something to the effect of, "Nah, don't worry about it, Pop. I'll be fine."

He went onto the racetrack without the protection of his shoulder harness. He didn't figure he needed it.

The race started and Weatherly tried to press toward the front. But early on, he ran into transmission problems in his Bud Moore–owned Mercury. Weatherly had to come into the pits to have a whole new transmission put in, and by the time he made it back onto the track, he was several laps down and was making circles only to gain as many points as he could for his championship defense.

Suddenly, on lap eighty-seven, something went terribly wrong. As Weatherly headed into turn six, his brakes failed and his car slammed into the steel retaining wall driver's side first. Weatherly's head, which would have been held in place had he chosen to wear his restraining shoulder harness, snapped violently outside the car and hit the retaining wall at high speed. He was killed instantly.

There had been horrendous wrecks and racing deaths prior to this one, including two in one family within a remarkably short span of time.

In October of 1956, NASCAR's top driver was Herb Thomas. He had won Grand National points titles in 1951 and 1953 and had captured an astounding forty-eight race victories over a seven-year span, more than any other driver. Entering the final four races in the '56 season, he was ahead of Buck Baker in the points standings and seemed headed for another title when Speedy Thompson ran him off the dirt track at the Cleveland County Fairgrounds in Shelby, North Carolina. That sent Thomas's car flying across the track and into a guardrail, which caused him to spin back onto the track right into the path of several onrushing cars. Thomas was rushed to Charlotte Memorial Hospital with a fractured skull, a badly lacerated scalp and massive internal injuries. He was given only a 5 percent chance of surviving, but miraculously did so after slipping in and out of a coma for three months. He eventually raced again, but was never a factor and retired in 1962 after ten seasons.

At least Thomas had survived. At the Southern 500 in Darlington in 1957, popular and talented driver Bobby Myers had run into a stationary Fonty Flock after Flock's car spun out and sat against the outside wall. Myers's car flipped end over end, metal pieces flew every which way and Myers was dead by the time rescue workers reached him. Fonty Flock survived, but never raced again. Six months later, Billy Myers, Bobby's brother, was running a race at Bowman-Gray Stadium in Winston-Salem, North Carolina, when he suddenly pulled off the track, stopped his car and died instantly from a heart attack.

But as great a driver as Thomas was, or as popular as the Myers brothers may have been, those terrifying incidents did not have the impact that the loss of Weatherly had on the sport. Weatherly was a star. He was colorful and dynamic. He was Curtis Turner's sidekick, blossoming as a driver once his partying buddy was no longer in the racing picture. He was the two-time defending points champion.

And now he was dead. The racing community was stunned.

Bud Moore did not know what had happened until after packing up his tools and heading back to the garage area, after which he was summoned to the office of Les Ritcher, head of Riverside Speedway. Moore had figured Weatherly was fine; that the car was just banged up, it had been a bad day and the team would go out and do better next week. That was the way racers and their teams thought. The really bad things always happen to someone else.

"Joe was killed in the wreck, Bud. His head hit the wall. He's dead," Ritcher told Moore.

Moore slumped against the wall. He was speechless.

That summarized how the entire NASCAR family felt. It was a dark day, and more storm clouds were gathering.

"It was a real shock," Muhleman said. "He was the first big-name driver in stock car racing who was killed. It was the first time any of us realized that even the best drivers could get killed the same way they did in Formula One or Indy racing. You just didn't think they could die at this."

On the eve of the 1964 World 600 in Charlotte, Fireball Roberts sat at a poolside motel with fellow driver Ned Jarrett and talked about what the future might hold. Roberts candidly admitted that he was planning to retire as a driver at the end of the season. He had lost a little of his edge. There were times when he didn't even feel like getting behind the wheel, he told Jarrett, and it had never been like that.

But Roberts was thirty-five, had won thirty-three races while usually competing only part-time and a major beer company had contacted him about being their spokesman. He was planning to quit as a driver after the season and take the job, which would pay him an annual salary of $50,000. He had never earned that much as a driver, with career-high race winnings of $73,060 in 1963 netting him the standard driver's take of roughly 40 percent—or slightly less than $30,000.

"Of course the money was low, but it was relative to the times," Muhleman said. "It was not as good relatively as it would become in later years, but it was good. You could win five thousand or six thousand dollars for winning a race, and those were big numbers back then."

Jarrett listened to Roberts that night and wondered about his own future. He was roughly five months away from turning thirty-two himself and wasn't yet ready to retire from driving, but knew that he probably had more time at the wheel behind him rather than ahead of him.

"Fireball was thirty-five at the time and we didn't know how long we could continue to go," Jarrett said. "We compared ourselves to other athletes in other sports, and they would start losing reflexes and some of the things that helped to make you a good driver by the time they were in their mid-thirties. Fireball had the opportunity to be a spokesperson for a big beer company for what was a whole lot of money back then, and that's what he was planning to do. I couldn't blame him. It made sense."

Jarrett wasn't the only one Roberts had spoken to about retiring. He had talked with fellow drivers Banjo Matthews and Neil Castles, good friends who had been hearing Fireball say some of the same things Jarrett did on the eve of the race that May.

"I've got plenty of money socked away and I've got this beer deal. I don't need to do this anymore," Roberts told them.

They all sensed that the thrill was gone for Roberts, who once had thrived on going as fast as he could and pushing the envelope like few others in their sport dared. Roberts also mentioned that he had been taking courses in public speaking and planned to supplement his postdriving income by getting into radio broadcasting. That way he could stay in touch with the sport he still loved without risking his neck all the time.

The morning of the race, Matthews assisted Roberts in putting on his custom-fit, tailor-made racing uniform. Unlike the other drivers, Roberts did not have his uniform treated with the flame-retardant material of the day because he had complained that he was allergic to it and that it made him break out into a rash. He also battled asthma and had complained that the smell of the fire-retardant solution made it difficult for him to breath during a race. After obtaining a written note from his physician backing up his claims, NASCAR granted Roberts permission to drive while wearing a cotton uniform not treated with the fire-retardant solution others were required to wear.

Even with the uniform cut to his comfort, something didn't feel right to Roberts that day. According to a passage later recorded in *The Stock Car Racing Encyclopedia* by Peter Golenbock and Greg Fielden, Roberts moaned to Matthews that he didn't feel up to racing.

"Glenn," said Matthews, "get your ass up and go get in your car and go home."

"I can't do that," Roberts protested.

"Why not?"

"Because all these people are here to see me race," Roberts said. He meant not only the fans, but also Ford and all his sponsors.

"I feel obligated to them," Roberts said.

So he climbed into the car and got ready to race. Early in the event, on just the seventh lap, Junior Johnson and Jarrett touched and set off a horrific chain reaction that would engulf Roberts. As it unfolded, Max Muhleman was upstairs doing color commentary on the radio along with Fonty Flock and Sammy Bland. Everyone was trying to figure out exactly what had happened.

"We were on the frontstretch, and the crash happened on the backstretch," Muhleman said. "We could see cars spinning—and then a huge plume of black smoke. It was obviously a gasoline fire, which was always bad news.

"I always looked for Fireball's car first whenever something happened in a race because we had become close friends and we were actively writing the book. I did a quick look for it, and I couldn't see it."

Muhleman exchanged knowing glances with Fonty Flock.

"It's Fireball," Flock said.

"Oh, I'm afraid you're right," Muhleman said.

Jarrett, meanwhile, was right in the middle of it the whole time.

"Junior was trying to pass me," Jarrett said years later, still moved by the haunting memory of the incident. "We started in front of Fireball. Junior got on the inside of me going into turn one, and we bumped together. Plus there was a bump in the track. Of course, we didn't have spoilers back then. You still had the air turbulence and it didn't take a lot to make a movement on the racetrack.

"Either when Junior hit the bump or a combination of that and the air turbulence caused him to move up a portion of the lane. I was pretty close to him and we touched and it sent both of us spinning. Fireball was behind us. He tried to maneuver past us or maybe he got hit from the rear, I don't know. But anyway, he lost control of his car too."

What happened next was horrifying.

"My car spun to the inside retaining wall, backward. And when it did, it burst open the fuel tank," Jarrett said. "As it skidded down the wall, it created sparks and caught it on fire. And Fireball's car spun to the inside, hit the inside retaining wall, also hit me and his car also caught on fire. As it headed on down the track, his car hit an abutment, an opening, in the inside retaining wall that was there to let traffic go across the track. When he backed into that, it tore the firewall and everything out of the car and then it flipped it upside down. That was before the day of the fuel cell. So that allowed the gas tank to burst open. With the firewall torn out of there, that allowed raw gasoline to flow inside the car."

Fireball Roberts was on fire, trapped inside not so much his car but a uniform that was doing nothing to help prevent a catastrophe.

"The difference between his car and mine . . . mine burnt up

156

totally also, but mine remained upright," Jarrett said. "The cockpit of my car didn't catch fire until probably a minute or two after I was out of it. With his, the flames went in there immediately. He was not injured in the wreck at all. He was in the process of coming out of the car when I got there. Our cars probably came to a rest thirty feet apart. So I ran over to help him."

When he got there, only seconds after the whole incident had begun to unfold, Roberts cried out to his friend.

"My God, Ned! Help me! I'm on fire!"

Jarrett did what he could.

"I grabbed him by the shoulders and we stood there on the track and tried to get his uniform off," Jarrett said. "But he was a class individual and he was wearing a tailor-made uniform, which was not good that day. It had zippers on the sleeves and zippers on the legs and on the sides. It looked nice, but it was very hard to get off."

Roberts also tore at the clothing, trying to get it off. Rescue workers arrived and tried to help as well, but by the time they got everything under control Roberts was burned over 80 percent of his body. Still conscious and in terrible pain, Roberts was rushed to Charlotte Memorial Hospital via helicopter.

Jarrett, who suffered severe burns on his hands while pulling Roberts from the wreckage, still thinks that Roberts would have been fine had he worn protective clothing.

"On whatever clothing we were going to wear on race day on the tracks that were a mile or more longer, NASCAR normally required all of us to dip it into a solution that they had that would flameproof the clothing," Jarrett said. "I still believe to this day that had it been flameproofed he would still be here, at least as far as that accident was concerned. Everywhere there was an opening—at the sleeves, at the neck, at the bottoms of the legs—that's where the damage was done. All the places where there were openings in his uniform, that's where he was burning. . . . We ripped his uniform off him by the time the safety crew had got there, but the damage had already been done."

Humpy Wheeler was in Indianapolis at the time of the race, doing some tire testing for Firestone at the Indianapolis Motor Speedway in preparation for the Indianapolis 500 that was to be run one week later. Max Muhlemen phoned him.

"Fireball has been in a horrible accident," Muhleman told Wheeler. "He is not expected to live."

Roberts hung on in the hospital for another six weeks. Muhleman tried to visit him, but was denied entry.

"Immediate family only," he was told.

There were days when he received reports that his friend was getting better. One of the interns who had helped give Roberts a warm bath told him that he had been washing off the gangrene and an upbeat Roberts had joked with him.

"Look at me. I'm the Jolly Green Giant," Roberts had told the intern.

Eventually, though, Roberts contracted pneumonia and blood poisoning after an operation to remove burned skin failed on June 30, almost six weeks to the day after the accident. Roberts slipped into a coma. He died on July 2, 1964.

Coupled with the loss of Weatherly only six months prior, Roberts's death shook NASCAR to its core.

Muhleman was so shaken that he left the newspaper business, never to return. He took a public relations job in Los Angeles with Ford just to get away from the suddenly dark, foreboding world of stock car racing.

Jarrett would race two more seasons, winning his second points championship a year later. But he never forgot the chilling events of the day when he pulled his friend from the burning car at Charlotte Motor Speedway.

"It certainly was a sad day for the sport of auto racing," Jarrett said. "Of course there were two good things that came out of that. It's too bad that someone had to lose their life to point out the need for something, but fuel cells and flameproof cloth came from that accident. Firestone went to work immediately after that and built fuel cells. Up until then, we just used the regular metal gas tanks that were used in regular cars. And DuPont went to work and developed flameproof cloth.

"So some good did come of it, but the sport lost a star too. It was so sad."

Muhleman saw Roberts's death as the end of a glorious era.

"I saw those guys in the late fifties and early sixties as absolute heroes. They were spectacular at what they did and they were colorful," Muhleman said years later. "I never once envied anyone else for what they were writing about when I was covering stock car racing. Ernest Hemingway was my writing hero at the time and maybe he had more good material, writing about bullfighters versus stock car drivers. But I'm not sure stock car drivers of that era weren't even more colorful than the bullfighters he wrote about.

"Make no mistake. That was an era of fabulously dashing, swashbuckling, daredevil, full-speed-ahead, face-to-the-sun heroes. They were fantastic . . . they had compelling stories to tell, and they were compelling stories themselves. Things have changed today. Some changes have been for the better and some, I wistfully say, we're the poorer for."

A White Man's World

The mid-1960s were proving to be turbulent times for the nation; American involvement in the Vietnam War was escalating, and antiwar protests were growing more heated. The civil rights movement was gathering momentum, even though it was still reviled in the Deep South. NASCAR, meanwhile, was suffering its own turmoil: by the end of 1964, Fireball Roberts and Joe Weatherly were dead and Curtis Turner, the third member of the original triumvirate of top stars in stock car racing, was still serving the lifetime suspension sentence handed down by Big Bill France for trying to unionize the drivers back in 1961.

It was around this time that Wendell Scott surfaced on the Grand National tour. Like many other drivers of his day, Scott had cut his teeth on short dirt tracks near his home in Danville, Virginia, winning more than two hundred races. Encouraged by his success, Scott believed that he needed to seek new challenges, and decided to try his hand at a higher level of racing. But there was one major difference between Scott and his fellow racing competitors: they were white, Wendell Scott was African-American.

NASCAR was a white man's sport in a white man's world, and there was little or no sympathy for Scott when his NASCAR efforts met with resistance. A handful of other drivers accepted him for what he was—a man, like them, with a burning passion for driving race cars and possessing the physical skills to do it at unusually high speeds. However, many hated him simply because of his skin color and tried to make his life miserable whenever he showed up at a racetrack.

Scott usually traveled to races at night, when he figured it would be easier to avoid the usual harassment he received upon arriving at a venue. When hungry, he couldn't walk to the concession stand like other drivers and order a hot dog or a bag of chips; black men weren't served at concession stands in those days, especially in the South where most of the races were being held. So Scott would head to a grocery store to buy food that he would bring into the track, only to be told he couldn't use the front entrance of the store like the white folks. He had to go to the back door, where he would tell a compassionate clerk what he wanted and it would be brought out to him.

Whereas other drivers felt comfortable leaving their race cars unattended at times, Scott never enjoyed that luxury; especially before qualifying runs, he had to stand constant guard over his car to prevent seemingly endless efforts to sabotage his vehicle.

He constantly battled financial problems; only occasionally would a minor sponsor come forward with any money, and opposing drivers were forever conspiring to put him and his inferior equipment into the wall on race day. They wanted him to quit and never come back.

But Scott refused to be intimidated. He kept quiet and kept racing with a dignity and strength that eluded his tormenters. Week after week, Scott showed up with his own car, having worked on it himself with patchwork parts, and tried to race with the big boys.

Scott usually maintained his silence when confronted by adversaries, but one time, he decided to do something about a long-time critic who had repeatedly attempted to run him off tracks and frequently shouted obscenities at him and challenged him to fight. As the two drivers passed through one of the flat turns circling the football field at Bowman-Gray Stadium in Winston-Salem, Scott's antagonist rammed into his No. 34 Chevrolet in a blatant attempt to knock him off the track and out of the race. After regaining control of his car, Scott pulled alongside the other driver and stared him down through the driver's side window. Then he slowly lifted a handgun to the window, pointing it at the other driver.

The coward never bothered Scott again.

Because of crushing racism, less-than-reliable equipment and having to maintain his entire racing operation with very little help from anyone else at all, Scott seemed to have no chance of winning on the Grand National level. But on December 1, 1963, on a half-mile dirt track at Jacksonville Speedway Park the unthinkable happened; Scott actually won a race, beating Buck Baker to the checkered flag by two laps.

When a race official told the beauty queen, who was white, of course, that she would have to kiss a black man in Victory Lane, she literally ran from the premises. Officials feared a riot from the rowdy crowd if they awarded Scott the victory, so they called Scott over and told him they were giving the win to Baker, even though they knew Baker had not won.

It was the most deplorable moment in racing history's most shameful chapter.

Even the battle-hardened Scott was stunned. This was a new all-time low. Had he not won the race fair and square? Had he not kept his mouth shut and played by white society's warped rules? Didn't he deserve this moment in the spotlight?

One month later, NASCAR covered its tracks by declaring Scott the official victor of the race after what it called "a scoring check." In a behind-the-scenes, makeshift ceremony held so as not to attract too much attention, officials handed Scott a small trophy made of stained wood that was thickly varnished. It was a bittersweet moment for Scott, but it did not dampen his passion for racing. He proudly displayed the trophy on a shelf at home and kept on driving.

He was his sport's Jackie Robinson with one major exception: even as times changed in the real world and Robinson, who broke baseball's color barrier in 1947, became a hero who helped change the way people think, Scott's tale went untold and ignored. It would be decades before the racing community stepped forward to honor Scott properly, and apologized for the hard road it had forced him to travel. Furthermore, whereas Robinson's entry into Major League baseball paved the way for countless other African-Americans to follow, Scott remained the lone member of his race to participate at NASCAR's highest level as a driver for the next twenty-three years.

Scott would race for ten more years after his one and only Grand National victory at Jacksonville, but he never again suffered the humiliation of winning a NASCAR race.

The mid-1960s was a troublesome time for NASCAR in other ways as well. The unfortunate, untimely deaths of colorful figures such as Roberts and Weatherly had been damaging enough—as had the retirement of Lee Petty—but two other early driving legends in Junior Johnson and Ned Jarrett called it quits too.

Junior Johnson hadn't quit running moonshine completely until 1959, according to his buddy Willie Clay Call, and Call should know; he stayed in that business until 1971. For Johnson, even a stint in jail wouldn't convince him that there was something wrong with the way his daddy and longtime buddies like Call had earned a living. Johnson's moonshine running had led him down a different path, but he remembered well the lessons learned outrunning revenuers.

"Moonshiners put more time, energy, thought and love into their cars than any racers ever will," he once said. "Lose on the track and you go home. Lose with a load of whiskey and you go to jail."

Johnson never lost with a load of whiskey and often bragged about how the revenuers had never been able to catch him on one of his moonshine runs. He did, however, suffer the misfortune of being caught by them while tending to a family still. Though he won five times on the Grand National circuit in 1955, Johnson continued working for the family business on the side. He came home from a race once during the 1956 season to find his father Glenn sick with a bad case of the flu.

"Would you go into the woods and get a fire started under one of the stills, son?" the father asked. Junior Johnson never said no to his father, even though he was a grown man by that time. "Of course I did what he wanted," Johnson would later say; it just so happened, however, that the law had that particular still staked out that morning.

"You got me," Johnson admitted when the revenuers emerged from their hiding places in the woods and arrested him. Johnson served nearly a year at a federal prison in Chillicothe, Ohio, for the crime, missing half of the 1956 season and all but one race of the 1957 season as well.

He returned in 1958, beginning a remarkable string of eight straight seasons with one or more victories, totaling forty-five wins. He won six races in 1958, seven in both 1961 and 1963 and had his best season in 1965 when he captured ten poles and won thirteen of thirty-six starts. He never did win a points championship, thanks to his win-at-all-costs-or-blow-out-trying style; his highest finish in the points standings was sixth in 1961.

"Junior would go as hard as he could for as long as he could," fellow driver Tim Flock once said. "He would never, ever slow up no matter how far he was ahead. If the car didn't break or crash, you couldn't catch him."

After seven starts in 1966, Johnson decided he had had enough. He still loved racing and planned to stay involved, but he didn't want to keep driving. Fifty wins had given him all the thrills he could handle and he wanted to pursue other challenges.

"I think I enjoyed working on the cars more than I did driving them. I kind of got burned out on the driving," Johnson said. "It just didn't do anything for me after I won so many races. I decided to turn the driving over to someone else."

Ned Jarrett was meanwhile deciding that he had experienced all he was willing to behind the wheel. In many ways he had been the antithesis of Johnson as a driver; careful with his equipment and consistency personified, he had followed up his 1961 points championship with another driving title in 1965. Whereas Johnson never made more than forty-one starts as a driver in any season he raced and often entered fewer than thirty events per year, Jarrett piled up the points in the championship race every year by usually entering fifty or more.

When he won his first points championship in 1961, Jarrett won only one race but finished in the top ten in thirty-four of forty-six starts. His best individual season might actually have been 1964, when he won fifteen races and posted forty top-five finishes in fifty-nine starts, but he finished second in the points standings that year to a young driver by the name of Richard Petty, who entered a remarkable sixty-one races, winning nine, finishing second in fourteen and third in twelve more.

Many believed that Jarrett's appetite for driving had waned after he pulled Fireball Roberts from the flaming wreck in Charlotte in 1964, leading him to retire two years later after making just twenty-one starts without a victory in 1966. But Jarrett denies this, pointing out that he believes his best season came right on the heels of the '64 Fireball tragedy. In 1965 he won his second points championship by winning thirteen races, finishing second in thirteen more and third in ten others; in thirty-six of fifty-four starts that year, he finished in the top three. He also won nine poles in 1964 and '65, proving he could run as hard as anyone when he wanted. But Jarrett's real strength was pacing himself, as evidenced by his performance in the 1965 Southern 500. Leading by a remarkable fourteen laps over his nearest competitor—

second-place finisher Buck Baker, who lagged 19.25 miles behind—Jarrett had continually turned his engine on and off during the final twenty laps to prevent it from overheating.

"I guess when you look at Curtis Turner and Junior Johnson, they were very dramatic to watch. And they were good for the sport," Jarrett said years later. "You need that type of person in the sport. It wouldn't do for everyone to have been like me or Lee Petty, although we would like to feel like we made contributions to the sport along the way.

"Back in those days, the equipment wouldn't stand for the way Curtis Turner or Junior Johnson drove; the technology wasn't there. But when they were in the race, they were fun to watch, and it presented an extra challenge to compete against those guys, the way they drove their race cars. Part of the challenge was not necessarily to be able to drive the car into the turn as fast as they did and still make it, but to beat them in a different way: by being smoother and taking care of your equipment."

Jarrett was one of the biggest fans of the wild driving styles favored by the likes of Turner and Johnson, but he was smart enough to know that it wasn't *his* style.

"Those guys on dirt, they were fun to watch," Jarrett said. "It was an absolute thrill to watch those guys drive on dirt. But a car will go faster straight than it will sideways. I was the type of driver who tried to keep the car as straight as I could. That was not very dramatic to watch. Those guys would be throwing that thing sideways and spitting rooster tails [of dirt] into the stands and that sort of thing; yeah, that was really something to watch. But the challenge to me was, hey, I could beat 'em. I want to keep that car straight because it will run faster straight than it will sideways. I figured that out pretty early."

They were two racers with vastly different backgrounds, driving styles and personalities, but when Jarrrett and Johnson decided to retire in 1966, they proved that different strokes work for different folks. When it came to getting to Victory Lane, their lofty career statistics were exactly the same: fifty Grand National victories apiece; when they retired, only Lee Petty had won more.

The departure of two more top drivers left a void in NASCAR. Big Bill France had noticed a drop in attendance at many of the races following the passing of Roberts and Weatherly in 1964 and decided on July 31, 1965 to reinstate Curtis Turner and Tim Flock in an effort to boost ticket sales, but it was too late. Curtis Turner had lost four years of his prime sitting out France's "lifetime" suspension, and Flock, who had been considering retirement when the suspension originally came down, had remained bitter toward France over what he considered his unfair banishment and had no interest in returning.

Turner, on the other hand, had begged France for years to allow him to return, but once France finally relented, Turner was no longer the dynamic talent he once was. He did, however, possess enough guile to revisit his glory days one last time in typical Turner style.

Turner made his return on October 31, 1965 at North Carolina Motor Speedway in Rockingham. It was the first race ever at the newest superspeedway, although the Rock, only a 1.017-mile circuit, was much more intimate and far less intimidating than Daytona or Charlotte. In true dramatic Turner fashion, stock car racing's original bad boy won the five-hundred-mile race in a 1965 Ford—beating out up-and-coming star Cale Yarborough and Marvin Panch for the victory. Yarborough was the only other car to complete the five hundred laps in the race, with Panch, who completed 498 laps, finishing third. Turner won $13,090 for the victory, but it was his last hurrah.

Turner continued to party with the best of them, but his wild lifestyle and his increasing age—he now was forty-one—had taken its toll on his body, and his skills had eroded. It wasn't like the old days, but his heroics and excesses were not forgotten; everyone seemed to have a Curtis Turner story or two.

Earlier in his career Turner had once stayed out all night partying before the Firecracker 250 at Daytona on July Fourth. The race was one of the few at the time televised on tape delay, and ABC was hoping for a good show. The TV executives were horrified when Turner showed up obviously drunk one hour and twenty minutes before the race was to kick off. They watched as Turner staggered into the garage area, still in a suit and tie, went straight to his car, got in without changing and put his head back on the seat; almost immediately he was asleep, snoring loudly. At the time Turner was still considered one of NASCAR's top draws, and ABC wanted him to race, but as they left the garage area, the TV folks grumbled to each other in disgust.

"There's no way that guy is going to go off in this race," one of them said.

An hour and fifteen minutes later, Turner's pit crew woke him and made him put on at least a fire-retardant race suit over his party clothes. He rubbed his eyes, shook the cobwebs from his numbed brain and nodded.

"Let's race," he mumbled.

Remarkably, he ran near the front for much of the race before falling out. Bill France briefly suspended him again for alcohol abuse, but his offense was not the affront that it would be for a driver today.

By Turner's return to the arena after his so-called lifetime suspension, he could only occasionally give both fans and TV executives the show they really wanted. Realizing his skills were slipping, Turner made only one more half-serious run at returning to his old form, making twenty-one starts in 1966, failing to win a single race and finishing in the top five only four times. He started the combined total of only ten more races over the next two seasons before retiring for good after posting seventeen career victories and seventeen poles at the Grand National level.

Turner soon announced that he would pursue a new athletic career as a golfer, and no one doubted that he would be able to hustle a buck or two between drinks at the golf course. But on October 4, 1970, Turner died along with golf pro Clarence King when the private airplane they were flying in, an Aerocommander owned by Turner, crashed into the side of a mountain near Punxsutawney, Pennsylvania. Turner, the expert flyer, was not at the controls—leading many in the racing world to believe that he left King to pilot the plane while he retired to the back of the plane to sleep off his latest hangover. Turner's body was discovered half a city block away from the wreckage in the woods. King was found strapped into the pilot's seat; he was believed to have suffered a heart attack while at the controls.

With the departure of so many top names, there could not have been a better time for Richard Petty to emerge as a top driver. Lee Petty's son had been coming on since the beginning of the decade, but it wasn't until 1964 that he won the first of what would be a record seven points championships. By then he had already finished second in the points race on three occasions, including both the 1962 and 1963 seasons, when he won a combined twenty-two races in ninety-six starts. Lee Petty had taught his son well, beginning with the hard lesson learned in that first Strictly Stock series race back in Charlotte in 1949 when Lee Petty wrecked the family car, leaving them without a ride home to nearby Level Cross.

To understand the Petty racing family, one must first understand the no-nonsense Lee Petty, the racing family's unquestioned patriarch. Lee Petty grew up farming, not racing; during the Great Depression, he sold biscuits to survive and later owned a small trucking business. He did not lead a wild life like Turner and Weatherly and so many other early drivers; he was a committed family man who was deadly serious about doing whatever it took to win races.

In the mid-1950s he had fixed his Oldsmobile up with wing nuts and armored plating on the sides, so that anytime he brushed up against an opponent he would shred the opposing car's sheet metal—or, if he was really fortunate, its tires, which could cause an accident that would take the opponent out of the race altogether. As racing historians Greg Fielden and Peter Golenbock wrote in their *Stock Car Racing Encyclopedia,* "Charlton Heston's enemy had done that to him during the chariot race in *Ben-Hur;* Lee Petty did it for real."

Early on Richard Petty learned hard racing from his father. Once during a race on an old dirt track in High Point, North Carolina, a young Richard was working as a member of his father's pit crew; he would climb up onto the hood to wipe the mud off the windshield as the rest of the crew worked to change tires and put gas in the car. Once, after the tires had been changed and the car had been refueled, Lee Petty mashed the pedal to the floor and charged back onto the track—with a terrified Richard still clinging to the hood of the car, holding on for dear life. Lee Petty drove one lap around the track before depositing his frightened son back in the pits, later cussing the boy out for not getting out of the way fast enough after getting the windshield wiped. Richard was twelve or thirteen at the time; by the time he was fourteen he was considered his daddy's crew chief and he knew exactly what to do.

By then Lee Petty was completely out of farming and racing was the family's full-time business. "Everyone around us, they were farmers, so they would come home and milk the cows and plow the fields," Richard Petty once told Mark Bechtel of *Sports Illustrated.* "I'd go to school and then come home and work on race cars."

By 1958, Richard, only twenty, was driving against stock car racing's top competition. In his very first start at the Grand National level, Lee Petty taught young Richard yet another lesson: as they jostled for position on the track, dad ran son right into the wall, knocking him right out of the race. Lee Petty went on to take the victory.

As Richard celebrated what he thought was his first NASCAR victory at Jacksonville Speedway Park in November of 1960, his father was behind the scenes protesting that his oldest son had actually been one or more laps down when the checkered flag was waved. Race officials looked into it and decided that Lee Petty was right and awarded the win to the runner-up—Lee Petty. Richard Petty was credited with 197 laps completed in the two-hundred-lap event and was awarded a fourth-place finish.

Both Pettys drove for Petty Enterprises, and Lee Petty, a frugal man, actually cost the family first- and second-place money by protesting. The money then was modest, however: Lee Petty ended up with $800 for winning while he would have earned $525 for second place behind Richard, whose fourth-place prize was a mere $275.

Richard credited much of his rising popularity in the mid-1960s to the fact that he drove a Plymouth. There was at the time an intense rivalry between Ford and Chevrolet, even amongst fans, and Petty reasoned that when a Ford driver fell out of a race, there was no way that a Ford fan was going to pull for someone driving a Chevrolet, and vice versa. Therefore, they almost always would pull for the guy in the No. 43 Plymouth by default. Eventually fans rooted for Petty so often that many ended up sticking with him as their primary driver.

In truth, the Plymouth engines weren't as powerful as those developed by Ford and Chevy; Petty would do fine on the short tracks, but he often got blown away by Junior Johnson's Chevys or Fred Lorenzen's Fords on the superspeedways. That changed in 1964 when Plymouth gave him a 426-cubic-inch hemi called King Kong. To illustrate how powerful the engine was, Petty's qualifying speed for the '64 Daytona 500 was 174.418 miles per hour—obliterating the previous qualifying record by more than thirteen miles an hour. He rolled to thirty-seven top-five finishes in sixty-one starts that season and thought he now had what it took to run with the big boys no matter where they went racin'.

But Bill France burst his bubble, announcing that King Kong would be outlawed for the following 1965 season, arguing that it wasn't a "generally available production motor."

Chrysler and Petty Enterprises were furious. Chrysler responded by pulling out of NASCAR altogether and Richard Petty said that he would refuse to drive any other make of car. In an additional form of protest, Petty dropped the hemi engine into a dragster, painted OUTLAWED on the side of it in large block letters and raced it all over the South for $1,000 per night in appearance money.

One night in Georgia, tragedy struck when Petty lost control of the dragster and it soared into the stands, killing a young fan. For a time, Richard Petty was distraught; the death of the young fan gnawed at him, as did NASCAR's actions against him. He was pleased when a compromise was reached between Chrysler and NASCAR prior to the 1966 season, allowing him to return full-time to the Grand National circuit after he ran only a very limited schedule in 1965 with old Plymouths, still managing to win four of his fourteen starts.

By 1967, long after his father had retired as a driver and the likes of Junior Johnson, Ned Jarrett, Curtis Turner, Fireball Roberts and Joe Weatherly were absent from drivers' seats as well, Richard Petty won a remarkable twenty-seven of forty-eight starts. He won ten in a row during one stretch, establishing a NASCAR record that probably will never be broken. Though many of his wins came on short tracks against lesser competition during an era when there were as many as sixty Grand National events in a season, they were still legitimate victories, and his race winnings exceeded $150,000. Petty's magnificent run began only four years after Fred Lorenzen (dubbed "the Golden Boy" because it was anticipated that *he* would become the sport's next huge star) had stunned the racing world by becoming the first driver to collect more than $100,000 in winnings during the 1963 season.

It wasn't solely Richard Petty's dominance, though, that made him—rather than Lorenzen—the megastar NASCAR so desperately needed at the time. Instead, it was the way Richard Petty carried himself, especially around his growing number of adoring fans, that earned him the nickname "the King."

He had a way of endearing himself to anyone he met, talking with reporters whenever they wanted and mingling with fans. He was the first driver to assiduously sign autographs and fans flocked to him for the chance to chat him up and come away with more than just a signature. After meeting Petty they felt like they knew him, if only a little, and that meant a lot.

"You've got to figure, the first race I drove in, I think one person asked for an autograph and I thought that was a big deal," Petty said years later. "The second race, it was two people. The tenth race, ten people, and then soon it got to be hundreds. One day I'm sitting in the grandstand, and then the next day I'm signing autographs. I grew into it and never really thought about it. I just figured that's the way it's supposed to be."

Without knowing it, Petty grew into the role of his sport's greatest ambassador at a time when one was needed so desperately. There were other great drivers who arrived at about the same time: David Pearson, Cale Yarborough and Bobby Allison, to name a few, and they became the next generation of stars, assuming the mantle from Johnson and Jarrett, Roberts and Turner. But it was Richard Petty who led the way.

For the next three decades and beyond, he would set the standard for style on the track and sportsmanship away from it, never losing sight of the fact that the fans were putting money in his pocket. The King's philosophy was simple: That guy who paid for a ticket to sit in the stands and watch the race isn't much different than I am, so I'd better pay attention to him and show him some decency and respect.

"The deal is like this: I think you have all these guys, all these drivers, and they all worked to get where they're at. They're common people," Richard Petty said. "None of them were born with silver spoons in their mouth and just got put out there in the driver's seat on the track. So I think the fans think these are hard-working people like themselves. I think they can identify with those guys because they think they're their kind of people. They're not on a different platform."

Richard Petty was careful never to act like he was superior to his fellow racers, even when he began winning more races than anyone else, making a habit of walking around the garage area before each event and talking with virtually every driver and crew member.

Driver Benny Parsons remembers his first event at Asheville-Weaverville Speedway in North Carolina in 1963: he had heard of Richard Petty and respected the family name, and was more than a little nervous about trying out for a full-time Grand National ride under the watchful eyes of Holman-Moody and Ford Motor Company. Parsons was sitting in his race car shortly before the event was to begin when Richard Petty walked up and stuck his hand out. "Hi, I'm Richard Petty. Who are you?" Petty asked Parsons as the two shook hands. Parsons had been around racing long enough to know how cutthroat the competition could be at most places, and he was stunned by Petty's friendly gesture, but Petty thought nothing of it.

"I was twenty-two years old at the time, a nobody," Parsons said. "You would have thought that Richard Petty had better things to do than to walk around before a race and introduce himself to a nobody like me. I've never forgotten that he took the time to do that. Since then, I've always been a Richard Petty fan."

Petty continued to be so accommodating until both he and the sport grew so big that it became impossible to make the rounds before the race without getting mobbed.

"It was a deal where you could do it because there weren't that many people around," Petty said. "I'd go around and talk to all the owners, all the drivers, all the crews. That was just me. Everybody didn't do it, but some others did. I just liked that. That was my personality. It's an unwritten rule of how you're supposed to conduct yourself with the media and the fans. It builds on itself and it has helped make the sport popular."

Richard Petty's popularity would continue to grow, and he maintains decades later that his fan appeal increased because he was able to defy France's iron-fisted control of the NASCAR Grand National circuit.

"This is not NASCAR we're talking about; this is personnel,"

Petty said. "NASCAR can't dictate to the driver or the crews on how to act, how to dress. They've never approached that. It's a good thing they don't—because the drivers . . . don't like to be told what to do all of the time.

"The thing is, a new driver coming in is going to follow the way I did things. . . . They pick somebody out and say, 'He's done it. He's made a success out of himself and that's how he has handled himself. That's the way we're going to do it.' "

Meanwhile, Big Bill France was by the end of the 1960s moving ahead with plans to add yet another superspeedway—this time in Talladega, Alabama. Drivers, Richard Petty included, were skeptical about the plans for this new track; as if it were possible, it seemed Talladega would be more dangerous than any track built before it, and they didn't share France's enthusiasm for the new venue.

France vs. Petty

In time, Benny Parsons was one of the new driving stars himself; and the affable Parsons would eventually become one of the sport's great ambassadors as an announcer on NASCAR telecasts. But before he moved to the broadcasting booth, Parsons established himself as a driving legend.

In the late 1960s, Parsons was just beginning to make a name for himself. An early media favorite because of his interesting background, Parsons was a native, appropriately enough, of Parsonsville, North Carolina. When Benny was a child, work in North Carolinian Appalachia was difficult to find and Harold Parsons, Benny's father, eventually left the area along with wife Hazel to find employment in Detroit. It was a move that would later pay off for Benny's racing career, but as a boy the move saddened him; he told his parents that he did not want to move and they agreed to let him stay behind in the care of Julia Parsons, his great-grandmother.

They lived together in a clapboard house built in 1890. There was no electricity or running water—although, when he was nine, Benny Parsons climbed the hill behind the house and dug a ditch that allowed him to at least run a gravity-fed water line into the home.

"We dug a trench and built a reservoir and we did have some running water then. But there was no pump, so there were no toilet facilities. We had an outhouse," Parsons said.

The young Parsons intensely admired his great-grandmother, and he kept busy raising chickens and pigs. He also farmed an acre of land and tended to a cow that provided much-needed milk. If coffee, sugar or salt were required, Benny would trade eggs for those "luxuries," which is what he and Julia Parsons considered them.

It was a spartan existence, but it was all Parsons knew, and he remained happy, coming to believe that those hardships helped shape his character.

"It was the way life was for me at the time," he said years later. "I didn't know any different. You know, I guess in a perfect world it would have been different for me. But it's not a perfect world. I may have turned out better off because of it."

Benny Parsons's parents made certain that he knew they had not abandoned him, staying in touch by telephone and letters. Shortly after completing the gravity-fed water line into the house in the summer of 1950, Benny and his great-grandmother excitedly left for Detroit to visit Benny's parents. It opened young Benny's eyes to a whole new world—one that included electricity, televisions, indoor plumbing, bathrooms and cars. Especially cars.

Harold Parsons had a love for cars and racing that he quickly passed on to Benny; occasionally he would come home and take Benny to Hickory Motor Speedway or to the track in North Wilkesboro to see a race. "When I was in sixth grade, we started going to Detroit and spending the summers there," Parsons said. "We went to the races every Friday night up there. It was a quarter-mile dirt track—a quarter-mile, oil-soaked dirt track. They'd start the feature three abreast—three abreast on a quarter-mile track! When they made it through the first corner, I was crushed. I just knew I was going to see a bunch of wrecks."

Benny Parsons liked racing, but it was not all he enjoyed. His father bought him a battery-powered radio that he could listen to even after he returned home to North Carolina in the fall and there was no electricity. Each fall he left the modern luxuries of Detroit behind and returned to the home in Parsonsville, where kerosene lighting and outhouses were ways of life. Now, though, he had his beloved radio with him, and he could take a little piece of the world with him back to the hills of North Carolina. "Racing wasn't the only sport I took a liking to at the time," Parsons said. "In football season, you also are listening to the radio and Notre Dame is playing football and you want to be the quarterback for Notre Dame. In baseball season you want to be another Ted Williams. I never got into basketball, but I'd listen to football and baseball on the radio and you'd envision yourself playing those sports."

Like many young folks his age at the time, he did not know what he wanted to do after high school; he tried college, but lasted only one semester at North Carolina State in nearby Raleigh. "I just wasted my daddy's money," he said. "But at least I realized I was wasting my daddy's money. So I went to Detroit and went to work for Chevrolet in one of those plants up there. I worked five weeks and got laid off."

By then his father was reasonably well-established in the Detroit area, owning a gas station and a taxicab service that included "fifteen or twenty cabs," according to Benny. He went to work for his father for the next eighteen months, learning as much as he could about his father's business. Chevrolet called Benny back to work and he returned to the plant for a while, but left again when his father asked him to come work for him full-time.

"I went to work as a mechanic, changing oil and changing tires." Parsons recalled. "I did whatever it took as far as the mechanical aspects of keeping those cabs running. I did also have my cab driver's license because I had to road test those cars. On holidays, when drivers were hard to find, my dad and I would both go out and drive and try to service the customers. But my primary job was being a mechanic."

It would prove to be great experience, and it steered Parsons in the direction of his life's calling. One day in May of 1960, Benny Parsons was working at his father's gas station when two men stopped by with a race car on the back of a truck.

"It was a 1960 Ford. Being from North Carolina and having read the *Winston-Salem Journal* all the time and being that much of a fan, I was like, 'Wow, a race car!' " he said. "I knew what it was and it impressed me, where it wouldn't have impressed a lot of guys. They had just stopped to use the bathroom and they knew of my dad." Parsons was curious about these men, and struck up a conversation.

"Where are you guys headed?" he asked.

"Anderson, Indiana. Do you want to go?" they replied.

Parsons, nineteen at the time, decided he did want to go; he went in and told his father, and left immediately. Over the next couple of years, he learned little by little about the racing business while traveling to various events with the two men, Wayne Bennett and Dick Gold.

"It was totally by chance. I happened to be there when that truck and car stopped by the gas station, only because those guys had to go to the bathroom," Parsons said years later. "They were just two guys who lived there in Detroit and loved to race. One was a driver and the other helped him out financially and mechanically. I started going around to races with them. I didn't drink, but most of the guys who hung around did, so I became the truck driver. I didn't know anything about auto racing, but I would roll a tire and hand them a wrench and all this other stuff. I'd do what I could."

Parson's worked for Bennett and Gold for more than two years before he seriously considered the idea of driving. In the winter of 1963, Gold stopped by the gas station again and asked Benny a simple question that would change his life.

"Did you ever think about driving a race car?" Gold asked.

"Yeah, I guess I've thought about it from time to time," Parsons replied.

"Well, I had to buy this old race car. It needs some fixing up, but if you want to try it, I'd be willing to let you drive it."

"What did you pay for it?"

"Fifty dollars."

Parsons agreed to take a look at the car and consider driving it. They went to Gold's house, where he had the car pulled into an old wooden garage.

"When he swung the door open, it was completely dark. But I looked closer and saw the car. My first thought was, If he paid fifty dollars for this piece of junk, he got cheated," Parsons said.

"It was a 1954 Ford and it had roll bars in it, and the engine ran. We went to the junkyard and got some sheet metal to hang on there and painted it. Wayne Bennett helped me set the car up to go around the corners. They let me put a tow bar behind the truck and haul my car, so it was a sweet deal. Their car was a yellow ninety-eight, so I made mine a yellow ninety-eight too."

Soon Parsons was winning races, and at the end of the year, Dick Gold pulled him aside again and mentioned how great the other yellow No. 98 car was, the one that he had been driving at the half-mile track while Parsons cut his teeth in the piece of remodeled junk on the quarter-mile track.

"Why don't we sell you the good car? We're thinking of either quitting or building a new car," Gold suggested.

"How much?" Parsons asked.

"Fifteen hundred dollars."

This was no fifty-dollar investment; $1,500 was a whole lot of money in 1963—especially to Benny Parsons, who had come from such a modest background—but Parsons wanted that race car. He went to his father and asked for some financial assistance, and he agreed to help Benny acquire the car.

"My dad helped me and I got together the money and went racing. We won like the first four races I was in," Parsons said. "That was on the half-mile dirt track in Detroit. I also went to a three-eighth-mile asphalt track up north of Flint, at Dixie Speedway at a place called Birch Run. I won a couple more races up there and won some on other half-mile dirt tracks; that's what got everyone's attention."

Getting the newer car had made Parsons understand more than ever that being competitive in racing depended on having the right equipment. It was the same then as it had always been and always would be; the drivers with the best backing were going to be the most successful.

One day in 1964, Parsons and a friend were working on his race car, and got the grand idea that they would go see Jacques Passino, who was then the head of Ford Motor Company's racing program, to convince him to sponsor Benny's ride.

"He's a big shot. Worldwide, and here we are, dressed in our boots with grease under our fingernails. But we got in to see him." Once inside Passino's office in Detroit, Parsons got right to the point. Parsons, imploring the executive to help his fledgling racing enterprise, argued: "Listen, I can drive one of these cars you guys are making. But I'm never going to get a chance unless I can get some money so I can go out and compete."

"I'll think about it. Call me in a couple weeks," Passino said.

"He probably thought we were crazy. I don't know. But maybe the fact that we marched in there and said, 'Give me some help,' was all it took," Parsons said.

Parsons wanted a little assistance to help him run the ARCA circuit in the Michigan area, but Ford had something else in mind. The officials at the motor company didn't even wait for Parsons to call them back, calling him a few days later and stunning him with an offer.

"What would you say if we told you we had a Holman-Moody car ready for you? We want you to run a Grand National race at the track in Asheville, North Carolina. What do you say?"

Parsons felt he couldn't say no, even if he had his reservations about the opportunity.

"I didn't feel like I could compete with those guys down

South," he said later. " If I had had any sense, I would have said, 'No, because I'm not ready to run on a half-mile pavement track.' "

It was while sitting in his new fancy Holman-Moody car on the track at Asheville-Weaverville Speedway, nervous and sweating as he waited for the race to start, that he had that first encounter with Richard Petty. The friendly ease with which Petty handled himself had a calming effect on the jittery Parsons.

Meeting Petty and sitting behind the wheel in a Holman-Moody car made Parsons feel like he had hit the big time. He was twenty-two years old. "Oh man, this is a big deal! I mean, I'm a factory driver now," he told himself as the race began on August 9, 1964.

What Parsons didn't know was that Ford had gotten together with John Holman of Holman-Moody and said that it would back one new team, and they wanted Holman to test out two drivers in that race: Parsons and Cale Yarborough. While the more experienced Yarborough did well and even led several laps, Parsons spun out twice and looked very much like a nervous rookie with limited experience running on asphalt. It wasn't until later that Parsons learned he had flunked his tryout, and when he returned to Detroit, he went to see Passino again.

"Hey, I know I didn't do so good in that Moody car. I know I don't deserve that ride. But I still need some help from you guys to run the ARCA circuit," Parsons pleaded.

Passino wasn't very compassionate, explaining that Ford's only concern, even on the less prestigious circuits, was results. To get Ford's backing, you had to produce, you had to run out front and make the Ford Motor Company look good.

"You go out and get your stuff together, and after you lead ten ARCA races, call me back. Until then, forget it," he told Parsons.

Parsons was determined to get back to racing's highest level, and he and a couple buddies put together an old car and took it to an ARCA race in Springfield, Ohio.

"The course was about a half mile and it had rained. I qualified and sat on the pole and led the first ten laps. Whatever happened to that car after that, I don't know. But it was like, 'Okay, one down and nine to go,' " Parsons said.

Whereas Ford and Chrysler returned to full participation in NASCAR by 1963, General Motors made a conscious decision to stay out of the game. Big Bill France was pleased to have Ford and Chrysler return with their millions—particularly Ford, which by the mid-sixties was spending between twenty and $25 million on motorsports annually, with roughly 35 percent of that targeted specifically for NASCAR; Chrysler's budget was by comparison only about $7 million annually. At the same time, Firestone and Goodyear were spending millions in a speedway tire war, with conservative estimates indicating that between the 1963 and 1968 Ford, Chrysler, Firestone and Goodyear combined to pump more than $200 million into auto racing (that despite Chrysler's abandonment of NASCAR for a year over the controversial banning of its hemi engine made famous by Richard Petty). At least $80 million of that staggering total went toward striving to consistently put a winning product on the Grand National stock car circuit.

France loved having that giant sum pumped into the sport, but wished he could lure General Motors back into NASCAR as well to keep Ford and Chrysler from always butting heads. As France once put it to writer Brock Yates of *Sports Illustrated* when discussing the era: "If I had three manufacturers in racing, I would have had a potential majority. But with just two, it was always a standoff."

France enjoyed not only the millions of dollars flowing into his sport, but also all the free publicity; the big motor and tire companies churned out reams of public relations materials designed to promote not only their cars but their drivers as well. But with their money, the companies wanted more say in what was happening on the tracks, and France felt his authority waning.

The big companies constantly bickered with one another— Ford sniping at Chrysler and vice versa; Firestone and Goodyear did the same. During this era, France and his NASCAR officials collected more illegal aluminum hoods, rigged bumpers and acid-dipped body panels than at any time before or since. The big companies all wanted the same thing: they wanted the most successful cars or tires, and the manufacturers in particular were willing to do anything to get the folks they were backing to Victory Lane.

Furthermore, the manufacturers harbored a belief that average Americans were looking for improved speed and performance in the automobiles that they purchased themselves. If a Ford, for example, could safely go two hundred miles per hour on a racetrack, surely that brand could handle anything on public roads; if the tires could handle those speeds, then there was little question that they would perform admirably for regular consumers.

France's grand vision of NASCAR all along had been to put cars on the track that at least resembled those in the showrooms of car dealers across the country. However, in their relentless pursuit of faster speeds, Ford and Chrysler were developing cars that bore no resemblance to mass-production automobiles. Both manufacturers had their racing divisions instead develop vehicles that were actually specially crafted aerodynamic racing sedans—grotesque machines such as Ford Talladegas, Dodge Daytonas and Plymouth Superbirds. They pushed France to accept them and encouraged him to build yet another superspeedway, which he didn't mind at all. What the manufacturers had in mind was obvious: They wanted the cars to go faster, and they needed new, bigger venues to do it.

With Daytona International Speedway approaching its ten-year anniversary and universally considered an unparalleled success, France eagerly accepted the challenge of building a similar facility in eastern Alabama, near Talladega. As they had been of Daytona earlier, the drivers were immediately skeptical.

They had again been considering unionizing, only this time they recognized the need to do it quietly and with more discretion than the reckless and desperate Curtis Turner had shown just eight years earlier. In August of 1969, on the Thursday evening before the Yankee 600 at Michigan International Speedway, eleven prominent NASCAR drivers met in Ann Arbor, Michigan, to discuss their prospects. The central figure in the meeting was Richard Petty, and other top drivers attending were Bobby Allison, Donnie Allison, Cale Yarborough, Lee Roy Yarbrough, Buddy Baker, Charlie Glotzbach and David Pearson. Their approach further differed from Turner's earlier effort in this fashion as well: the top drivers were in agreement that something needed to be done, whereas Turner was forced to talk many of his skeptical colleagues into following his lead and had been motivated by his behind-the-scenes deal with the Teamsters.

Petty and several other drivers had been privately discussing the possibility of forming a union for some time, but they kept the discussions to themselves, mindful of what had happened to Turner once he went public with his union plan in 1961. Simply put, they feared the wrath of Big Bill France and did not want any publicity until they felt they were ready to present a reasonable plan.

The meeting in August of '69, resulted in the formation of the Professional Drivers Association, or PDA; their stated purpose was to improve the conditions for drivers and crews throughout the world of automobile racing, but was concerned mainly with NASCAR's practices. The Grand National drivers were seeking simple amenities, including paved areas at tracks where mechanics could work on their cars, decent washrooms for race participants and a pension plan. Looking back, the goals were very similar to Turner's—with one very important exception: the PDA's effort was in no way tied to the Teamsters, who were allegedly connected to the Mob. It was a saner approach toward attempting to improve conditions, but there was no question that it also was designed to weaken Bill France's continued grip on the sport.

Petty told reporters at the time that "the Professional Drivers Association will devote its effort to the betterment of the sport by seeking to work in harmony with NASCAR, the promoters and others involved in auto racing." Predictably, France was not amused and had no plans to work with or even recognize the newly formed PDA.

"We're not planning to change NASCAR. We'll post our prize money and the members of this new group can run if they want to. If not, that's their business," France said.

Later, when pressed by reporters, France added: "NASCAR has been pretty great to this bunch. I drove in a day when there was zero prize money posted and the track operators were rinky-dink guys who were not responsible people. . . . These fellows have gotten to be big heroes and they have apparently forgotten how they got there."

The budding controversy came at a difficult time; France was only a month away from opening the Alabama International Motor Speedway in Talladega, a fact that had contributed to the timing of the PDA's announcement.

Furthermore, the sport had been making strides to distance itself from its redneck, moonshine-running image of the past in order to appeal to a broader fan base around the country. NASCAR seemed poised to build on nationwide popularity for the first time in its twenty years of existence. Sensing this, France had hoped to use the inaugural race at his new track in Talladega to showcase the sport, which was to be the biggest and fastest track in America.

However, many drivers were unenthused, as they had been when the superspeedways had opened at Daytona and Charlotte; several of them had tested the track and thought its surface was too rough, its banks too steep.

Despite their objections, France was committed to the track and wasn't going to postpone the inaugural race to make any changes so late in the game. He believed that NASCAR needed another Daytona-type facility to keep the manufacturers happy and to continue to fuel the sport's growth. Drivers at the time were exceeding 190 miles per hour at Daytona, and felt they were stretching their luck at those speeds; France's plan at Talladega was to build a similarly designed 2.66-mile track that had two notable exceptions—a longer straightaway to encourage higher speeds, and banking in the turns that were two degrees greater. Apparently, ten years' worth of technology allowed for two extra degrees in the turns, as France had once said he settled on thirty-one-degree banking at Daytona "because that's as steep as they can lay asphalt."

Sports Illustrated wrote of Talladega that "the new track seemed sure to produce tire-frying, eye-bulging velocities well above two hundred mph."

Knowing France was preoccupied with successfully opening Talladega, the drivers decided to take a hard stand; citing universal concerns over safety in general and what they perceived to be unsafe conditions at the new Alabama International Motor Speedway specifically, the PDA announced that its members would boycott the first race at the facility.

Typically, France responded with a power play of his own, announcing that the race would go off as scheduled, with or without the likes of Petty, Yarborough, Pearson and the rest of the sport's new up-and-coming stars.

Only one Grand National driver refused to join the PDA-backed boycott: Bobby Issac, a quiet and moody thirty-seven-year-old man who had cut his driving teeth by hanging out with Ralph Earnhardt in the Sportsman division. Ironically, Issac had a hot temper and a history of drawing fines from NASCAR officials for rough driving and fighting. France so greatly appreciated Issac's support that he later presented him with a gold Rolex watch, inscribed with the words *Winners never quit, quitters never win.* It was an obvious dig at all the other drivers who he believed had quit on him in his hour of need, feeling that they were disloyal and greedy.

To prove his deeply held belief that the Talladega track was safe, France pulled a publicity stunt the likes of which has never been attempted by the head of any other professional sport. At fifty-nine years of age, he told the media that he could drive a stock car on the Talladega track at high speeds, and backed up his assertion by borrowing a Holman-Moody Ford and turning several laps, the fastest recorded at 176 miles per hour.

"If a man my age who hasn't driven competitively in years can go one hundred seventy six miles per hour here without any problems, surely the top drivers in our sport can safely go even faster," he reasoned.

But France wasn't done grandstanding; he then submitted an entry for the inaugural Talladega 500 and asked PDA board member Bobby Allison if he could join the drivers' union since he was going to run in the event. Of course, France had no intention whatsoever of running in the event, but if permitted to join, he could disrupt the new union from within.

When practice sessions began, Bobby Allison turned the fastest laps, going more than 197 miles per hour. The PDA expressed concerns over tire safety, because no tire had been constructed to withstand such speeds and it appeared that the Talladega track would require five hundred miles of flat-out driving, and as qualifying approached the tire problems increased. Some teams found that their tires lasted as few as three laps before literally falling apart. Drivers also complained that their cars were "bottoming out" as many as a dozen times each lap.

France finally seemed to acknowledge the potential for disastrous problems when only nine cars attempted to qualify for the first fifteen starting positions. Tires continued to blister after only short runs, and Goodyear and Firestone, under heat themselves, tried to assure competitors that better tires were on the way—as if they magically could devise and produce a vastly improved product in a matter of days, if not less. An informal test was attempted in which drivers Donnie Allison and Charlie Glotzbach drove on sets of tires from both companies. The results were the same: neither tire company appeared to have a product that was ready to withstand the rigors of a five-hundred-mile race at Talladega.

W. R. McCrary, then the general manager of racing for Firestone, admitted his company's tires would not "live on this track and we won't consider running a tire that will hurt the drivers." Goodyear seemed poised to make a similar announcement when France intervened, taking Dick Ralstin, Goodyear's public relations manager, behind closed doors and convincing him to make another announcement instead.

"Goodyear will bring in another tire by race time on Sunday," Ruslin said.

That Friday night, Richard Petty called a meeting of the PDA. It was decided that they would force a meeting with France the following morning, at which they would request that France postpone the race until the safety concerns could be addressed more completely, which seemed, under the circumstances, a reasonable request. But France would have none of it.

"The track is safe at a racing speed of approximately one hundred seventy-five miles per hour," France told the drivers. Since practice speeds had been posted at well over 190 miles per hour, the drivers were incredulous. Was France getting his figure from his own publicity stunt behind the wheel?

"Who's to say what the racing speed would be on this or any other track? Winning might require us to race at one hundred ninety or one hundred ninety-five miles an hour. The track is not safe at the speed we would be required to run," Petty argued.

This led to a brief discussion about running at less than full speed, but the drivers agreed that it was a ridiculous suggestion. First of all, no one believed that everyone in the room would adhere to this sort of gentlemen's rule, and it could be even more dangerous on the track if some drivers ran "flat-out" while others held back and ran slower.

"We came to race. We came to run wide open," Petty said. "We feel this track isn't ready and the PDA has decided we will not race."

Cale Yarborough, the PDA vice president, stood next to Petty and added: "A piece of iron can't stand that kind of pounding for five hundred miles. We're breaking things on the cars that have never been broken before."

France was unmoved.

"We will have a five hundred-mile race here tomorrow, and the prize money that has been posted will be paid. Whether you run for it will be up to you to decide," he told the drivers.

"You built this place too quickly, Bill. It's not safe, not running on these tires," Petty argued.

"Richard, if you don't like this track, load up your car and get out," France replied. The meeting was over, but at a subsequent convening of the PDA they made the joint decision that if France would ignore their concerns, that they would refuse to drive in the event.

Petty made the PDA's stance public with a news conference later in the day, while Yarborough stood at the King's side; but as of late Saturday afternoon, they still held out some small hope for a reasonable solution. No Grand National driver had yet left the speedway as darkness approached when suddenly a voice boomed over the public address system.

"All those who are not going to race, leave the garage area so those who are going to race can work on their cars!" Big Bill France decreed.

Within minutes, a truck motor could be heard firing up, and Richard Petty's famous No. 43 car was pulled from the garage area, followed by thirty-two more cars. The drivers had taken their stand, and France had again refused to budge even an inch.

The first race at Talladega went off as scheduled, as France used NASCAR Grand Touring teams to fill the field, while a rather disappointing crowd of sixty-five thousand sat in attendance, far less than the over one hundred thousand originally anticipated.

France tried to make the fans understand by handing out a printed statement to each person who entered the track, explaining the situation as he saw it and offering fans the chance to attend a second race at either the Talladega track or Daytona International Speedway free of charge. It was an unprecedented two-for-one deal, and it was France at his best—extracting the positive from a dire situation.

Most fans who had been fuming over the absence of the big names were pacified by the offer, figuring they would get to see Richard Petty and the rest of the boys race the next time they came, and that it would then be free of charge.

But would they? The last time France had dealt with a driver uprising, he had banned the circuit's most popular driver for life; would he dare do the same to Richard Petty and his PDA cohorts?

He would not, and it's doubtful France ever gave it much serious consideration. He knew Richard Petty was a rising star, and that potentially great rivalries, so important to any sport, were developing between Petty and David Pearson and Cale Yarborough and Bobby Allison. More than anything else, he knew NASCAR needed Richard Petty and his growing legion of fans. He needed to mend his relationship with the drivers but in a way that would relinquish none of his own control.

His solution was to add what he called "a good faith pledge" to standard entry forms for future NASCAR Grand National events. Though only two paragraphs, it essentially removed any possibility of another mass exit by disgruntled drivers and their teams on the eve of a race, stating that Grand National cars entered in an event "must remain and be raced unless withdrawal is approved by the NASCAR Competition Director."

"I think a driver is obligated to race after he qualifies," France told reporters.

Veteran driver Buck Baker was virtually retired in 1969, starting only one race, but he still had a powerful voice that he knew would be heard by the other drivers (including his son Buddy, who happened to be on the PDA board of directors), and Buck used that voice to tell journalist Chris Economaki that his son and the drivers who had opposed France were out of line.

"Things must have gotten a little plush for these guys," he told Economaki. "They must want it a little better than it is."

That was exactly what the younger drivers wanted, but Buck Baker remembered fondly the good ol' days, even though, in reality, they had not been great at all for drivers who had risked a great deal for very little reward. But back in his heydey, when he signed an entry blank to run in a race, Buck Baker made sure he ran.

"Today it's different. They've made the money and the fame too fast," Baker opined, adding that the drivers wouldn't realize how good they had it "until they walk down the street one day and no one knows who they are."

France also had his detractors, and it wasn't only the drivers who comprised the core of the PDA. Larry LoPatin, president of American Racing, an organization that controlled five speedways, told Economaki in an interview that France's "tyrannical" handling of the Talladega controversy was not an acceptable solution to the problem. He protested that France's response to what seemed to be legitimate safety concerns was to put less-experienced Grand Touring drivers on the dangerous Talladega track. He thought France had shown that he was consumed only with putting on a good show for stockholders who had helped him get the new track built and was not at all concerned with the safety of his drivers. He thought France had first put the most experienced stock car drivers in the world at risk and when they protested, he then put at risk drivers who had no business operating at the frightening speeds Talladega made possible.

According to France's critics, he had made two mistakes that doubly indicted him for unnecessarily imperiling NASCAR drivers.

LoPatin went on to cite France's many conflicts of interest; along with being NASCAR's president, he also was chief executive of the superspeedways at both Daytona and Talladega. How could the manager of speedways where events were to be held also make all the rules of racing; and if he were to continue operating in dual positions, how could he do so without comprehending the need for understanding and compromise?

France's best response to the criticism was pointing to the fact that the inaugural race at Talladega went off without incident. It was won by Richard Brickhouse, a supposed PDA member who announced he was breaking his ties to the newly formed union over the Talladega public address system on the morning of the race. France met the thirty-year-old driver in Victory Lane and said of him and the other drivers who competed: "You guys who raced here today were the real winners." He hoped Brickhouse, who was driving in only his second Grand National season, would become a star—but he never won another race in his short-lived career.

The first Talladega 500, however, was an accident-free event. Much to most everyone's surprise, Goodyear's late shipment of new tires held up, although critics wondered if the real drivers might have pushed them harder by driving at consistently faster speeds. To France, though, the accident-free race validated his conviction that the Talladega track was safe.

Richard Petty and Big Bill France were not done feuding. After Talladega, France expanded his good faith pledge on entry forms for races the next season, and Petty and several other PDA members refused to sign the forms bearing the new clause, instead signing their names to entry blanks only after scratching out the controversial text.

"Bill wants to keep control of one hundred ten percent of the sport, and it can't be done. Stock car racing has outgrown a one-man operation," Petty said.

But Petty would face another problem: Chrysler, the manufacturer for whom Petty drove, sided with France and told him to sign the entry form as it was written. Car owners checked into the legality of NASCAR's language on the forms and found everything to be binding and in order, which upset PDA members even more because it meant NASCAR could force car owners to appoint substitute drivers if the PDA staged another boycott.

Petty, a winner so often on the track, had lost, and there was nothing else he and his fellow drivers could do. France, predictably, had won again because he continued to play with a deck he stacked to his advantage every time.

France had all his big stars back in line and back at the track for the 1970 season. He also sent word to Detroit that the days of the aerodynamic supercars were over, decreeing that NASCAR would lower their speeds at the superspeedways with restrictor plates. It was a small concession to the drivers that perhaps they had been right all along about the questionable safety of Talladega, though France would never publicly admit as much. In the end, France got what he and the sport so desperately needed: a new track, higher speeds and new driver rivalries. Among the new up-and-coming driving stars was one Benny Parsons. He never again talked with Ford Motor Company officials about getting help to run in the ARCA series, though he dutifully kept his promise to lead ten races in the 1964 season. In December of 1967 he was invited to a party by Ford, where much to his surprise he discovered his name on a list of Ford drivers that included such open-wheel greats and part-time NASCAR drivers as Mario Andretti, A. J. Foyt and Parnelli Jones.

"I didn't know why I had been invited to the party. I didn't know why my name was on the list," said Parsons, who was still living in Detroit at the time.

He found out a short while later when a Ford official called him up and asked, "What would you say if I told you we had a Holman-Moody car ready for you to take to Daytona Beach? You'd have to go down to Charlotte and pick up the car. And you'll have to put the engine together. When you get there, we'll give you an engine and everything you need."

Like the last time Ford surprised him with a proposition, Parsons was in no position to turn the opportunity down. "So I go down and get this car," he said. "They give me a frame with a body hung on it. No fenders, just a roof and quarter panels. No doors, no fenders, no hoods. They take everything from the car and throw it in my truck and say, 'Here you go.'

"We had never seen a car like that before. I didn't have the first clue on how to fix it up. So I went back to Detroit, and when I pulled up with it everybody said, 'This is ridiculous. You need to call them up and tell them you can't make it. You can't do it.' "

Parsons considered giving up, but then realized something that would change his life forever.

"I finally figured it out. This was a test," he said. "This was a test to see how badly I wanted to race. Now, if I want to race, I'll get to Daytona. If I call them up and say, 'Sorry, we can't get this car ready in time. We can't make it,' then I really didn't want to do this that bad. I decided it was something I wanted to do badly enough. So we had twenty-one days or something to build an engine and get this car ready to go."

Parsons's father gave him the time off from the gas station and cab business that he needed. He scoured the city's junkyards for parts and spent endless nights for three weeks in a two-car wooden garage behind a friend's house, putting the ride together.

"How do you test someone? You back them up to the wall and give them an impossible task and say, 'Do it.' That's what they did to me. It was an impossible task," Parsons said. "I was working at the gas station, I had a two-year-old child; we had nobody that worked full-time on the car, everybody had another job.

"That was how badly I wanted it at the time. It turned out the impossible just took a little more determination, but we got it done."

He took his makeshift car to Daytona and sat on the pole for the ARCA race, running at more than 180 miles per hour. It was the type of feel-good story that NASCAR needed, and Parsons was poised to provide. Parsons wasn't yet driving on the Grand National circuit, but soon would be because of his dogged persistence.

France may have feuded with many of the big-name stars toward the end of the sixties and would continue to do so for years to come, but Parsons and others like him were living proof that there were other potential driving stars out there just waiting to be discovered. First, though, most of them had to prove that they wanted it badly enough to pay incredible dues. And as Richard Petty and the rest who had tried to stand up to France came to understand, there would be dues to be paid even after they had made the so-called big time.

In the meantime, France was now facing other hinderances. Sponsorship money, the driving force in the sport then as today, was drying up and the various controversies were doing little to present NASCAR in a positive light that would help solicit new money.

Junior to the Rescue

Junior Johnson retired as a driver in 1966, but never left the sport; he continued to operate as a car owner, occasionally butting heads with Big Bill France while coming to a kind of mutual respect with the man at the same time. Johnson may have been a country boy raised in the world of moonshine, but he proved to have a business acumen that belied his background.

There was no bigger business in 1971 in the state of North Carolina than tobacco, not even moonshine, that backwoods industry whose last significant remnants were finally beginning to fade. Most of the sponsors over the first twenty-two years of NASCAR had been, predictably, automotive-related companies: Champion spark plugs; STP, the oil additive that was synonymous with Richard Petty's No. 43 baby blue-and-red Chrysler; Goodyear and Firestone; Purolator; the Pure Oil Company. And, of course, the automobile manufacturers.

But the feuds among the big auto companies and between them and NASCAR's governing body kept driving them in and out of the sport. When a rule went against them, the auto makers often responded by quitting the sport; they usually didn't stay away for too long, but sometimes the boycotts lasted for years. When France outlawed the special aerodynamic sedans that had been built specifically for racing, and then announced in 1970 that he would require restrictor plates on cars at the superspeedways, the Detroit Big Three began to shy away from sponsoring cars on NASCAR's Grand National circuit. The automotive industry was being forced by the federal government to spend more and more money on emissions control and safety research, leaving less and less to spend on racing programs.

It was a critical time in NASCAR's history. Just when the sport needed more sponsorship money to pump it up and fuel its growth, it was receiving less. And at the same time, the cost of operating a racing team was skyrocketing, as owners were spending more on parts and fuel. Furthermore, racing teams were now building and maintaining many more cars during the season than they had in the past.

Like most car owners, Junior Johnson was feeling the pinch. One evening, he was having dinner with a friend who worked at the Hanes Hosiery Company. Hanes had been dabbling in NASCAR, but wasn't ready to plunk down the kind of sponsorship money that would make much of a difference in the long run. Johnson had been thinking about something else and wanted to run it by his friend: He had noticed that the big tobacco companies had just been booted off television by the government, in one of the early salvos of its ongoing antismoking campaign. Now Reynolds had a little advertising money left over in their budgets that they might be willing to spend. Why not spend it on a NASCAR Grand National race team?

"I been readin' in the newspapers that R.J. Reynolds Tobacco Company is lookin' to spend some of that money the government says they can't spend no more on television advertising. Do you think Reynolds Tobacco would be interested in gettin' into racin'?" Johnson asked.

"Well, I know those guys. Let me make a call about that," his friend replied.

He called Johnson soon thereafter to say that he had arranged for a meeting at Reynolds with Ralph Seagraves, an acquaintance of Johnson's who also had grown up in the hills of North Carolina. Seagraves asked Johnson exactly what he was looking for in terms of sponsorship money.

Johnson swallowed hard. He was going to go for it. The newspaper had mentioned that Reynolds had millions to spend. Why not ask for a big chunk of it?

"Oh, I don't know. How about five hundred thousand dollars or six hundred thousand dollars to sponsor my race team? It might even take a little more, say eight hundred thousand dollars?"

Seagraves smiled.

"Look, we just got booted off television. To be quite honest, we're looking to spend a whole lot more than that. We were thinking more along the lines of eight hundred million dollars or nine hundred million dollars."

It takes a whole lot to shake Johnson up, but on this occasion, his jaw almost dropped to the floor. He later remembered thinking, *That's* some ungodly figure you're willin' to spend. But he quickly gathered his thoughts and knew what to do.

"Well, let me put you in touch with Bill France Sr., because he'll have some ideas about helpin' you to spend a lot of that, I'm sure," Johnson said.

"That would help," Seagraves said. "I know you know Bill pretty well. Could you call him for us?"

"Sure, I'll call him and tell him to call y'all."

Johnson did that as quickly as he could. He told France, "Bill, I met with these people from Reynolds Tobacco Company and was tryin' to get some sponsorship money out of 'em. But Reynolds is interested in doing something a lot bigger than what I had in mind."

France thanked Junior and told him that he would take it from there.

"He listened and took the call," said Johnson, "and I never really did have anything to do with it after that."

It was a historic moment for NASCAR, forged in large part by the former moonshine runner with little formal education but an uncommon knack for getting important things done. France would be forever grateful. Reynolds agreed to sponsor the very first Winston 500 at Talladega, in May of 1971. It was an entertaining and exciting race won by Donnie Allison, Bobby's brother, who was driving for the Wood brothers. Bobby, driving a Holman-Moody Mercury, finished second, and Buddy Baker, driving for Petty Enterprises, took third. It was a perfect day to showcase so many of stock car racing's top teams and drivers in front of the eyes of a potentially huge new sponsor.

The boys at Reynolds had gotten a taste of big-time stock car racing and they liked it. They wanted to do more. They agreed to sponsor what was to be called the Winston Golden State 400 in June of 1971 at Riverside International Speedway in Riverside, California. This time Bobby Allison won in a car he owned himself.

Reynolds had taken the bait. The company had a huge advertising budget, and had very few places where it could legally spend the money. The tobacco industry was becoming an outlaw industry, and its marriage to NASCAR, the outlaw sport, seemed perfect. The two parties desperately needed each other to survive and to thrive in an increasingly politically correct world where neither felt it belonged.

The folks at R.J. Reynolds talked with France about doing more. France suggested that they use the Winston cigarette brand to sponsor the Grand National driving points championship each year, and officials at Reynolds readily agreed to do it. Thus, the name of the competition was changed to the Winston Cup Grand National championship, and later to the Winston Cup series.

The landscape of the sport had been altered forever.

In the early 1970s, money problems were springing up everywhere in NASCAR. The strong-willed and determined survived; the weak-minded and easily frustrated gave up and found something else to do for a hobby or a living.

Benny Parsons had passed the Ford test that allowed him to run at Daytona, a place where he always seemed welcome. It was, of course, the place where he had taken pains to get himself noticed several years before. In 1965, he had shown up there to run an ARCA race with yet another makeshift car and with no flameproof uniform to wear while driving it. At the time, with a few exceptions like the other "test" he had failed in 1963 at Asheville-Weaverville Speedway, his only driving experience was on the small dirt tracks near Detroit, where drivers had no idea what a flameproof uniform was.

"I get to Daytona and find out you have to have a flameproof uniform to drive," Parsons recalled. "The only uniform I had ever had was a T-shirt and a pair of white pants. At the time, all of the people that handled gas also had to have flameproof clothing. So they had a big black kettle—a huge kettle, like when your grandmother boiled clothing. They boiled water in it and put this chemical in there that rendered clothing flameproof."

Parsons took one look at the kettle of witch's brew and knew what he had to do: He dispatched a crew member to the nearest JCPenney department store to buy a pair of white coveralls. When the fellow returned a little while later with the goods, Parsons took a close look at it; the "uniform" looked a little large, but that was okay.

"We put it in the kettle, it rendered it flameproof and that was my uniform," Parsons said.

There was one problem. It looked like shit.

"I was about a forty-two at the time and this outfit was a forty-eight. It was all the guy could find at JCPenney. I had to roll the sleeves up. It was kind of baggy—and it looked even worse after we dipped it in that kettle," Parsons said.

Parsons didn't care. He was running at Daytona, and it so happened that he ran well in that race.

"I was running third and on the last turn beat the guy I thought was leading to the line and thought I had won my first race at Daytona. I thought I had won my first race at Daytona! I got back around to try to find where Victory Lane was because I had no idea," Parsons said.

When a NASCAR official approached, Parsons thought the guy was about to congratulate him and give him those much-needed directions to Victory Lane. Instead, the official shook his head and asked, "What are you doing?"

"I want to know where Victory Lane is because I just won this race," Parsons replied.

"You didn't win anything. You were a lap down."

Parsons was stunned.

"When the caution flag came out during the race, you went into the pits. You pitted before the pace car picked up the field. You were lapped in the pits because you pitted too soon."

Parsons was disappointed, but he knew they might be right. He was used to running shorter races on dirt tracks where you didn't even have to pit.

"I had never made a pit stop in my life, so maybe I did pit too soon. I have no idea. But I always thought my uniform had something to do with it. It looked terrible. No way they wanted someone wearing something like that getting his picture taken in Victory Lane. I set ARCA back about fifty years."

Nonetheless, he was credited with third place, and for the first time in his life the press came looking for him to find out just who he was. That is when the legend of Parsons the ex-cab driver was born. In truth, he had only driven his father's taxis on holidays when the regular drivers couldn't or wouldn't work.

"People writing stories on that race said to themselves, 'Benny Parsons finished third. Who is he?' They went to my application for the race, and where it said 'occupation' I had put down 'taxi cab business.' They were like, 'Oh, he's a cab driver. What a great story.' That's how that all got started. But I never actually told anyone I was a cab driver."

He was a great story no matter how it was told.

Once he started getting some support from Ford toward the

end of the 1960s, he became more competitive, but he still struggled at times. He was constantly working on his race car to try to make it better; once, he worked so long in Detroit that he suddenly realized he had left very little time to get to the track in Dayton, Ohio, for qualifying. It was a straight shot down Interstate 75, but he would have to hump it.

"We left Detroit at like eight o'clock in the morning to go to Dayton, Ohio, to race," Parsons said. "There was no way we were going to make it, but we've got to. I needed the money. I needed to run well."

He and his crew members were driving a truck that was pulling the race car behind.

"At the last traffic light in Detroit, we broke a brake line in the truck," he said. "The truck had a race engine in it. We didn't stop; we ran down I-Seventy-five as fast as we could go with no brakes. I can't believe the things that people did to go to the racetrack back then. You can't believe the things I've done."

Parsons arrived in Dayton too late to qualify.

"We had to start at the rear of the field, and then we busted a rear tire and it was a disaster," he said.

When Ford decided to back off in its racing program in 1970, Parsons was despondent. He was making maybe $10,000 a year racing in features that usually paid $400 to win. What little he made always went back into the race car. Without Ford's help, he would be dead in the water.

"Now I'm in a panic because I'm out of business. I'm not racing for a living, and I survived [in the racing business] off what the race car made," he said. "If I cleaned house and won a feature and a heat in the dash [events at a short track], I couldn't have made much more than five hundred dollars. So I'm making no money, but I was doing exactly what I wanted to do. What I thought was that I was building for a future.

"As it later turned out, I was. But at that time I thought it was over. I thought I was out of business. Ford had been giving me engines and gears and I wasn't paying for it. That's what I lived on."

One of Parsons's contacts at Ford reached him and gave him the lowdown: "You can take the equipment you have and race with it, but I won't supply you with any more parts. You can keep the stuff you've got, but this well is drying up. You'd better find a new one to dip into."

"And just where am I going to find something like that?" he asked.

"Listen, Benny, what you need to do is hook up with L. G. De-Witt."

"Who?"

"L. G. DeWitt. He's a guy who's got a car down South. He might be able to take you on and help you out. He might be looking for some driving help right about now."

On the way back from Daytona to Detroit, Parsons and his wife already had planned to stop in North Wilkesboro, North Carolina, to visit with family. DeWitt's operation was located nearby, and Parsons decided to look him up. DeWitt had a car that he owned and operated on the Grand National circuit.

"I hear you might be looking for a driver," Parsons said to De-Witt.

"Well, we have a driver. It's Buddy Young. Right now he's injured. He crashed at Riverside [in California], but we think he's going to be okay to keep racing. Thanks anyway for asking," De-Witt replied.

Parsons figured he had played his hand and that was it. He returned to North Wilkesboro. He was in his uncle's barber shop when Junior Johnson's brother Fred called on the telephone looking for him.

"They're looking for you down at DeWitt's place. They want you to drive that car," Fred Johnson said.

Parsons called DeWitt's shop.

"I thought you didn't need me. I thought Buddy was going to be okay to race."

"He couldn't get a doctor's release. We want you to drive the car."

Parsons went straight back to DeWitt's shop, they adjusted the seat to fit his frame and they were off to race first at Richmond and then at Rockingham. This time, Parsons had enough experience that he didn't feel out of place on the bigger tracks. He was ready for the big time. The weekend after that, DeWitt came to him and told Parsons that he wanted him to drive the car full-time.

"I went home and packed up the bags and came back to North Carolina," Parsons said.

He was making $150 per week driving the car, plus expenses. He also got 10 percent of whatever the car earned in each race. Benny Parsons could not have been happier.

His dogged determination really paid off three years later when, in 1973, he won the points championship. It paid $70,000, but most of that got pumped back into the DeWitt racing operation. Parsons's driver's share was a princely $4,000.

Parsons wasn't the only driver of his day who fought incredibly long odds just to keep himself in a race car on a NASCAR track.

Cale Yarborough had grown up in the small southern town of Sardis, South Carolina, just a gear shift from stock car racing's first superspeedway in Darlington. By the time Yarborough was ten years old, he had circled every inch of the perimeter of the 1.366-mile track in search of a break in the wire that would let him sneak into the place. He eventually found what he was looking for, and at age eleven got to witness his first Southern 500. At age twelve, he competed in his first race—not a stock car event, but a soap box derby. It wasn't nearly enough to satisfy his growing appetite to drive things that go fast.

"There's no motor in it. Those soap box cars just don't go fast enough," he complained to his mother Annie Ray Yarborough.

Shortly thereafter, young Cale's life changed forever when his father Julian Yarborough was killed in the crash of a small airplane. But the terrible tragedy did nothing to quiet Cale's need for speed. As a member of his local 4-H Club, he roped a calf, raised it and then sold it—all to raise money for an old car he just had to buy. Then he built a shed where he could work on the car, and spent long hours rebuilding it so he could race it at dirt tracks in nearby towns like Sumter and Hartsville. Along the way, he wrecked and rebuilt that old jalopy and wrecked and then rebuilt countless others like it in that makeshift shed, where a single bare lightbulb hung at the end of a long cord and burned long into the night on many occasions. He often had to beg his mother to give him money to fuel his increasingly expensive racing habit.

By the time he was eighteen, Yarborough had found his way into the big superspeedway at Darlington many times. He often hung around the garage area near his close friend, older driver Bobby Weatherly, only to get shooed away by officials. One time in 1957, when NASCAR officials were preoccupied with other pre-race duties, Yarborough slipped behind the wheel of Weatherly's Pontiac and actually drove in a Grand National event. It was a dubious beginning to his career: He started forty-fourth, and finished forty-second after experiencing mechanical trouble, earning himself a whopping $100.

As the years passed, Yarborough did many wild and crazy things, only some of which involved driving a race car. He developed a friendship with Tiny Lund, and the two of them were constantly playing practical jokes on each other. They would be driving along on public roads away from the track, when Yarborough would get to bragging about something he used to do as a kid back in South Carolina, like wrestling alligators or bears. Lund would pull off the road and have him prove it. Yarborough would dive into swamps to take on unsuspecting alligators, or would fish water moccasins out of their homes with his bare hands, just to prove a point. He later developed a fondness for skydiving, and eventually made more than two hundred jumps from airplanes.

Another time, Yarborough wrestled a pet bear given to him by one of his pit crews. He almost failed to win that battle. But Yarborough gave the impression that he could have gone into battle in a bloody war, led a suicide charge up a hill against over-whelming odds and still somehow emerge without a scratch. He once made an emergency landing of an airplane in a field even though he had no prior experience as a pilot; he also lived through getting struck by lightning—not once, but twice.

It wasn't until Yarborough moved to Charlotte, just north of the South Carolina border, that he finally began to make a name for himself as a stock car driver. He first found work at Holman-Moody, where Ford Motor Company was having its race cars built at the time. It wasn't glamorous: Yarborough swept floors, turned wrenches and did whatever menial work was assigned him. At the same time, he kept reminding anyone who would listen that he was a darn good race car driver and all he needed was a chance. He was working as a member of a pit crew when he finally got that chance, and he turned in an impressive showing.

Soon he was running races fairly regularly on the Grand National tour. He won his first race in 1965 and firmly established himself as an up-and-coming star by winning six of twenty-one starts in 1968. But it wasn't until the 1970s that he really began to hit his stride, finishing second in the points championship in both 1973 and 1974, when he won four and ten races, respectively.

About the same time Yarborough was establishing himself, so was Bobby Allsion. Bobby liked to tell the story about how, at age fourteen, he was working under the hood of an old T-model Ford that belonged to the headmaster of the Catholic school he was attending. Even at that early age, he already had gained a reputation as someone who could tune up engines.

Noticing young Bobby's feet sticking out from underneath his car, the headmaster stopped and asked, "Mr. Allison, have you found the problem?"

"No, not yet," he replied quietly.

The headmaster did not hear him.

"I say, Mr. Allison, have you found the problem?"

Allison thought he had just answered the question. Frustrated that he hadn't yet figured out what was wrong with the car and irritated with the questioner for interrupting, the novice mechanic now answered plenty loud enough for the headmaster to hear:

"Hell, no! I haven't found the problem yet, okay?"

Then he realized to whom he was speaking. He popped his head out from under the car and began to apologize profusely to the headmaster, whose scowl spoke volumes. Bobby Allison was already building a reputation as someone who spoke his mind and often got himself in trouble because of it.

In his early formative years, Allison worked weekends at his father's hydraulic car lift business and gave little or no thought to driving a race car for a living. But after an uncle took him to a modified stock car race at the fairgrounds dirt track near his hometown of Hueytown, Alabama, Allison was hooked on the sport. From that moment on, he seemed to spend every spare moment studying the race cars and their drivers. He found himself with an overwhelming urge to race.

He worked to buy his first race car, which doubled as a vehicle to get him to school during the week. After a while, once race officials realized how young he was, they required a parental permission slip to let him run in events. His mother, who had no idea he had been running in races on previous Saturday nights, balked at the idea. Night after night, Bobby begged her to sign the permission slip. She finally relented, thinking it was a one-time deal. Bobby thought otherwise; he took it as a sign of perpetual parental permission.

He never asked for permission again. When he wanted to enter a subsequent race, he borrowed the driver's license of a friend and raced under the assumed name of "Bob Sunderman." That worked for a while, until Bobby's father saw his son's photo in the local newspaper; imagine his surprise when he saw his grinning son, identified not as Bobby Allison but as Bob Sunderman, celebrating yet another victory at the local dirt track.

"If you're going to race, use your own name," he told his son. It was the same thing Ned Jarrett's father had once told him.

His mother took longer to win over, but eventually she too gave in to his new obsession.

Humpy Wheeler remembered one time when young Bobby Allison was racing at Bowman-Gray Stadium in Winston-Salem, North Carolina. It was before Curtis Turner was banned, and while Turner was a big star at the time, no one had any idea who in the heck this Bobby Allison was. At first Allison made them remember him for all the wrong reasons.

"Bobby showed up on the circuit in a little Chevelle, and this was when the rest of the guys were running big cars. We had big Fords, big Plymouths and big Dodges," Wheeler said. "And here comes this little maroon-and-white Chevelle. It was sort of almost a joke at the time.

"He was a rookie driver, almost by himself. He had his brother Eddie with him and that was it. But, boy, was he competitive."

That much quickly became clear as the race progressed and Allison's little Chevelle kept trying to press Turner's big ol' Ford for the lead.

"No one knew who Bobby was at the time," Wheeler said. "He was a guy who won a prolific amount of short-track races, but so what? So did most of the people running that race.

"They were at Bowman-Gray, the flat quarter-mile track, which was hard to pass on. But Bobby kept trying. Turner was driving a Ford, and the track wasn't but thirty-something feet wide. Turner could block a racetrack better than anybody I've ever known."

Eventually, though, Allison wore Turner down and briefly took the lead—much to the surprise of everyone but Bobby. It didn't last long, though, as Turner ran him down and simply ran him off the racetrack. A star of Turner's magnitude wasn't about to let a rookie driver in a weak car get the best of him.

"So Curtis got by the last few laps. That was like an elephant versus an ant with the little old car Bobby had," Wheeler said. "And so Curtis won the race after he knocked Bobby out.

"They didn't have a winner's circle there. They just had the start-finish line, and that's where they had the victory celebration. Curtis's car was sitting there."

All of a sudden, Bobby Allison's Chevelle came rushing back into the picture before Turner could properly set off his latest victory celebration.

"Here comes Bobby driving his car backward wide open," Wheeler said. "You knew exactly what was going to happen because you'd seen it a hundred times on some little quarter-mile dirt track. He slammed right into Curtis's car."

Bobby Allison jumped out and wanted to fight, but Turner backed off. He thought this newcomer was crazy—just crazy enough to be dangerous.

"Curtis Turner was a lover, not a fighter," Wheeler said, laughing at the memory. "He would do anything to get away from that, so he kindly let some folks step in and break it up."

Wheeler and the others who witnessed the Bowman-Gray incident found Bobby Allison very hard to forget.

"He loved to race more than any human being I've ever known," Wheeler said. "He would race seven days a week. Sometimes he did if he could, wherever it took him. And he had an abandon on a racetrack that was pretty extraordinary, particularly when he got to running on the superspeedways."

Allison started winning regularly at the Grand National/ Winston Cup level about the same time Yarborough did. They soon developed an intense rivalry.

But at the turn of the decade in 1970, as good as they were and as often as they charged to the front in races, neither Yarborough nor Bobby Allison stood as Richard Petty's fiercest and most consistent challenger for supremacy on the track. That honor belonged to one David Gene Pearson from a little piece of scorched earth called Spartanburg, South Carolina. Pearson was by the late 1960s becoming a force with whom all the other drivers had to reckon. He rarely raced a full schedule, and when he did the results were predictable.

"Richard Petty's greatness came out because he beat—most of the time, or at least some of the time—two other great drivers in David Pearson and Bobby Allison," Wheeler said. "Pearson was a product of a textile mill environment. He was very quiet and reserved, very pragmatic, never had much to say.

"You never saw Pearson in a race—particularly at a super-speedway—until the end. The last ten percent, he'd show up. Where was he the rest of the time? He was buried back there in eighth or ninth or tenth, just waiting."

Waiting to pounce on the leaders. While Allison and others liked to run out front as early and as often as they could, Pearson picked his spots and then rushed toward the front at the end.

"Bobby Allison was different. Bobby was combative," Wheeler said. "He was a tremendous, tremendous competitor. David Pearson was too, but Bobby was more where you could see it all the time. There was nothing hidden about it. He was quite a communicator."

Pearson often preferred to let his car do the talking. He won fifteen of forty-two starts in 1966 and won his first points championship, finishing first, second or third in twenty-five of those starts and in the top ten in eight others. Two years later, racing for the Holman-Moody operation, he won the first of back-to-back points championships, and the numbers were even more incredible: in 1968, he placed in the top ten in thirty-eight of forty-eight starts, won sixteen races and finished second in twelve others; in 1969, the year the drivers refused to drive at Talladega, he won eleven races, finished second eighteen times and third on nine occasions. He also combined to win twenty-six poles in the two remarkable seasons.

Pearson had come a long way from his modest beginnings in Spartanburg. The first car he ever purchased was a 1938 Ford that was such a wreck that his mother Lennie took one look at it and immediately offered him thirty dollars to remove it from the family premises. No dummy, Pearson took the money and obliged; after selling the junker, he had enough to buy a 1940 Ford that at least looked a little better—but he had to hide it from his mother so she wouldn't make him sell that one too.

He hid the car and worked on it at Mack's, a local Spartanburg hangout. He made a roll bar out of a discarded bed frame and fixed it up as best he could, and then went racing at local dirt tracks. Right away, he knew he wanted more.

He got his chance to race at NASCAR's highest level in 1960, after friends had founded "the David Pearson Fan Club" on a local radio station and begged the public to donate money toward his cause. Pearson was trying to raise enough to purchase an old race car from NASCAR regular Jack Smith. Despite his friends' well-intentioned effort, in the end he still needed to borrow $2,000 from his father, Eura, to make it work.

Running only selected races because of his tight budget in 1960, he still managed to capture Rookie of the Year honors. That landed him a ride the next season with Ray Fox Sr., a respected owner who put him in a Pontiac and told him that good times lay ahead. Just to be sure it didn't go to his head, young David Pearson kept a job with a heating and roofing company in Spartanburg to make certain he'd always have some money coming in.

Rides with legendary car owners Cotton Owens (with whom he won the 1966 championship) and Holman-Moody followed, along with impressive wins at the big speedways in Charlotte, Daytona, Atlanta and Richmond. Pearson was living a dream. This was what he always had wanted to do.

But the best was yet to come. After a brief down period at the start of the new decade, when Pearson wanted to back off a full-time schedule and soon found himself out of the mix at the declining Holman-Moody operation, he hooked up with the Wood brothers. It was a perfect fit.

The legendary A. J. Foyt had been driving for the Wood brothers, but Glen Wood, who headed the operation, wanted to select which races the team would run in. He and Foyt had trouble agreeing on which events to enter. To Glen Wood it was simple, and his philosophy fit with Pearson's.

"We run only certain events, but they're always the biggest events. We run the ones that pay the most money," Glen Wood told Pearson.

"I like the sound of that," said Pearson, who earlier in his career had been nicknamed "Little David" and "Giant Killer" because of his wins in the big races such as the World 600 in Charlotte, the Firecracker 250 in Daytona and the Dixie 400 in Atlanta.

Pearson knew it was a solid ride. After years of being with the best, and then bouncing around with little success in 1970 and 1971 when he couldn't find steady backing, a solid ride was exactly what he needed.

On April 16, 1972, Pearson made his first start for the Wood brothers at the Winston Cup Rebel 400 at Darlington Raceway in Darlington, South Carolina. Richard Petty was strong in his 1972 Plymouth, but Pearson held him off for the victory in his No. 21 '71 Mercury, capturing the first-place prize of $16,850. It wasn't the first time the two had dueled; they'd gone at it twice in 1967 at the same track, first at the Rebel 300 and then at the Southern 500, with Petty finishing first and Pearson second. But this time it was different. And this time, it signaled the beginning of a period that would mark the greatest driver rivalry in the history of the sport.

"The Bitch Hit Me!"

Nineteen seventy-two was a benchmark year for NASCAR in another regard, as Big Bill France announced he was stepping down as head of the organization. Oh, he would still be around; no one needed to worry about that. But he was leaving the day-to-day tasks and presidential title to his son Bill Jr. Though there were some doubters initially, the transition proved to be rather seamless.

In the twenty-three years since France had organized the first Strictly Stock race in Charlotte, the sport had come a long way. Superspeedways had been constructed in Daytona, Charlotte and Talladega. The recklessness of the former moonshine runners had been tamed. Driver rivalries had come and gone, but it had been proven that the talent pool was deep enough to ensure that new ones would emerge. Even the untimely deaths of some of the sport's biggest names did not slow the growth of the circuit, increasingly fueled by corporate sponsorship of the racing series and individual race teams.

It was in 1972 that Richard Petty landed the STP sponsorship for Petty Enterprises—a megadeal that would shape NASCAR's future. Once Petty had STP's ample cash flow to anchor his operation, other teams were forced to solicit more lucrative sponsorships just to try and keep up. This trend among racing teams coincided with the deal initiated by Junior Johnson and brokered between Big Bill France and the R.J. Reynolds Tobacco Company. Once R.J. Reynolds increased its presence in racing to great marketing success, the beer companies started lining up to get involved, including Falstaff, Miller, Coors and Budweiser.

It was no longer simply Grand National racing; it was Winston Cup racing. Suddenly, NASCAR had an influx of cash that it had never before enjoyed on a consistent basis. The sport seemed healthy and ready to expand further.

David Pearson certainly was ready to drive to a place he had been many times—and craved to get to again and again. That, of course, was Victory Lane. From the start, the driver's teaming with the Wood brothers was a natural if occasionally odd fit. Pearson was the fun-loving, handsome, daring driver who had a reputation with the ladies. Glen and Leonard Wood were about as straitlaced as it gets.

But, oh, did they have stories.

Leonard Wood liked to tell about one time when he and his brother Ray were hauling one of the team's race cars back to Stuart, Virginia, all the way from a race in Riverside, California, in the 1960s. Marvin Panch was driving for the team at the time. This was in the days before fancy transporters and younger men were hired to drive them. The two brothers sat in the front of a truck with a simple trailer behind it. The race car was on the trailer.

It was a long, exhausting trip and by the time they got to Greenville, South Carolina, they were close enough to home to be feeling pretty good. They stopped for a bite to eat at a truck stop. As they left the roadside diner, they noticed a crowd had gathered around their trailer.

"There were a lot of people standing around the car, but that wasn't all that unusual when we stopped. Wherever we were or whenever it was, people always seemed drawn to the race car," Leonard Wood said. "So we didn't think nothin' about it. We got in the truck and left." About halfway between Greenville and Charlotte, they heard a loud rumble that caused the truck to start vibrating. Ray looked at Leonard.

"You can feel it in the truck. What is that?" he asked.

Leonard wasn't sure and eventually the noise ceased. They continued driving until they reached Gastonia, North Carolina, on the outskirts of Charlotte, when it happened again.

Leonard rolled down his window.

"I'm thinkin' it's got to be an airplane or something going overhead," he told Ray as he stuck his head out of the window for a better look. But he saw nothing in the sunny, cloudless sky––and again the noise and vibration stopped.

Exiting the highway as they reached Charlotte, the noise started up again. An exasperated Leonard Wood threw open his door and looked behind, where he noticed steam coming out of the exhaust pipe on the race car.

"Stop this thing!" he yelled to Ray.

Leonard hopped out and walked around to the trailer, where he could see the silhouette of a person sitting behind the windshield of the race car. Leonard peered closer.

"I looked in the window and this guy's got Marvin's helmet on and the motor's runnin'," Leonard said.

"Where do you think you're goin'?" he asked the stranger.

"I don't know," replied the man from behind the steering wheel. "But let's go."

Leonard Wood shook his head in disbelief. The misguided fan had hopped in the car as they left the truck stop in Greenville and had been periodically firing up the car as they cruised up the highway.

"About that time Ray comes around the other side, and we jerk him out," Leonard said. "The bottom line is that we let the sheriff's department take over from there. I think the guy had had a little bit too much to drink."

Another story Leonard Wood liked to tell occurred in 1972 when Fred Lorenzen, who had prematurely retired as a driver in 1967, was trying to make a comeback. For a time in his prime,

Lorenzen had been known as "the Golden Boy" and he had won twenty-six races from 1961 through 1967. But by '67 he had lost his enthusiasm for driving. He started only five races that year, with one win and one second-place finish. Soon after, he surprised the racing community by saying he was retiring—a decision he would later regret.

But by the time Lorenzen tried his hand at racing again a mere three years later, his skills seemed diminished. He started seven races in 1970 and won one pole, but finished in the top ten only once. He started fourteen races the next season, won another pole and had nine top-ten finishes—but only one higher than fourth. By '72, the whispers had begun that maybe he just couldn't win like he used to.

Lorenzen believed none of this; it was only a matter of time until he won again, of that he was certain. He was driving for owner Hoss Ellington in Atlanta that season when he headed to the garage area after only a few practice laps and Leonard Wood overheard Lorenzen talking about his ride with the man they called "ol' Hoss."

"She's just right. Don't touch it. My grandmother could drive that thing," Lorenzen assured Ellington.

The next day, about midway through the race, Lorenzen went to the rear and was running in last place. Ellington sidled up to Glen and Leonard Wood, knowing that they had overheard the boastful Lorenzen say that his car was just right less than twenty-four hours earlier.

"Say, you boys didn't by any chance get his grandmother's number, did you?" Ellington offered.

Lorenzen never came close to winning another race. After eight starts overall during the 1972 season—seven for Ellington—he retired for good.

Pearson loved good stories too and he loved to mess with Leonard Wood. One time the group was staying at a Holiday Inn in Griffin, Georgia. Pearson and several others were already at the hotel diner having breakfast when Leonard walked in.

Pearson leaned over and told him, "The waitress, she can't really hear too good. You need to really speak up loud."

When she returned to the table, Leonard began shouting his order into her ear, startling her. Pearson broke out laughing. He had known all along that the woman's hearing was fine. "I didn't really sound off all that loud, but I did put my order in pretty forcefully—much to my great embarrassment," Leonard Wood said.

Barney Hall, a longtime announcer with Motor Racing Network, used to travel with Pearson and the Wood brothers quite a bit and they became close friends.

"And when Leonard couldn't find David, he would find me," Hall said.

It happened often.

"You know where David's at?" Leonard would want to know.

"Yeah, I think so."

"Well, tell David we need to go and practice."

So off Hall would go, searching for Pearson. The Silver Fox might be in the company of a good woman, or relaxing by the hotel pool; upon finding him, Hall would try to persuade the reluctant Pearson to return to the track.

Hall: "Leonard says you need to practice."

Pearson: "Aw, I don't need no practice. But I'll come along anyway."

When they would catch up with the Wood brothers, Pearson would repeat his protest.

"I don't need no practice," he'd tell Leonard.

"I know *you* don't. But the car does," Leonard would fire back.

All joking aside, Pearson deeply appreciated the fact that the Wood brothers hired him to drive in 1972, after he had been down on his luck. His departure from the Holman-Moody operation had not gone well.

"The reason I quit Holman-Moody was on account of money," Pearson said. "Ford Motor Company got out of racing for a while when I was with them, and John Holman wanted to cut my salary as a result. I was getting fifty percent [of all winnings] for driving. I always did get fifty percent for whoever I drove for. And he wanted me to drive for forty percent."

Holman was adamant that Pearson take the pay cut, and Pearson was just as stubborn about refusing it. Inevitably, the tension boiled over and their partnership was dissolved.

"John, if that ten percent is going to make you or break you, you ain't gonna stay in business no way anyhow," Pearson said. "So I might as well leave now."

Holman told him to go ahead.

"I wasn't going to drive for that cheap," Pearson said years later.

When he began driving for the Wood brothers, Pearson knew right away that they were men of their word. Whatever they said they would do, they did, which appealed to Pearson's nature. He came from a mill town where a handshake and a promise meant something. After driving for the Woods for a couple of seasons, Pearson was talking with Hall over dinner one night, and voiced his high esteem for the Woods' integrity. "I'm amazed at how good they are as people," Pearson told Hall. "I would rather have a handshake and a promise from Glen and Leonard Wood than I would a contract from most other car owners."

That didn't mean the Silver Fox was going to stop messing with their minds from time to time; Pearson was notorious for not showing what his car had early in races, and sometimes not even in qualifying. It used to drive Glen and Leonard Wood crazy, because they had no real idea of how well (or poorly) the car was handling.

"Aw, don't worry about it. We'll be all right," Pearson would tell them.

And unlike Fred Lorenzen's promise to Hoss Ellington, Pearson's predictions usually came to pass. There were many races where Pearson held off until the final laps of the race and then surged to the front, ultimately taking the checkered flag. His motto was that he would run out front when he had to—and when it paid.

"Go back and check the records, like in Charlotte where they were paying lap money, I would lead a lot," Pearson said in January of 2000. "I know they [members of his pit crew] would tell me what laps were lead money and I would get out front—and once they weren't paying, I would back off and let somebody else lead. Then they'd tell me that the lap money starts again in two or three laps, and I would go back up to the front. I was just saving my car."

Amassing forty-three wins and fifty-one poles while also running second twenty-nine times, Pearson credits much of his success during his seven-year association with the Woods to the brothers themselves. Glen Wood was the coordinator who kept the operation running smoothly; Leonard was the chief mechanic who kept the race cars roaring around the track, and was one of the first to make constant adjustments during the course of races.

All Pearson had to do was win.

"A lot of times the car wasn't capable of running any better than wherever we finished, even when I was running hard," Pearson said, "but that's how smart the Wood brothers were. We were changing that car all along and nobody ever knew it. They would measure tires and change the wedge and change the tire pressure and things like that; we were doing that at least a year or two before anyone else started doing it.

"Every race I drove for the Wood brothers, I always felt like I could win the race. I don't remember going to a race, unless maybe it was Martinsville, where I thought we didn't have a car good enough to win."

And even then, he won at Martinsville in April of 1973. But that particular race was an exception to the rule, because Martinsville—which originally opened in 1947 as a half-mile dirt track, with the legendary Red Byron winning the first NASCAR-sanctioned race there—was a short track, and the Wood brothers' cars didn't excel on short tracks. They rarely even entered such races, but Martinsville was too close to their home base of Stuart, Virginia, for them to pass up the chance to make some good local news.

"Well, I did win at Martinsville. But I was lucky," Pearson recalled. "We didn't have a short-track car. Every car we had was a superspeedway car. They was too big, too heavy, too wide—or wasn't wide enough—to run a short track with. But we were lucky enough to win Martinsville; that's how I felt about it—that we got lucky. That's the only race where I went in thinking I really didn't have a chance to win it."

Though the points championship was captured by Benny Parsons, the '73 season really belonged to Pearson. He started only eighteen races and won eleven of them, including a record ten superspeedway victories in a row, often dueling with Richard Petty; the stage was set for the two to put on a show the likes of which the Daytona International Speedway had never seen before—or since.

By February 15, 1976—the sunny afternoon on which the eighteenth running of the Daytona 500 was held—Pearson and Richard Petty had firmly established themselves as the top two competitors in their sport. In the previous thirteen seasons they had finished one-two in a remarkable fifty-seven NASCAR races, with Pearson winning twenty-nine times, Petty twenty-eight. Longtime NASCAR journalist Bill Robinson once wrote, "What could be more beautiful than Petty and Pearson, side by side, flat out and belly to the ground, racing toward a hurrying sundown?"

While the two drivers respected each other, there was no love lost between them. In the 1975 Daytona 500, won by ex-cab driver Benny Parsons, Petty had infuriated Pearson by towing Parsons in his draft until he could get within striking distance of Pearson, who was leading the race at the time. Petty was eight laps down and could have simply gotten out of Parsons's way and left him to catch the Silver Fox unassisted by aerodynamics. When Cale

Yarborough and Richie Panch forced Pearson into an unfortunate spin on the backstretch late in the race, Parsons took advantage— courtesy of Petty—to pass and go on to the victory. Pearson eventually had to settle for fourth behind Parsons, Bobby Allison and Yarborough. It was particularly frustrating for Pearson because he had to that point never won a Daytona 500, suffering the same hard-luck fate that would famously befall Dale Earnhardt years later.

So when he prepared to compete in the 1976 event, Pearson arrived at Daytona carrying a monkey on his back; the Silver Fox had built his reputation by winning big races at all the big tracks—including several wins in lesser events at Daytona International Speedway—but he hadn't yet won NASCAR's biggest race of all. Petty, on the other hand, had enhanced his immense popularity with the fans by winning five previous Daytona 500s.

In some ways, Petty and Pearson were alike; they were both southern gentlemen who spoke in a soft drawl that could charm anyone they pleased. But whereas Pearson shied away from media attention, Petty sought it out. One day in the garage area, Pearson watched as Petty approached a television reporter.

"You want an interview?" Petty asked.

The surprised reporter accepted the offer, and ended up speaking with Petty for several minutes before the King went on his way. Score one more sound byte for the journalist, and chalk up who knows how many new fans for Richard Petty.

Pearson shook his head in amazement. "I never would've done something like that," he said years later. "That probably hurt me in the long run. I saw Richard do that more than once. I think Richard did it the right way."

Speed Week leading up to the 1976 race was eventful and full of controversy. One week before the race the top three qualifiers had their times disallowed because they stood accused of cheating by NASCAR and were convicted without a trial. There never was due process with NASCAR; Big Bill France autocratically established and enforced the law, and tolerated no dissent.

The top qualifier, A. J. Foyt, was furious after his apparent pole-winning speed of 187.477 miles per hour was thrown out; NASCAR officials said that they found "sufficient evidence" of the use of nitrous oxide—the "laughing gas" that dentists had used for years—to enhance the combustion on Foyt's Chevy during his exceedingly swift qualifying run. Youngster Darrell Waltrip, a relative newcomer on the NASCAR scene—who quickly had made many enemies because of his propensity to talk too much within a fraternity where taciturn silence was the norm—also had his qualifying time (second only to Foyt's), thrown out after openly admitting that he had concealed his own little bottle of the laughing gas. And Dave Marcis, who sported wing-tip dress shoes every time he climbed into a car, had the third-fastest qualifying time disallowed because his chief mechanic, the legendary Harry Hyde, had allegedly attempted to create increased downforce and engine temperature by illegally tampering with the radiator on Marcis's car.

Foyt could not believe his time was being disallowed; he angrily lectured Bill France Jr., the relatively new president of NASCAR, about his innocence and the injustice of the ruling. Folks who wondered how Big Bill's father would have handled the touchy situation soon found out when Bill Sr. was called in to restore order in the garage area after Foyt's outburst. He had earlier enlisted the help of his longtime friend and noted bigot, Alabama Governor George Wallace, to serve as grand marshal of the race, and made it clear that he wanted order restored before his esteemed guest arrived in Daytona Beach.

"Governor Wallace told me to make sure all these sonsabitches are legal by the time he gets here, and I'm gonna do just that. Right now," the elder France snapped.

Sports Illustrated later reported that ten minutes later, Big Bill "emerged from behind closed doors with his arm around the neck of a suddenly compliant Foyt, who was saying, 'Yessir . . . yessir . . . yessir.'"

The disqualifications stood and all the sonsabitches were in line by the time Governor Wallace arrived to perform his prerace duties. The three offenders were permitted to requalify, but the pole for NASCAR's most prestigious race was inherited by Ramo Stott—a full-time bean farmer and part-time driver from Keokuk, Iowa, who had in the previous eight seasons entered only twenty-nine races, registering a handful of top-ten finishes. No one believed that he would be left running up front for long.

Stott gave way quickly and soon enough the 1976 running of the Daytona 500 became a race for the ages between Petty and Pearson.

Petty led as the race headed into its final stages; for the twelve laps that preceded the white flag signaling one lap to go, Petty was in front with Pearson right on his bumper, stalking the lead. Once the white flag dropped, each of the estimated 125,000 fans in attendance expected Pearson to make a move—and that Petty would then attempt to counter it.

Eddie Wood, Glen's son, was on the radio with Pearson, serving as the spotter for the Wood brothers' team high atop Daytona International Speedway that day. "They go outside and get the white flag," Eddie Wood said. "They go into [turn] one, he didn't say anything. They go through two—and coming off of it he said, 'I'm gonna try it here.' They head for three, and we can't see anything. We're watching the crowd, and we know he's doin' something because of the way they're reacting."

This was the era of the slingshot pass on the superspeedways, the day of unrestricted engines and bulky body styles that made the simple aerodynamics of the signature move irresistible to the second-place car and virtually impossible to avoid by the leader. But then, of course, the process could be almost immediately reversed if executed properly. The bulky lead car would create such a tremendous wash of air that once the second-place car pulled out into it, the trailer literally shot past the helpless front-runner.

As the two drivers headed into turn three toward a quickly setting sun that afternoon at Daytona, Pearson executed the slingshot pass to perfection and vaulted into the lead.

"I got him!" Pearson shouted into the radio. Eddie Wood allowed himself a little smile.

But Pearson had made a slight mistake. He drifted too high in turn three, and Petty went low to retake the lead.

"The crowd kind of settles down a little bit as they get into three," Eddie Wood recalled. "But he gets up a little, and Richard goes to the bottom and gets under him as they come out of three and start heading for four."

"He's under me!" Pearson said on the radio.

Eddie Wood's smile disappeared.

"And the crowd gets up again," Eddie remembered. "That lasted for a second, it seemed like. Then . . ."

Pearson's voice boomed over the radio again.

"The bitch hit me!" Pearson exclaimed.

Through turn four, Petty actually had pulled ahead by half a car length. But as they exited the turn, this time it was Petty who drifted high. The right rear of his famous No. 43 Dodge caught the left front of Pearson's celebrated No. 21 Mercury—turning it nose-first into the wall before Pearson spun into the infield and on toward pit road, where he came to rest facing the wrong way at the entrance to the pit areas.

Petty had his own problems; his car fishtailed for two hundred yards or more down the frontstretch and then turned head-on into the wall as well.

Even as he was spinning out of control, Pearson remained calm behind the wheel of his Mercury. He rammed in the clutch as he hit the wall, revving his engine in a last-ditch effort to keep it running no matter what was going to happen next. Petty made the serious error of ignoring his clutch as his car bounced off the wall and slid to a stop in the grassy infield less than a football field short of the finish line and his sixth Daytona 500 victory. As a result, his engine died. He desperately set about trying to restart it, to no avail.

"At this time, David was spinning back, heading toward the infield," Eddie Wood said. "And he says, just as calm as can be,

'Where's Richard?' He's very calm. And then he asks again, 'Where's Richard?' "

Young Eddie Wood, who had been marveling at Pearson's ability to control his emotions, refocused on the task at hand and answered frantically.

"He's up here. He's up on the track—and now he's stopped! Keep on comin'!" Eddie said.

"I'm comin'," Pearson replied.

As Petty struggled in vain to restart his stalled Dodge, Pearson's battered Mercury limped on past. Working the starter over and over, Pearson was able to keep his engine running and the wounded vehicle—which only seconds earlier had been purring at nearly two hundred miles per hour—crept ahead a few feet at a time.

"Keep on comin'!" Eddie Wood shouted into the radio again.

Pearson didn't need to reply this time.

"He kept on coming, right on by him," Eddie said. "Right to the finish line."

Petty's crew illegally pushed his listless Dodge across the finish line; since no one else was on the lead lap at the time and he had completed 199 laps in the two-hundred-lap race, he still was awarded second place. Maurice Petty, Richard's younger brother and engine man, led a charge on Pearson's car as it crawled down pit road heading for Victory Lane.

"He's all up in David's window," Eddie Wood said. "They stopped in pit road and I never did find out what was said there."

Pearson said of the incident: "It really was pretty simple. He asked me what happened and I told him. The bitch hit me. Word for word."

Petty's crew seemed to be looking for a fight until Richard climbed out of his car and calmed them down. "If you want to blame somebody, blame me," he told them. "It was my fault." But Petty never did say anything directly to Pearson. Neither driver figured he had to.

"He knew what happened. He didn't have to say nothin',"

Pearson said. "He was probably faster than I was that day. If he hadn't come up into me, he would have won the race. He was that much faster than me. What happened, he was trying to block me more than anything. But he got into me. And, of course, both of us wrecked. I was lucky and kept my car going."

Years later, on the fiftieth anniversary of NASCAR, *Sports Illustrated* named the 1976 Daytona 500 the greatest race in the circuit's history. Recently reflecting on all that he had accomplished in his storied driving career, Petty said with some reluctance, "The race I'll be remembered most for—and the one I'll remember most— is the one I lost."

Three years after the epic Pearson-Petty duel at Daytona, the 1979 Daytona 500 was run under similarly memorable circumstances. It was the first five-hundred-mile race to be televised live and in its entirety, and NASCAR put on one hell of a show. For the special occasion, CBS-TV introduced some revolutionary techniques that soon would be taken for granted on race telecasts, including setting "speed shot" cameras low on the retaining wall near the start-finish line to allow fans watching at home to experience the rush of seeing cars rocketing by at speeds pushing two hundred miles per hour. Suddenly, you no longer had to be there to "feel" the power as cars zoomed by, producing the thumping, deafening rumble that rattles the brain.

In 1979 Cale Yarborough was at the top of the racing world, having won an unprecedented three points championships in a row while driving for car owner Junior Johnson. During this incredible span from 1976 to 1978, he won a total of twenty-eight races and finished second eighteen times, earning a reputation as a driver that never gave up and never quit chasing the leaders until he either ran out of laps or there was no one left to catch.

By this time, Petty's career was faltering a bit. He hadn't won in forty-five races, and like many before him who won early and often and then slumped badly, there were whispers that maybe he just didn't drive as hard as he used to, that his skills had faded. The shine was off the Petty-Pearson rivalry too, as they hadn't finished one-two since June 12, 1977 at Riverside, California. They had done so a total of sixty-three times, with Pearson coming out on top thirty-three times to Petty's thirty—but never would finish that way again.

The 1979 Daytona 500 did not belong to them either; that race was owned by the Allison brothers, Bobby and Donnie, and Yarborough—though none of them would go on to win it.

Donnie Allison was the lesser-known of the Allison brothers, but was an accomplished driver in his own right. He seemed to have hard luck, though, and he had a reputation for stubbornness. He was outspoken and opinionated and had a quick temper that could explode if someone disagreed with his point of view. He long ago had set about to make a name for himself in racing, in large part because Bobby, the older of the pair by two years, had once told him that he would never be a race car driver.

Donnie Allison's passion for proving his brother wrong ran deep; he once sold a shotgun his father had given him for thirty-five dollars, which he used to buy parts for his race car. In their younger days, Donnie and Bobby would buy bushels of peaches and eat them for breakfast, lunch and dinner so they could stretch their money and keep their beloved cars running.

That, of course, was long before the 1979 Daytona 500. Donnie Allison had been running at the Grand National/Winston Cup level since 1966, with his first win coming in June of 1968 at North Carolina Motor Speedway in Rockingham, North Carolina, when he drove a Banjo Matthews—owned Ford to victory over second-place Bobby, who finished two laps down.

Donnie Allison won a total of ten times between 1968 and 1978, but never escaped Bobby's shadow and rarely cruised easily to victory. What turned out to be his last career victory, in Atlanta in November of 1978, came only after the win initially had been awarded to Richard Petty in the afternoon race. Scorecards, which then were kept by hand, were checked and rechecked and Donnie

Allison headed home to Alabama, thinking he had finished third. Finally, it was determined that Donnie had passed both Petty and Dave Marcis—but both of the younger Allison's scorers had been wrong on their lap counts! He almost got screwed out of the victory by his own crew members! It wasn't until nearly 8:00 P.M. that night, when Donnie Allison was contacted by phone at his home in Alabama, that he learned he actually had won the race.

By 1979, even Bobby realized that Donnie was a pretty good driver, and Donnie thought he had a legitimate shot at the biggest victory of his checkered career in NASCAR's signature event. Bobby Allison and Cale Yarborough, however, were to play huge roles in determining Donnie's fate that gray day in Daytona.

There was some uncertainty that the race would be run because of overcast, rainy weather that forced fifty laps to be run under caution to dry the track. Officials were nervous about the weather because CBS needed the event to go off on time; a delay could have been disastrous and might have discouraged the network from ever committing to cover NASCAR live again.

"If that event didn't go off on time, they were all going to lose a lot of money," driver Darrell Waltrip observed years later.

On lap thirty-two of the event, both Allison brothers and Yarborough were involved in a wreck that sent them to the pits to try and get their cars fixed. Donnie Allison's ride was salvaged and he lost only one lap. Yarborough's car survived the wreck, but it cost him three laps. Bobby Allison was the big loser in the crash, as his car could not be fixed well enough for him to possibly get back into contention. He eventually got back on the track, but could not make up the ground he needed.

Bobby Allison thought Yarborough was to blame for the incident (interestingly, Donnie Allison later told reporters that he thought Bobby was actually responsible for spinning all three drivers out), so while Donnie Allison and Yarborough made up for lost time, Bobby Allison stewed about the earlier mishap, convinced that Yarborough caused the crash.

As they headed into the final lap, Yarborough and Donnie Allison had not only made up all their lost laps but were dueling for the victory. Halfway down the backstretch, Yarborough, running second, attempted a slingshot pass of the younger Allison, who moved down on the track to successfully block him and close off the inside lane. But Yarborough refused to back off; he continued to try to pass on the inside, and a series of broadside slams brought the crowd of 125,000 to its feet.

After repeatedly making contact, Donnie Allison drove Yarborough onto the infield grass. In his attempt to recover and get back on the track, Yarborough had to make a hard right—directly into Allison. Both cars then shot up the banking, out of control, and slammed into the outside wall before sliding down and coming to a rest in the infield.

"I had Donnie set up for the slingshot move on the last lap," Yarborough said years later. "When I pulled out to go by him, he just ran me off the racetrack. It was that simple. It had been raining all night. The infield wasn't nothing but mud. I hit that and was out of control."

Three other drivers remained on the lead lap at the time: Richard Petty, Darrell Waltrip and A. J. Foyt. Prior to the wreck, they had little or no chance of catching Allison and Yarborough—in fact, Petty, running third at the time, was half a lap behind when the checkered flag went up—but suddenly they were dueling for the lead. Notified by their spotters via radio, they went low in turn three to avoid the wreck and began racing one another hard for the win.

Petty won by a car length over Waltrip, who was running on seven cylinders and struggled to keep up, but the show was far from over. As Petty crossed the finish line, Bobby Allison stopped his car at the site of his younger brother's wreck with Yarborough. By then Donnie Allison and Yarborough were out of their cars and arguing heatedly over who had caused the crash. As the elder Allison pulled up to the chaotic scene and the national television cameras continued to roll, the incensed Yarborough approached

Bobby, who remained sitting in his car. He accused him of slowing to try to block him on the last lap, even though Allison was several laps down. Bobby tried to argue that he had been well ahead of the duo when the wreck occurred and that he had nothing to do with it.

But there weren't many words exchanged before punches started flying.

Talking to reporters about the incident later, Donnie Allison recalled: "Cale said something and hit Bobby with his helmet [through the window]. I knew what was going to happen next. I'd seen that look on Bobby's face before. Bobby beat the shit out of him."

Bobby later insisted that all he did was stop at the scene of the accident to offer his brother a ride back to the garage area.

"Donnie said, 'Go on,' so I started to put my car in gear," Bobby Allison told Ron Green Jr. of the *Charlotte Observer* on the twenty-year anniversary of the fabled race. "Then Cale started to yell at me. More words went back and forth and he ran to my car. He hit me in the face with his helmet and I saw a couple of drops of blood on my leg. I knew I had to get out or I'd be running from him for the rest of my life.

"I got out and he went to beating on my fist with his nose."

Asked who won the fight, Yarborough later said: "The fireman that finally pulled us apart."

By then, Petty had made it back around the track and was getting ready to head off to Victory Lane.

"I slowed down to see what was going on and I could see helmets flying and all that," Petty said. "But I don't think we cared much about what they were doing." He had just lucked into his sixth Daytona 500 victory.

"I wasn't involved in the race. I just happened to win it," the King later joked.

While much of America was snowed in by heavy storms in the Northeast and Midwest, television viewers watched the first live telecast of NASCAR's biggest race in record numbers. Network executives were surprised but pleased to learn that the race earned a 10.5 rating, which meant more than the traditional race fans in the southern states had tuned in and liked what they saw.

Talking about the significance of the race with reporter Ron Green Jr. years later, Petty reflected on what that one day meant to NASCAR's national growth.

"Even if you weren't a race fan, everybody got caught up in the emotion of the deal," Petty said. "That was a big stimulator for the sport because it took it out of the Southeast. That's what made it all work. We already had the South. Now we got the North, the Midwest and the West. It hit an untapped market."

Yarborough added: "It had a big impact on racing. It was the first live start-to-finish coverage on CBS. The whole eastern part of the United States was tuned in. Nobody had nothing else to do but watch the race. When it was over they said to themselves, 'Man, this is some kind of sport.' I think it hooked a lot of people."

David Pearson wasn't a factor that day at Daytona; by 1979, his run with the Wood brothers was coming to an end. Despite their mutual respect for one another, they had begun having some difficulties communicating and winning races. After winning ten of twenty-two starts in 1976, including the thrilling victory at Daytona, the team had won just two of twenty-two starts the following season and four of twenty-two in 1978. That would have been fine for lesser teams, but Pearson and the Wood brothers alike had grown accustomed to greater success.

On April 8, 1979, their frustration boiled to a head during a fateful pit stop at the running of the Rebel 500 in Darlington, South Carolina.

"Earlier in the race I got oil all over the windshield, so I couldn't see where I was going," Pearson said. "I rubbed the wall—and when I came in after that for a pit stop they still didn't clean the windshield. Somehow or another, it didn't get cleaned." So he went back on the track, but he still couldn't see very well.

"Next time I come in, I have to have it cleaned because I can't see where I'm goin'!" he shouted into the radio. When it came time to pit again, Pearson repeated his request.

"Fine," they radioed back from the pits, "but when you come in, you've got to beat Darrell [Waltrip] out."

What happened next is still confusing to this day, but this is Pearson's account of the bizarre events that followed:

"They was talkin' about how I had to beat Darrell out and stuff like that. So I come in and Glen hops over the wall and is cleaning the windshield. Well, I didn't see the guy squat down to take the left-side tires off. They didn't say they were going to change four tires, they just told me to beat Darrell out. So when I came in and they changed the right-side tires and they dropped that car down, I took off. When they dropped that jack, that was my signal to go. When Leonard ran around the front of the car, I took off."

The problem? There were no lug nuts on the left-side tires.

Pearson beat Waltrip out of the pits—but didn't get much past the end of pit road before his left-side tires fell off and the car grinded to a halt. For the Wood brothers team, which had built its reputation years earlier by revolutionizing the way pit stops were made and the precision with which they were executed, it was a most embarrassing situation.

"I was embarrassed like everyone else," Pearson added.

By 6:00 P.M. that evening, the driver and car owners had announced they were splitting up. An era was over. Pearson insists to this day that the split was coming anyway, and that the Darlington incident had little or nothing to do with it.

"A lot of people talked like our split was bad, that it happened because the tires came off at Darlington," Pearson said. "But that was just a misunderstanding. That's not why we broke up. It was just time to split up. We've always been friends and always will be."

Jaws, the Intimidator and Million-Dollar Bill

Proving once again that the sport could survive and produce new driving stars as old ones faded, NASCAR did not miss a beat even as Richard Petty became less and less competitive and his great rivalry with Pearson faded once Pearson parted ways with the Wood brothers. There were a number of established stars still driving to fill the void—Cale Yarborough and Bobby Allison, for example—but there were new stars emerging who would carry the NASCAR torch through the 1980s and into the 1990s.

Among them was Darrell Waltrip, who had burst onto the scene in 1972 immediately running his mouth, if not his cars, wide open; he talked so much that Yarborough nicknamed him "Jaws." Waltrip had been around since 1972 and his first victory came in May of 1975 in a car that he had built himself. Until he started racing with the proper financial backing, the fast-talking native of Owensboro, Kentucky, was known more for his self-promotion off the track than for his exploits on it.

By the mid-1970s, he had been backing up his boasts with victories; he began winning regularly in 1975, and it was Waltrip who won the Rebel 500 in 1979 at Darlington as the wheels were coming off Pearson's storied career. He did so by holding off none other than Richard Petty over the final four laps, running full-throttle into the corner in the outside lane of turn three before slamming on his brakes and diving low to pass Petty on the inside in a brilliant move.

Waltrip had been beaten out of the pits during the race by Pearson, only to have Pearson's left-side tires come off soon thereafter. Despite all that Pearson had accomplished in his career, Waltrip was hardly apologetic about Pearson's demise; for weeks afterward, Waltrip walked around the garage areas and entertained at cocktail lounges with his own rendition of Kenny Rogers's hit song "Lucille," with a refrain that went: "You picked a fine time to leave me, loose wheel . . ."

Waltrip had angered many veteran drivers from the first day he stepped into their exclusive world. He saw them not as legends to be admired and respected, but simply as fellow competitors who could—and would—be beaten. He honestly believed he was the best driver on the track whenever he got behind the wheel.

"I'm gonna make these folks forget all about Richard Petty," he boasted once.

Like Petty, who knew the value of exploiting the media, Waltrip took self-promotion seriously. But whereas Petty came across as humble and was more intent on popularizing the sport, Waltrip seemed more interested in lauding his own accomplishments, which initially turned off fans and fellow drivers alike.

Waltrip made no apologies for his brashness; when he came onto the scene, television was just beginning to make what would be a huge impact on the sport. Every time he saw a camera in the garage area, he saw an opportunity.

"I'd watch some of the other guys get interviewed on TV and I'd say to myself, 'Man, if they would just look at the camera, open their mouths and talk, maybe people would get to know them and the sport a little better. Maybe they'd get their message across,'" Waltrip said. "So that's what I decided to do. And, man, whenever that red light went on, I went to work."

It helped that he worked hard on the track too, and often enough backed up his ballsy predictions; occasionally, however,

Waltrip faltered and his arrogance would come back to haunt him during a race. At North Wilkesboro in 1979, Waltrip wanted to pass Bobby Allison and was convinced that he had the fastest, winning car—which maybe he did—but Allison kept expertly blocking his path. Finally, as he grew increasingly frustrated, Waltrip started ramming into the back of Allison's car. The rugged Allison, as everyone knew, was not one to take this affront lightly.

Waltrip's own crew warned him to back off on the radio.

"Quit doing that! Back off! You can't do that to Bobby Allison!" Waltrip refused to heed their advice.

"Aw, he'll take it. He ain't got no choice. There ain't nothin' he can do about it," Waltrip radioed back.

About that time, as if on cue, Bobby Allison took his foot off the gas and let the younger driver go by; the incensed Allison then sped up again and put Waltrip into the wall and out of the race.

The hard lesson did little or nothing to slow Waltrip or his mouth. By 1981, he was driving for none other than Junior Johnson after an expensive contract dispute with Digard Racing Company, with whom he had won a total of twenty-six races between 1975 and 1980. To get out of the deal, Waltrip ultimately had to agree to pay Digard owners Bill and Jim Gardner $325,000 to settle the dispute out of court.

The old-school Johnson and the new-school hotshot Waltrip clicked instantly. They didn't always completely understand each other, but they clicked.

"I had more fun with Darrell than any other driver I ever had," Johnson said. "He was always like a little kid, because he would go off and get to playing with something he wasn't supposed to be playing with. It was fun to get him back into his place most of the time."

Waltrip was at his best in 1981 and 1982, winning twelve races each season and back-to-back championships while driving Johnson's Buicks. Finishing second both years was Bobby Allison, who had driven briefly for Johnson in 1972 in a union that had soured quickly. Waltrip remembers one race at Riverside when he and Allison were battling to secure their places in the points championship race.

"Back in those days at Riverside, if you run off the track, you could get a flat tire real easy. We didn't have radial tires," Waltrip said. "And Bobby had a bad day. He had about six flat tires."

As soon as the race was over, reporters rushed to ask Allison why he thought he had gotten all those flat tires.

"Well, you know, I believe Junior hired one of them Wilkes County sharpshooters to sit up in turn six and shoot my tires out," he deadpanned.

One of the reporters went back to Johnson to report what Allison had said. "Shows how smart he is. I wouldn't a been shootin' at his tires," Johnson replied.

The other excellent newcomer of the early eighties was Dale Earnhardt, Ralph's son. While Waltrip's approach was more irreverent off the track than on it, Dale Earnhardt's driving was more old school than even the legends of NASCAR remembered from their roughest driving days. Early in his career, he had to scratch out his very existence and that struggle was something he would never forget.

Nicknamed Ol' Ironhead and the Intimidator for his aggressive, stubborn driving style that infuriated many and even terrified a few of his fellow drivers, Earnhardt was twenty-four years old when he began driving full-time in 1975 as a way to make ends meet for his struggling family. Earnhardt was a country boy from Kannapolis, North Carolina, who often borrowed money from friends on Thursday night so he could race on the weekends at dirt tracks—with the small matter of whether or not they would be paid back on Monday hinging on whether or not he won enough to settle up. And Earnhardt didn't merely want to win enough to pay them back; he wanted to have a little grocery money for his family left over. It wasn't an easy life.

Pete Wright, who over many years worked as a shop man and pit crew member for Junior Johnson, Donnie Allison, Waltrip,

Ken Schrader and others, remembers one night in the mid-seventies when he was at the Martinsville track for a Modified race. The driver Wright was working for was running close to the front in the race when his clutch started slipping, which led Wright to spray it with a fire extinguisher in an attempt to fix the problem. No one ever said the cure-alls used in the heat of a race were always scientific.

"I'll never forget this," Wright said. "There was this car owner, Charles W. Reed, who had a pretty good Modified car but hadn't done as good as us in the race. After the race, his driver come in and parked right beside us. They had run like a dog; they were terrible. This car usually wasn't that bad; it usually would be somewhere closer to the front."

Wright watched as Reed walked over to his car.

"Get out of my car! You'll never sit in this car again!" Reed shouted.

The driver in the car looked down dejectedly and did not reply.

"You'll never be a race car driver! Get out of the car!" Reed repeated. "You're wasting my time and my money!"

The driver, one Dale Earnhardt, climbed out and left the scene, speaking nary a word.

"At that time," said Wright, "he was struggling like a lot of guys. He was doing what he could do. And he obviously wasn't the driver Charles wanted at the time—but it didn't make him quit."

Dale Earnhardt had been trying to make it in racing off and on since dropping out of school in the ninth grade to devote more time to it. That decision did not sit well with his father Ralph and the two, who had been distant much of the time while Dale was growing up anyway, found their relationship even more strained; it was racing that drew them closer together.

In the early 1970s, Ralph Earnhardt built engines for Dale and his son did the chassis work. Driving in Modified races at short tracks mostly in North Carolina, Dale won twenty-six events during their second year together and even more the following year. Suddenly, the father-son bond that had been missing for so many years began to cement. Ralph Earnhardt was a man of few words, but he did give Dale one piece of advice that the younger Earnhardt would never forget.

"Establish your territory," Ralph told Dale in a brief dissertation on how to survive on a racetrack.

Dale Earnhardt was beginning to do just that on and off the track when the elder Earnhardt died suddenly of a massive heart attack at age forty-five. Dale, then nineteen, was grief-stricken and lost in the wake of his father's tragic passing and would later describe the next year, 1974, to friends as the worst of his life. He had a wife and two children, though the marriage would not last. They moved from run-down mobile homes to cheap, cockroach-infested apartments, wondering at times how they would feed the kids. He wanted to devote more time to racing, but couldn't afford it; he worked installing insulation, rebuilding car engines and doing anything that would put food on the bare cupboard shelves.

None of the work was steady and after moving from one temporary job to another, he found work one winter as a subcontractor with the boilermaker's union in the North Carolina coastal town of New Bern. That December, he worked long hours right through the holidays, including Christmas Day, helping to make welding repairs to machinery in a paper mill. The job was hot and the mill stunk, as paper mills do. Earnhardt hated every second of it and longed to get back behind the wheel of a race car.

He continued to race occasionally, and shortly after the welding job, he quit the conventional workforce and tried to build a career by racing full-time. He lost his first wife to divorce, married and divorced again and continued to struggle until Roland Wlodyka, Ron Osterlund's general manager of Winston Cup racing operations, agreed to give Earnhardt a chance to drive the team's second car for a race at Atlanta in 1978. Their primary driver at the time was Dave Marcis, and he clearly would have top priority, but at least Earnhardt (who had been buying parts from Osterlund's shop for years and eventually persuaded Wlodyka to give him a shot) would be competing for a real team in a real car.

Earnhardt had driven in eight previous races at the Winston Cup level prior to that Atlanta race, but never with equipment that was as good as he had that day. Surprising everyone but himself, he ran hard and close to the front all afternoon, finishing fourth. That earned him a full-time ride with the Osterlund operation for the next season, and the Intimidator was born.

In 1979, he won four poles and his first Winston Cup race; he finished in the top ten in seventeen of twenty-seven starts and won Rookie of the Year honors. He was on his way, but he wanted more—much, much more.

When he was congratulated for winning Rookie of the Year honors, Earnhardt would routinely tell friends and teammates: "That ain't shit. I don't give a shit about winnin' that. Next year I'm gonna be Winston Cup points champion."

Amazingly, he did it. No one else before or since has won Rookie of the Year honors and a points championship back to back, but perhaps success, after all those years of grinding, came too quickly at stock car racing's highest level. En route to the 1980 points championship, Earnhardt won five races and finished in the top ten in a remarkable twenty-four of thirty-one starts. In his next four seasons, however, he would win just four more races—and rarely finished in the top ten.

By midseason the next year, Osterlund stunned Earnhardt by selling the team to coal magnate J. D. Stacy without consulting crew or driver—and in May, Earnhardt quit to take a ride vacated by Richard Childress, a NASCAR veteran who had never won and wanted to put a more talented driver in his seat. It was the beginning of what would be a long and fruitful relationship, although their initial partnership was brief.

"You've got the talent to be driving for someone who can provide you with better equipment," Childress told Earnhardt prior to the 1982 season.

Thus, Earnhardt ended up driving Fords in 1982 and 1983 for Bud Moore, the legendary former driver and car owner who would remain involved in NASCAR for nearly all of its first fifty years. Still, Earnhardt struggled to rediscover the success he had enjoyed in 1979 and 1980.

The Intimidator prospered again when he reunited with Childress in 1984, and started making his black No. 3 car famous. Always known as a fierce competitor who would do virtually anything to win, he soon enhanced his reputation as a hard-charging driver and led many to wonder if he had some kind of death wish. The same complaints made about Curtis Turner two decades earlier soon were being levied against Earnhardt. Was it safe to race with him on the track when he resolved that he should be running out front? The answer was obvious: probably not.

The third driver to emerge as a bona-fide star in the 1980s was Bill Elliott, who had been racing in some form or another since he was sixteen years old and had a family tree firmly rooted in the moonshine business, which made him a good story and helped enhance his popularity with fans. Elliott hailed from tiny Dawsonville, Georgia, where stories of moonshiners in their "trip cars" outgunning the revenuers, were still told long after such duels on backwoods country roads had become a thing of the past.

They told stories of the "trippers" who would gather at Harbin's gas station every night, and wait for the call to go into the hills and pick up their loads of illegal whiskey. Fully loaded, in more ways than one, they would tear off up old Route 9 to Atlanta, or maybe go all the way to Gainesville, Florida. The service station was open 'round the clock, and so was the service the trippers provided.

Bill Elliott grew up listening to stories of how the trippers, on a slow night, would place a diversionary phone call to the only sheriff in town; once the law was out of their way, they would showboat right there in the middle of town, racing and doing 180-

degree spins just for the hell of it. Bill Elliott's father George once claimed that Dawsonville was the rightful birthplace of stock car racing.

"NASCAR doesn't want you to know there was a history of stock car racing before there was NASCAR. But this is where it was," George Elliott told *Sports Illustrated* during a 1998 interview.

There is some truth to what George Elliott said; many of the earliest driving stars—guys like Lloyd Seay, Bernard Long and Roy Hall—came from Dawsonville. But as Bill Elliott and his two brothers Ernie and Dan grew older and became part of Dawsonville's racing tradition, George Elliott, owner of an auto parts store and a junkyard in town, guided them toward safer and more organized forms of stock car racing.

"If they were going to be driving fast, I wanted them doing it in the right place," he told *Sports Illustrated*.

When Winston Cup events came to Atlanta, the Elliotts would pile into the family car and head to the speedway. At the track Bill dreamed of racing against the likes of Richard Petty, David Pearson, Cale Yarborough and Bobby Allison; then he would go home and race in the makeshift course he and his brothers often laid out in their daddy's junkyard—a rusted Oldsmobile marking the inside of turn one, a wrecked Chevy truck marking turn two and so on. Other times, Bill would head for the hills, where they still made moonshine and occasionally the trippers would plot out a makeshift track of their own and hold races in pastures in the mountains of northern Georgia.

George Elliott soon fielded cars for Bill and his brothers at area racetracks and discovered that Bill had the greatest knack for driving, whereas Ernie and Dan preferred working on the cars. In time, Ernie would build the engines and Dan the transmissions for the cars that Bill would then drive. As George Elliott grew more and more financially secure—he eventually owned several small businesses, including a Ford dealership—he began entering Bill in bigger events. Running in their first Winston Cup event in February of 1976 at Rockingham in North Carolina, the Elliott team finished thirty-third and earned $640 in a beat-up old Ford Torino purchased off none other than Bobby Allison. It may not have seemed like much to others, but the Elliott family was thrilled both with the car and the thirty-third place finish.

Eventually, though, it became obvious that George Elliott did not have the financial wherewithal to continue backing Bill's Winston Cup efforts. Harry Melling, a businessman from Jackson, Michigan, who had caught the stock car racing bug and wanted to become more involved in the sport, agreed to buy the Elliott race team at the end of the 1981 season. By 1983, Bill Elliott had a real car and was driving a full schedule for the first time. In the last race of the season at Riverside, in his one hundred seventeenth start at the Winston Cup level, Bill Elliott finally won.

He won three more times in 1984 to set the stage for a fairytale year in 1985, when Awesome Bill from Dawsonville would become Million-Dollar Bill Elliott. He won eleven of twenty-eight starts, including the ones that counted the most. He opened the season by winning the Daytona 500, and then won at Atlanta and at Darlington. He was truly awesome in the May race at Talladega, winning the pole position with a speed of 202.398 miles per hour and making up five miles on the leaders during the race by turning lap after lap at more than 205 miles per hour to win after he had fallen behind because of a broken oil line. "As far as I'm concerned, 'Bill Elliott' is just another way of saying 'fast,' " Harry Melling said at the time.

R.J. Reynolds Tobacco Company, the generous sponsor of the Winston Cup series, was offering a one-million-dollar bonus to any race team that could win three of what were termed NASCAR's four major races—the Daytona 500, the May race at Talladega, the six hundred-mile race at Charlotte and the Southern 500 at Darlington. Elliott had won the first two; all he had to do now was win one of the last two at Charlotte and Darlington.

He suffered brake problems and failed to win the six hundred-miler in Charlotte, but came back to win the Southern 500 and the bonus in its inaugural year. The drama of a million-dollar bonus won by a simple country boy who had been thrilled a decade earlier simply to enter a Winston Cup race and walk away with $640 captured the imagination of racing fans and further increased Elliott's popularity. The sport had another Everyman Made Good to promote among its growing fan base.

As popular as Elliott was, fans were reluctant at first to embrace Waltrip and Earnhardt. In fact, they loved to hate them, often throwing chicken bones and other debris at their cars as they passed by on the track, which actually could cause serious problems if the bones landed in the wrong place and got caught up in the car's grille or engine.

But as the 1980s wore on, their on-track rivalry heated up. Fans grew more accustomed to Waltrip's habit of boasting and then backing it up, and some of them began to appreciate it, the way football fans had cheered Joe Namath, the brash New York Jets quarterback who once guaranteed a Super Bowl victory and delivered it against overwhelming odds. There still were many fans that hated "Jaws," but now a growing number of them were lining up behind him as well.

Similarly, Earnhardt enjoyed a surge in popularity. Like Elliott, fans could identify with him because of his background, and his win-at-all-costs style, while infuriating some, endeared him to a large measure of fans at the same time. Notorious and feared, embraced and admired, Earnhardt became both a huge draw and NASCAR's signature personality. Fans either loved Earnhardt or hated him, but they all wanted to see what he was going to do next.

Humpy Wheeler, who by that time was running Charlotte Motor Speedway, had a theory on the popularity of the famous driver of the black No. 3 car. "I think the thing that has made him so popular is that he is really a reincarnated Confederate soldier," Wheeler said in 2000. "I mean, if I'm from Central Casting and we're doing a reenactment of Gettysburg, and I want a guy to lead Pickett's Charge up the hill . . . [he] would look exactly like Earnhardt. Sort of that slightly cocky, don't-talk-about-mymustache-or-I'll-whip-your-butt kind of guy. Gentle around women but rough around men. Knows his place, doesn't talk a lot and says it with his steering wheel."

In the Deep South, where NASCAR's roots remain, the reincarnated Confederate soldier bit played well and helped sell tickets and television rights. The Miller 400 in February of 1986 illustrated the lengths to which Earnhardt was willing to go to stay out front once he got there. With three laps remaining in the race, Jaws was running second to the Intimidator and was looking to make his own move to get out front.

Driving then for Junior Johnson, Waltrip came on the radio and told Johnson in the pits: "I'm going to make my move down the backstretch! I'm going to pass him on the backstretch!" Johnson, who had been imploring Waltrip to make an attempt to pass in one of the corners, warned his driver to be careful; he didn't want Waltrip to make the pass and then get directly in front of Earnhardt for fear that he would try to simply knock him out of the way.

"All right, but don't you clear him! Because the second you think you've cleared him, he'll turn you!" Johnson replied.

Waltrip heard the first part of Johnson's message, but ignored the second. Jaws shot inside of the Intimidator on the backstretch and attempted to clear him. As the two cars entered turn three, Earnhardt caught the right rear quarter panel of Waltrip's Chevrolet and turned Jaws enough so that he had no choice but to slam head-on into the outside guardrail. The impact was frightening not only to Waltrip, but to everyone who watched the incident unfold.

Earnhardt wrecked too, but seemed to care little about that. His malicious maneuver took out not only Waltrip but also Geoff Bodine and Joe Ruttman, who had been running close behind the two leaders. Johnson was furious afterward; Junior had driven hard in his own day, but not so dangerously, at least not in his mind.

"You can't race with a fool like that!" Johnson said of Earnhardt as he rushed to make certain that his own driver was okay. "It was no different than if he had put a loaded gun to Darrell's head and pulled the trigger."

Earnhardt made it clear that he wasn't about to stop taking aim at folks who interfered with his burning desire to reach Victory Lane. Leaning casually against his own wrecked car after the race, he remarked to reporters: "Helluva show, wasn't it?"

The winner that wild afternoon in Richmond was Kyle Petty, Richard's only son. He had been running in fifth place when Earnhardt effectively eliminated the four in front of him. All he had to do was negotiate his car through the wreckage that was piled up in turn three, and then he went on to win his first Winston Cup race under caution. Since entering Winston Cup racing in 1979 under intense scrutiny and burdened by enormous expectations, Kyle Petty had been a flop. For that one afternoon, at least, he was the best left standing on the track in what remains one of the more bizarre finishes in Cup history.

The circumstances served to fuel perhaps the most intense rivalry of the 1980s: Waltrip versus Earnhardt. Prior to that day, Waltrip had won fifty-two races to Earnhardt's fifteen since the Intimidator's rookie season in 1979. Along the way, Waltrip often rubbed Earnhardt the wrong way intentionally with verbal jousts, once suggesting that drivers "ought to get ten bonus points for taking Earnhardt out of a race."

That kind of talk stirred Earnhardt's competitiveness; he was a throwback, so much so that even rough-and-tumble veterans like Junior Johnson were wary of him. But at least he knew where he came from and which drivers deserved his respect. Earnhardt thought Waltrip was a loudmouth who didn't appreciate all that racing offered in terms of an improved lifestyle.

For instance, while Waltrip made fun of David Pearson's demise, Earnhardt respected the Silver Fox greatly and was much more reverent of what NASCAR's forefathers had done before his arrival in racing; after all, his father Ralph had been one of them. When Dale Earnhardt crashed hard at Pocono, Pennsylvania, early in his career and car owner Rod Osterlund needed a relief driver in a hurry, the call went out to Pearson to drive the following week in the Southern 500 at Darlington—the site of Pearson's pit fiasco only five months earlier. Pearson won, and won the Rebel 500 over Benny Parsons at Darlington the following spring, but those two triumphs, the one hundred and fourth and one hundred and fifth of Pearson's career, would be his last.

Pearson continued driving until 1986, but retired in April of that year because of recurring back problems. The great irony in the timing of his announcement was the fact that he did so just before a race at Charlotte Motor Speedway, one of his favorite tracks, after he had been tabbed by the Wood brothers to drive for an injured Neil Bonnett.

By then, there were new stars in the NASCAR orbit and at least one of them, Earnhardt, drove with a fury reminiscent of the past. Wheeler said that Earnhardt had plenty in common with the greatest drivers of all time.

"The guy's got an uncanny ability to drive on slick racetracks. I think if you look back at the great stock car drivers—Petty, Earnhardt, Cale Yarborough, Waltrip—they had great ability too," Wheeler said. "When a race starts on any track, it goes through three or four phases before the end. It gets slick, or it gets cold and tight. It gets hot and it gets slick. Then cloud cover comes and it becomes a new racetrack.

"They all had the great ability to adjust to these changing conditions. You have to adjust chassis and stuff while this is going on, but the driver's got to be able to adjust too. And the one thing he's got to be able to do is drive a loose race car—because that's when it reverts to almost a dirt track like in the old days."

There is one other thing about Earnhardt that is impossible to overlook, Wheeler added. "Earnhardt has that ability to intimidate," he said. "People don't like to see that black car on their bumper. They just don't. Now Richard Petty, he was okay on your back bumper. David Pearson, he was okay. But you didn't want to see that black car."

Family Secrets

The wild wreck at Richmond in 1986 reignited Dale Earnhardt's sputtering career, and the Intimidator captured his second points championship. However, he really was not the most captivating driver on the circuit that season; neither was Darrell Waltrip, nor Million-Dollar Bill Elliott. The 1986 season belonged to Tim Richmond, an Ohio native who had cut his teeth in Indy Car open-wheel racing. In 1980, he competed in the Indianapolis 500 and was running in the top five when he ran out of fuel and had to settle for ninth, which was still good enough to earn him Rookie of the Year honors; shortly thereafter, Richmond fell in love with stock car racing.

He kicked around with various rides until 1986, when up-and-coming owner Rick Hendrick took him on and provided Richmond with one of the best crew chiefs in the business in Harry Hyde. Richmond always wanted to run wide open, while Hyde always tried to convince Richmond about the benefits of saving the car and sticking around until the end of the race. Richmond and Hyde's stormy relationship was the basis years later for the movie *Days of Thunder,* starring Tom Cruise as a young, reckless driver and Robert Duvall as a stubborn veteran crew chief, who clashes with the brash, headstrong driver.

Once, during a tire test at the North Wilkesboro track in North Carolina, Hyde talked Richmond into running fifty laps wide open and fifty laps conservatively; at the end of the test, Hyde approached Richmond.

"Well, by my calculations, your way would have put us about seven laps down over the course of a four hundred-lap race. My way, we would have probably won a four hundred-lap race," Hyde told the driver. His numbers got Richmond's attention.

But Richmond wasn't about to slow down much on or off the track and, in many ways, Tim Richmond's career paralleled Curtis Turner's: both were devilishly handsome and had insatiable appetites for women and alcohol, and each burned bright before their flames were too quickly extinguished. And then they were gone.

Driving for Hendrick, one of the sport's top car owners, Richmond won seven races in 1986. Each time he won, and even when he didn't, Richmond celebrated with gusto. He was known to show up at bars near a track the night before a race and party until closing time, and then would shout, "All right, everybody! Now it's back to my place!" But Richmond wasn't just drinking; he was using illegal drugs too, according to acquaintances. Once after winning a race, he arrived at the home of one of his many girlfriends holding the trophy in one hand and a bag of cocaine in the other.

"I won again, honey! Let's party!" he said.

Hyde, an irrepressible practical joker, loved to tease his young driver. One of his hobbies was to sit around on his property near Charlotte Motor Speedway and "plink" old aluminum cans with his .22-caliber rifles. One day when Richmond and a girlfriend showed up the driver asked to try his hand.

"Sure," Hyde said, "but I'll have to go into the house to get you some ammo."

The rifles reloaded, Hyde watched as Richmond's girlfriend proceeded to slowly get the hang of it, occasionally plinking a can or two, but Richmond grew frustrated, missing every time he pulled the trigger. "Something's gotta be wrong with this rifle you gave me, let me switch with her," Richmond said.

"Sure," Hyde said, "just let me reload it for you."

Richmond took the other rifle and kept on missing, Hyde teasing him with every errant shot. Finally, Richmond gave up and stormed out. Hyde smiled, knowing that he had given the girl real ammo, while Richmond had gotten a box full of blanks. On the track, though, Hyde respected Richmond's considerable talent. Once during a multicar pileup in the middle of a race, Hyde was having a hard time raising Richmond on the radio, and couldn't tell if his star driver had avoided the wreckage. "Tim! Tim! Did you come through it okay?" Hyde shouted into the radio. After several seconds of static, Richmond's voice crackled back: "I don't know! I'm still wreckin'!"

Once Richmond showed up for a race so hungover from yet another night of wild partying that several drivers threatened to boycott the event if officials let him get behind the wheel. Shrugging off their threats, he got behind the wheel anyway, as Turner had in a similar situation two decades earlier.

Richmond, whose style was a curious blend of haute couture and low country, romanced far too many women to count. But he was most taken with former model LaGena Lookabill Greene of Charlotte, who he pursued for six years, proposing marriage to her on three different occasions. She was a former Miss Hawaiian Tropic USA and Junior Olympic gymnast before becoming an actress, who had guest-starred on TV series such as *St. Elsewhere* and *Remington Steele.* She had graduated with honors from the University of North Carolina with a double major in psychology and art. Refusing Richmond's advances at first because she knew he had wandering eyes, she nonetheless couldn't forget him; not many people could once Richmond turned on the charm.

Most of Richmond's early driving experience had come in open-wheel Indy-style cars, but with his movie star good looks and engaging smile, Richmond ignored critics who said he didn't have enough expertise in stock cars and became a media darling.

The press initially ignored his obvious faults, and plentiful indiscretions, as is often the case with star athletes.

Richmond won four races from 1982 through 1984 before hooking up with Hendrick, who had more money and better cars and figured correctly that he had a budding star on his hands. Richmond won seven races in 1986, a staggering total against a competitive collection of drivers including Earnhardt, Waltrip and a dozen others who were used to getting to the winner's circle.

But Richmond was already dying.

His sordid lifestyle had caught up with him in the form of a disease that was only beginning to register any impact in the nation's consciousness; Tim Richmond had AIDS.

LaGena Lookabill Greene believes that he already knew he was afflicted with the disease when he asked her to fly to New York with him on September 10, 1986. In an elegant hotel suite overlooking Central Park, Richmond proposed marriage for the third and final time, promising to be a devoted husband and father. Greene accepted, and later said that afterward she and Richmond made love.

"I believed that by giving myself to Tim physically, our union marked the beginning of a lifetime of commitment," Greene told the *Miami Herald* in 1996, long after she too had been diagnosed with AIDS. "We never made love again. Now I see that day as the end of my life as I had known it."

They made plans to spend the following Thanksgiving together in Los Angeles, but Richmond didn't show up for the rendezvous.

"And he didn't call for the next two years and four months," Greene later told the newspaper.

At first NASCAR tried to hide the fact that Richmond had AIDS; when he inexplicably disappeared from the circuit less than a year after winning seven races in 1986, NASCAR officials insisted that he had pneumonia. Ironically, the sport had always celebrated characters like Richmond and laughed off their indiscretions; womanizing was generally admired among NASCAR's ranks and their fans. NASCAR wanted to protect its image, and therefore passed off Richmond's illness as pneumonia; but Richmond knew differently.

He wanted to continue racing, and lobbied NASCAR to let him in 1987. They finally relented and on June 14, 1987, he returned to the circuit and took the lead from Bill Elliott with forty-seven laps to go at Pocono, Pennsylvania, winning his comeback race in dramatic fashion. He won the next week too at Riverside, California, but it would be his last victory.

Other drivers thought that Richmond didn't look right, speculating that perhaps his health was failing him; most of them still didn't know the truth, that they were tradin' paint with a man who had AIDS. The ones who did know did not want to get on the track with him, and two months after winning his last race, several drivers filed official complaints with NASCAR protesting that his participation compromised their safety. Furthermore, Richmond's health was already deteriorating; prior to a race at Michigan Speedway, team members had trouble waking him from a deep sleep in his private bus only minutes before he was scheduled to qualify his Chevrolet. Finally, on September 9, 1987, less than a full year after he had taken the circuit by storm, Richmond resigned from Hendrick Motorsports.

In Charlotte, LaGena Lookabill Greene began receiving dozens of phone calls from women who wanted to know if the rumors about Tim Richmond having AIDS were true; they had also slept with him and feared for their lives.

"From those calls alone—only counting the ones from Charlotte—I could have started a support group of women exposed to HIV from Tim," Greene said in her 1996 interview with the *Miami Herald.* "There would have been about thirty in that support group. They told me they were exposed, that they had had sex with Tim and they were worried."

One of the women, Debbie Putman of Charlotte, North Carolina, died of AIDS at age thirty-five; Richmond would not survive even that long. His comeback after his diagnosis was short-lived, and he was out of racing altogether by 1988. By August of 1989, he was dead at age thirty-four.

Richmond's loss was not as deeply mourned as the deaths of other members of the NASCAR fraternity who had passed away. The popular Tiny Lund died at Talladega in a crash in August of 1975, and Buddy Baker, one of Tiny's many good friends in racing, was unaware of the tragedy even after he had won the race and was entertaining the media in the winner's circle. Baker later told author Peter Golenbock in his book *The Last Lap* that he was told of Lund's death so casually that he was shaken to the core.

"The car handled great. We really ran great today," Baker was telling the media.

"Oh, by the way, Tiny died today. What do you think about that?" Baker remembers one insensitive reporter asking.

Baker nearly fell out of his chair.

"Guys, you will have to excuse me. That's the end of the interview," he said. Later, he told Golenbock, "Tiny was a good friend. Racing means a lot, but it's just not that important."

Certainly, the cavalier reaction to Lund and Richmond's deaths was an inevitable byproduct of the racing environment; hey, deaths happen. It was as if the brave and gallant drivers were considered fallen heroes—casualties of war. A strange and morbid subplot in NASCAR's history, the circuit's relative indifference to death would come under increased scrutiny as auto racing became more visible in the coming years.

Of course, Richmond's death wasn't the first NASCAR had glossed over, nor would it be the last.

In 1970 driver Lee Roy Yarbrough crashed hard during tire tests at the Texas World Speedway, knocking himself unconscious. He soon began suffering lengthy memory lapses related to the crash, but was cleared to run again both in Indy Car and on the NASCAR circuit. He was also meanwhile drinking heavily, and by late 1972 he was out of racing altogether. Eight years later, he was committed to a mental hospital after attacking his own mother and attempting to choke her to death. He died in a Florida hospital in 1984 after suffering a violent seizure and striking his head, and some wondered if it might have been different had he gotten proper medical treatment for his initial concussion fourteen years earlier. Instead, he had continued to race (and crash) for two more years, almost certainly causing additional damage.

Lund died at Talladega, which the drivers had pronounced unsafe at its opening only six years earlier. In 1987, Bobby Allison, one of the circuit's most respected and experienced drivers, sailed airborne off the track—tearing down a good fifty yards of the frontstretch catch fence. He was only kept from going into the grandstands by two steel cables that reinforced the fence.

The Allison incident finally led to the end of unrestricted racing at NASCAR's two greatest superspeedways—Daytona and Talladega. Mostly out of fear for spectator safety, NASCAR mandated carburetor restrictor plates at both venues in an effort to keep speeds under two hundred miles per hour. It worked, but at the expense of some exciting racing. Drivers like Earnhardt hated it because it not only took away his ability to pass anywhere he damn well wanted on a track like Talladega, but it also reduced his ability to accelerate away from trouble when he spotted it.

Though NASCAR's restrictions made racing safer and smarter, that didn't mean resurrected Confederate soldiers were going to like it.

Through the years, no one more accurately personified NASCAR than Junior Johnson, who by the mid-1980s had evolved from moonshine runner to champion driver to successful car owner. After serving nearly a year in a Chillicothe, Ohio, federal prison for tending to the family still, he returned to the stock car circuit, and by the early 1970s was helping broker big-money deals between corporate sponsors and Big Bill France. By the end of the decade Johnson had so rehabilitated his image that his good friend

Enoch Staley, who ran the track at North Wilkesboro, called to tell him that he wanted to erect a wooden grandstand in Junior's honor. Johnson welcomed the honor, but was apprehensive when he learned that Staley's plan was to christen the Junior Johnson Grandstand with a half-gallon jug of Wilkes County's finest white lightning.

"I don't want nothin' to do with any of that stuff. It caused me enough trouble when I was a young feller," Johnson told Staley.

"Don't worry, Junior. I promise you won't even have to touch the jar," Staley replied.

When Johnson arrived at the small ceremony a few days later, he found the jar of moonshine tied by a long cord to the very top of the new grandstand. Junior grabbed the middle of the cord, pulled back and let it smash into a railing, where it shattered into hundreds of pieces. "He was right. I never had to touch it. But the smell from that stuff was pretty bad," Johnson later said. In 1986, President Ronald Reagan pardoned Junior for his booze-running as a young man, further evidence that Johnson and NASCAR had moved closer to the American mainstream.

Some suspected that the same Junior Johnson was not entirely reformed, however, particularly when it came to the tactics he'd use to cultivate relationships with reporters who covered his teams. When one reporter wrote a piece surprisingly critical of Johnson's ownership methods, he found himself surrounded by Johnson supporters as he left the press box at a track the following afternoon. Surrounding him, they began to threaten the besieged columnist.

"What were ya thinkin', writing those things about Junior?"

"We ought to kick your ass."

As they jumped the reporter, throwing him to the ground and acting as though they were going to start pummeling him, a car roared toward them and screeched to a halt, breaking up the fracas; it was Junior Johnson.

"Quick! Get in! Let's get out of here!" Johnson commanded.

The reporter scrambled to his feet and jumped in the car. Junior floored it, and they were gone. As the two men drove off, Johnson played the good cop. "What in the hell happened?" he asked.

"You won't believe it. They jumped me because of something I wrote about you," the reporter said.

Johnson smiled and acted terribly concerned. The reporter, who would later wonder whether Johnson had staged the whole thing, never again wrote a bad word about Junior Johnson.

If sometimes underhanded, Junior Johnson was fiercely loyal. Pete Wright was a member of Johnson's team in the mid-eighties, after defecting from the team run by owner Billy Hagan—where he had met future drivers Terry and Bobby Labonte long before they were big names.

"Bobby was a floor sweeper at Hagan's around 1981," Wright said. "He would work half a day at school, and then come in there and work. He would get out of school at three o'clock, and he would sweep floors and empty trash cans and stuff. I joke around with him about that now. I know how he got where he's at. Even when he was sweepin' floors and emptyin' trash cans, he always said: 'I'm going to be a driver. I want to be a driver.' " Wright ended up on Junior's team when Johnson came to him and asked if he would consider filling in as crew chief and jack man for Jeff Hammonds, who was having a knee operation and would be unable to jack for a while.

Wright, who had been a fan of NASCAR since he was a boy attending races every weekend in Rocky Mount, Virginia, could not resist the urge to join the great Junior Johnson's team. "It was the middle of the season. I didn't want to quit Hagan, but I did," he said. He quickly discovered that Johnson's pit crew, like the entire team, held high standards for their racing operation.

"I will never forget the first time I jacked for them, at Pocono in 1986. Back then, they had pit crew races during the race itself. We had won it at Hagan's in '83," Wright said. "Whoever spent the least amount of time on pit road in like twelve given races would win it. The time would start from when they entered pit road to when they left, including the pit stops and all. Junior's team really wanted to win it when I got there in '86. We all did because it was like a fifteen-thousand-dollar split amongst the pit crew if you won. Back then, that was damn good money."

So before that first race as a member of the Johnson crew, Wright found himself surrounded by tire changers Mike Hill and Sandy Jones, who were looking none too friendly. "Now listen, bud, don't make us wait on you today. Don't make us wait on you—because if you do, we'll get Junior to get somebody else to jack the car," they told Wright.

Wright nodded, but thought to himself: You bunch of damn hot dogs. You'll find out here what I can do.

"Darrell [Waltrip] was driving, and he comes in seventh, I believe," Wright recalls. "That was before they had pit-road speed [limits] and all that. When they come down pit road in those days, they came hard. And when they all left, he was leading. When they come back around, he was leading the race under caution." After the pit stop, Wright walked up to Hill and Jones as they finished wrapping up their air hoses.

"Boys, y'all are going to have to pick up the pace a little bit if you want me to jack for you," Wright told them. "I was in. From then on, there was no problem."

Wright soon discovered that Junior Johnson's team was a family operation from top to bottom. It wasn't only Junior who treated the workers in the shop like their own kin, but also Junior's longtime wife Flossie.

"Floss and Junior didn't have any kids, so we were their kids," Wright said. "You didn't go to the bank. If you wanted a new car, or to buy your wife something for Christmas or her birthday, you didn't go to the bank or use your credit card. You went to see Flossie, and she would help you. I mean, I wish I had a dollar for every meal I went up there and ate while I worked there for eight years. . . . I remember times when me and some people would go off to eat and come back, and she'd see us pull in. She'd call the shop wanting to know why we didn't come up to the house and eat."

The Johnsons' approach made the shop men forget about the long hours they put in virtually each and every week of the year at the garage in Ronda, North Carolina, Junior's lifelong hometown.

"You could stay there and work all night," Wright said. "I worked several all-nighters up there getting cars ready. But you didn't care because you knew they appreciated it."

There were many nights when Wright would look up the hill toward the Johnson house and see Junior staring down from a window up above.

"Junior stood up there in that house and looked down there on the shop," Wright said. "He could see in the shops from his house, see the lights on. You knew he wasn't up there talking about you or anything like that. He was up there appreciating what you were doing. He would come down and say, 'You need anything? Need me to go to the store and get you anything?'

"If you worked all night, you didn't even think about going home until you went up to the big house and ate breakfast with Floss. That was just their way of showing their appreciation. I was there a good month before I really started feeling a part of the family; but I had known Junior, or at least known of him, ever since I was a kid because of his moonshine days. I had family that made moonshine and moonshiners stuck together back then."

Waltrip would say years later that Johnson's impact on the sport cannot truly be measured because so much of his influence was felt primarily by the guys in the shops who have achieved their own measure of fame and success in NASCAR's garages.

"Drivers come and go, but so many mechanics have gone through Junior's doors, so many guys that have done so much in this sport . . . engine builders and car builders and crew chiefs . . . I can't even think of all of them," Waltrip said. "That's what we called the University of Ronda, and when you left there you had one of the best educations in racing that you could ever hope to get.

"Junior was an innovator. He never technically cheated or broke any rules because everything he did, no rules had been made pertaining to that particular [car modification] at that time. So Junior is more responsible than anybody else for language in the rule book. Because he would lay awake at night studying, [thinking], Okay, it says this but it don't say that. Then he would always have a little bit of an edge on everybody.

"He was an automotive genius, a mechanical genius, by all means, and [had] common sense. Junior could take a piece of metal, or a crankshaft or a rod, and say, 'You know what? If I did this or I did that, I think I could make this a better piece.' He was a hands-on guy who could touch it and feel it and then make it happen. He didn't have to necessarily run it through a computer or spend a lot of time designing it. He'd just do it based on how it felt and how it looked."

However, Waltrip's assertion that Johnson never cheated is absurd. Even Junior would admit to bending the rules whenever he thought he could get away with it.

"We all cheated. There's no question about it. We all cheated at one time or another," said Johnson, whose marriage with Flossie eventually fell apart—as did the family atmosphere that once permeated their home and race shop.

As NASCAR approached the 1990s, there were those who saw the need for the sport to become more inclusive and diverse. Unfortunately, those who understood the benefits of inclusions and diversity were not among NASCAR's elite. Too many of the circuit's insiders could not see past the Confederate flags and dollar signs being flashed in front of their faces each week, even as the sport continued to spread throughout the United States and further distance itself from its moonshine roots in the Deep South.

It was into this environment that Willy T. Ribbs ventured for a brief three-race stint in 1986. In some ways Ribbs seemed a dream for NASCAR; always looking for qualified drivers who could promote themselves, their sport and their sponsors' products, Willy T. appeared to be an advertising bonanza. Ribbs was handsome, had won a driving championship at the Trans Am level, knew how to handle a car and was a smooth talker.

He was also black. No other African-American driver had raced at NASCAR's highest level since Wendell Scott had been forced into retirement after suffering life-threatening injuries during a crash at Talladega in 1973.

Willy T. Ribbs? Sounds like a joint that sells barbecue, some laughed.

But Ribbs saw his venture into NASCAR as no laughing matter; he wanted to make a difference and stick around for the long haul.

"I had won the Trans Am national championship, and I was looking for a new challenge," Ribbs said. "Initially, I thought we would be able to get more sponsorship money. We thought we would be able to attract some corporate advertisers. We thought more of them would want to be part of making a positive change in the sport. It just didn't happen."

Ribbs's NASCAR driving career lasted all of three races, 516 laps and 540 miles in 1986. Driving a car for Digard Racing and team owner Bill Gardner, he ran at North Wilkesboro, at Riverside, California, and at Michigan, failing to finish any of the races before engine failure finished him first.

Ribbs said that he was received well by most of the drivers. "I'd say ninety percent of them were very professional, and some of the others chose to remain ignorant," Ribbs said. "I have no comment on them, other than to say that the other ten percent were part of the problem and not the solution. Where I got most of my resistance, though, was not among my peers or even the fans. It was more among the sponsors and some of the team owners."

Ribbs never did get to meet Scott, who died in 1990.

"I never did [meet Scott]. I wish I had. I think it's really sad that

I never got to meet him," Ribbs said. "I was not familiar with his background prior to my entry into NASCAR. I would have liked to have talked with him about his experiences.

"A lot of people back when he was racing had manufacturer's sponsors and other money coming in to back them. He had nothing. But in those days, the money was nice but not necessarily a requirement if you just wanted to run. Now it's so much bigger, you have to have the financial backing or you can't even get out there."

By 1986, Ribbs estimated that it cost somewhere around $3.5 million to $4 million to field a competitive NASCAR race team for an entire schedule.

"We were just operating on a shoestring, about three hundred thousand dollars total," he said. "Every time we had engine failures. We just didn't have the money to put a competitive car out there. It just didn't happen, and after the third race they had to close the doors to the shop. That was it. It was over."

Despite this hard reality, Ribbs held out hope at first that Digard Racing would receive financial assistance from someone. But the call never came.

"At that particular time, yes, I believed something would happen to keep it going for us," he said. "I believed in the American Dream. I didn't hold onto that for very long, not in NASCAR. The American Dream did happen for me, but it happened for me in Indy Car racing." (The American Dream came along, and the Fairy Godfather was Bill Cosby, who agreed to finance Ribbs's Indy Car effort.)

"People from CART/Indy Car and the organizers of the Indy 500 all treated me like a normal human being, not like a second-class citizen. It was totally different from my experience in NASCAR. I was accepted as a normal human being."

Years passed, and no one called to offer Ribbs another NASCAR ride. It led the bitter Ribbs to conclude that NASCAR simply does not want minority drivers. He does not believe that it can present itself to the American public as their next major sport until it changes its approach to race relations.

"The minority involvement is just not there," Ribbs said. "The only way you can tout yourself as a major sport is if all Americans are invited to participate. Until that happens, you are not a major sport. If they really believe that, they [NASCAR] are psychologically masturbating.

"They could change it. They know what they need to do. They know exactly what they need to do."

He argues that the sport's racial climate could change with one phone call, taking issue with NASCAR's arguments that there simply are no qualified African-American drivers, nor are there many programs in place to promote minority involvement.

"Why not give Willy T. Ribbs a call? So that argument doesn't fly. They know who's available. I'm still driving on the Trans Am circuit," Ribbs said in the year 2000. "If I got in with the proper practice program and a team that had some money behind it, I could still do it.

"Everything they say they're doing now to address the problem, it's all window dressing. If NASCAR wanted me in Winston Cup championship racing, I'd be in Winston Cup racing. . . . All they got to do is call one of the teams and say, 'Hey, look, give Willy T. Ribbs a call. Get him behind the wheel of one of your cars and give him a chance to race for the championship.' They call different people every single day, drivers who have had not near the success nor the name that I've had, okay? So all that other stuff is just that: stuff that represents a stall tactic."

Ribbs insists that he was well received by the fans he came into contact with during his brief foray into NASCAR.

"I had pretty much fan interaction and it was pretty positive, actually. I would even say very positive," he said. "I mean, man, they lined up for autographs—in the hills of North Carolina. They knew I could drive. They knew what I was driving too, though.

"I wasn't looking for any problems from the fans, so I can't say it surprised me. They just came flocking to my trailer. I found that to be encouraging at the time. Maybe the sponsors weren't watching the fans."

Ribbs will admit to being disturbed by the rows and rows of Confederate flags that he sees at NASCAR events even today.

"I guess that sort of sets the tone, doesn't it? You reap what you sow," he said. "No one has ever called me back from NASCAR. But I didn't expect them to."

Nonetheless, he doesn't buy the argument that African-American drivers would be shunned by a large portion of the paying NASCAR public, who want theirs to remain the last "whites-only" sport in America.

"That's the same theory they used when they argued against bringing Jackie Robinson into baseball," he said. "But exactly the opposite happened. The sport would explode and diehard fans would love it."

Oddly, Ribbs was hired to run in the NASCAR truck-racing tour not long after giving this interview, indicating that despite his justifiably harsh assessment of measures taken by NASCAR to address the total lack of diversity in the sport, there are some in the circuit committed to improving race relations.

Wonder Boy and the Good Ol' Boys

As the 1980s concluded and the 1990s began, NASCAR was in more desperate need of new star drivers' bitter rivalries to fuel the sport's growth and popularity as perhaps never before. Bobby Allison had been forced into retirement in 1988 after a terrible accident at Pocono International Raceway in Pennsylvania left him in critical condition for several weeks, and required months of intensive physical therapy. He left with eighty-four career victories, third on the all-time list behind only Richard Petty and David Pearson, but because of the accident he could no longer remember the details of all of them. Cale Yarborough retired as a driver the same year, taking his eighty-three career victories and an 0-1 record in Daytona fist fights against the Allisons into his new role as car owner. Dale Earnhardt and Darrell Waltrip had gone at it pretty good in the eighties and were still driving, but suddenly their rivalry didn't seem as heated as Waltrip's star began to fade. Even the King was still driving—but Richard Petty hadn't won a race since 1984 when he captured career win number two hundred at the Firecracker 400 in Daytona.

So who was left to carry the torch? Not Kyle Petty, Richard's son, who had a matinee-idol smile and had proven only to be a competent, if unspectacular, driver. Earlier in his career he lacked the dedication to the sport that his father and grandfather had displayed, and seemed too interested in other things away from the track. He often joked that he probably lacked their driving skills as well, although there were days when he appeared to be an outstanding racer. In 1992, he was in the hunt for a Winston Cup points championship, giving the legions of Petty fans hope that they could soon transfer their driver loyalty from Richard, who was about to retire, to his only son; Petty, though, would never fully realize his potential.

Another driver's son, however, was beginning to show signs of greatness, displaying rare skill, raw determination, fierce dedication and courage behind the wheel. Before he could speak, Bobby Allison's son Davey would point at his daddy's race car and make sounds like a revving engine. In grade school, he was reprimanded by teachers for drawing pictures of race cars when he was supposed to be paying attention to his lessons. As he grew into a teenager, the only way his parents could get him to concentrate on keeping his grades up at school was to ban him from the race shop until the marks at school were up to snuff.

Eventually, he started driving his own car on short tracks across the Southeast, winning his fair share and longing for a shot at the big time. His opportunity arrived in July of 1985 when Hoss Ellington enlisted the young Allison to drive his Chevrolet in a race at Talladega, and Davey came home in tenth. Afterward, his car was mobbed in the garage area by members of the media who believed that he was primed to become the sport's next superstar. It wasn't until 1987, when owner Harry Ranier tabbed him to replace the retiring Yarborough, that he gained a full-time Winston Cup ride—but success came quickly. He won two races that season and captured Rookie of the Year honors.

The next season, Ranier left the team and Robert Yates, the highly respected longtime engine builder and crew chief, took over as team owner; it was a good match for the young driver. Both were quiet, introspective men who were intensely competitive and possessed burning desires to win. Over the next four seasons, they teamed to capture fourteen poles and seventeen races, including the 1992 Daytona 500.

"We really get along well. I can see spending my whole career working with Robert Yates," Davey Allison told friends and family.

Likewise, Yates and those who worked with Davey had nothing but great things to say about the experience; everyone on the team seemed to mesh and get along. They hadn't yet won the Winston Cup points championship, but they sensed that they soon would win more than one. Davey Allison finished third behind Dale Earnhardt and Ricky Rudd in the 1991 points championship, and in 1992 he entered the final race of the season leading a five-driver battle for the coveted crown.

Running second in the points heading into that race was another strong candidate to be anointed NASCAR's preeminent superstar of the nineties—Alan Kulwicki. Unlike the likable Davey Allison, Kulwicki was a talented but difficult man who was so obsessed with perfection that he often drove those around him insane. A native of Wisconsin, he also was viewed by many NASCAR partisans as an outsider.

Yet there was evidence that he was something of a genius. He attended college and studied engineering, then put what he learned to practical use by inventing a number of automotive gadgets that were incorporated not only by his own crew, but all race teams. Unable to see the right rear corner of his race car in what was then the standard rearview mirror, he devloped a multi-angled mirror that enabled him to view the obscured area. He invented a baffled exhaust system for stock cars, and a wheel-balancing system that was used in Indy Car racing.

By 1984, after running successfully in several USAC stock car division races and American Speed Association races, Kulwicki ran his own cars in five NASCAR Busch series races. Two years later, still running his own team on a shoestring budget, he moved to Concord, North Carolina, home of the Charlotte Motor Speedway, and decided to give Winston Cup a try. Amazingly, with only one car and two engines, he completed 94.7 percent of the possible total number of laps in the twenty-three events he entered, earning Rookie of the Year honors.

He got his first Winston Cup win in 1988 and celebrated by doing what he called "the Polish Victory Lap," a clockwise lap around the speedway in Phoenix, Arizona. He captured four pole positions that year and six more the next, which prompted none other than Junior Johnson to approach him about giving up his own team to come and drive for him. It was a lucrative, long-term deal that Johnson offered, and Kulwicki would no longer have to worry about stretching his meager finances to remain competitive.

Kulwicki stunned the racing world by turning Johnson down, something that just wasn't done. Johnson wasn't pleased, and it did not seem to be mere coincidence when the primary sponsor Kulwicki had lined up for his own team in 1991 defected to Johnson only weeks before the season-opening Daytona 500. Kulwicki was able to enter that event only by virtue of a one-race sponsorship deal he cut with the U.S. Army, and he entered the next three by exhausting his own bank account. Eventually, Kulwicki won a pole position at Atlanta that year and a race at Bristol, which gained him a three-year sponsorship, relieving some of the financial pressure heading into 1992.

As the '92 season came to a close, Kulwicki was battling Davey Allison and three very popular drivers in Bill Elliott, Harry Gant and Kyle Petty for the points championship, which came down to the very last race of the season on November 15, 1992, with all five arriving at the event with a mathematical chance of winning the title.

Adding to the drama was the fact that it was the final race of Richard Petty's storied career. He remained enormously popular, even though he hadn't won since 1984 and, according to his most vocal critics, including Darrell Waltrip, the King had been "just riding around" for eight years. His critics, though, were far outnumbered by his admirers. The night before the race, the Hooters

500, a crowd estimated at 75,000 had turned out at the Georgia Dome to say good-bye.

Humpy Wheeler, president of Charlotte Motor Speedway, was one of the millions who were going to miss Richard Petty's No. 43 car driving around the track every Sunday—even though he knew, like the rest of the public, that Richard Petty wasn't really going anywhere. The King was going to continue to be around the sport as the head of Petty Enterprises, trying to help Kyle win his own championships. Richard Petty was retiring with two hundred career wins—ninety-five more than any other driver—and seven points championships, also a record.

More important than all the impressive numbers, though, was what he meant and would continue to mean to the sport as an ambassador.

"He was our Arnold Palmer," Wheeler said. "There was nothing spectacular about the way he drove, he just did it very gracefully. He had the ability to keep the people who were on his team together, mainly [crew chief and master mechanic] Dale Inman and his brother Maurice [who built the engines].

"The greatest thing about Richard Petty, and the thing we'll never, ever be able to repay him for, is the countless hours he stayed at those hole-in-the-wall tracks signing autographs and the wonderful, beautiful, graceful way that he accepted defeat. You never heard him whine—except maybe a little bit about David Pearson and Bobby Allison. But if he was out there and blew the engine, he'd come back smiling. He'd get back in the trailer and be mad as hell, but he had that great ability to be positive about everything. And to pay attention to the fans.

"I'm not sure that I know, even after being around the Benedictine monks at Belmont Abbey College [in North Carolina], any cleaner-living person than him, because I spent an enormous amount of time with him on the road. He was our number one guy in NASCAR."

Wheeler said that the Richard Petty Farewell Tour of 1992 at tracks around the country was the first indication that NASCAR was poised to reach new heights of popularity previously thought unattainable.

"The other extraordinary thing about Richard Petty, he never really made a lot of money racing if you really look at it. He got paid back on the greatest farewell tour any athlete in the history of sport has done," Wheeler said. "I think that's where we got the first glimpse that this thing was going to take off and just go to the stratosphere. The response, the outpouring of fans on that tour, was overwhelming."

It was so impressive that Wheeler received calls from agents for other prominent athletes who were retiring (including a representative of basketball great Kareem Abdul-Jabbar), inquiring how NASCAR had organized the Petty farewell.

"We were actually helping [Petty] with it," Wheeler said of the Charlotte Motor Speedway marketing arm. "We were doing a joint venture with him where we'd do a Richard Petty car every race . . . a Daytona Richard Petty [No.] forty-three . . . a Rockingham forty-three, so on and so forth.

"The first signal to us that this was going to be much bigger than we initially thought was when our souvenir guys ordered twenty-five thousand of these little cars, and took them down to Daytona for the first race."

Wheeler arrived at Daytona on the Wednesday before the race and sought out his souvenir guy.

"How's the car deal going?" Wheeler asked.

"Too good, really. There's none left," he replied.

Wheeler was stunned, but it was Daytona, and there had been qualifying the previous week. It was probably an unusual circumstance, he thought.

"Then the next race we sold out at Rockingham," Wheeler said. "The next race was Atlanta, and we really knew what was going on by then. But the cars didn't show up for Atlanta on time. People were mad."

Wheeler spoke with the manufacturer of the souvenir cars and was promised they would be in Charlotte by the Monday after the race, and he related the information to race fans who had asked for the cars in Atlanta and went away fuming.

"Well, I come out to work the Monday morning after Atlanta, and there's cars backed up down the highway [leading to Charlotte Motor Speedway]," Wheeler said.

Before the 1992 season was over, Wheeler had sold nearly one million of the cars, which sold for between seven fifty and ten dollars.

"The fan response was unbelievable," Wheeler said in the year 2000. "I mean, here was Richard in his final year, and he just couldn't be competitive. But the people, the outpouring was just unreal. It seemed like everything they did, all the souvenir stuff, it sold out. And it kept going.

"It was absolutely overwhelming. And even today, years later now, he's still a prolific souvenir seller."

It also helped, according to Wheeler, that in his finest hours Petty had some talented rivals to fend off.

"Look at boxing. Great boxers have great opponents. They have great wars. Rocky Marciano versus Jersey Joe Walcott, Tony Zale versus Rocky Graziano, Muhammad Ali and Joe Frazier. Richard Petty's greatness came out because he beat—most of the time, or at least enough of the time—two other great drivers in David Pearson and Bobby Allison."

The last time Petty ever did was at the 1984 Firecracker 400, a race that was started via radio by President Ronald Reagan from Air Force One as he was en route to Daytona International Speedway to attend the event. After landing at Daytona Beach International Airport adjacent to the track, the president pulled openly for Petty to win the race from a VIP suite at stock car racing's most famous track. Petty was forty-seven years old at the time.

The King was fifty-five years old when he climbed into the car for his last race at the 1992 Hooters 500 in Atlanta. Sadly, his final run lasted only ninety-five laps before he got caught up in a multicar crash and his STP-sponsored, red-white-and-blue Pontiac No. 43 caught fire as it spun into the infield.

"This wasn't the kind of blaze of glory I wanted to go out in," he told reporters later. "But I've been doing this for thirty-five years, and I'm still walking and talking. I've been fortunate."

With the Petty retirement sideshow out of the way early, it was left to the five contenders for the '92 crown—Davey Allison, Alan Kulwicki, Bill Elliott, Harry Gant and Kyle Petty—to fight it out for the points championship with all eyes upon them. Allison fell back early because of a tire problem, but had fought back to sixth place when suddenly, on lap 255 of the 328-lap event, he exited turn four and found that he had no place to go when Ernie Irvan (nicknamed One-Eyed Ernie and Swervin' Irvan for good reasons) spun in front of him. The ensuing wreck knocked Allison from contention, and he went on to finish twenty-seventh.

Gant and Petty kept running, but were back in the pack, finishing thirteenth and sixteenth, respectively, but without ever threatening to win.

That left Kulwicki and Elliott to decide one of the closest points championship battles ever. Elliott was the local favorite, as the native of Dawsonville, Georgia, always was when he drove in Atlanta. Furthermore, he was driving for Junior Johnson, another universal favorite of the NASCAR world, and Johnson hadn't earned a championship as an owner since winning three times with Waltrip at the wheel between 1981 and 1985. The great irony was that it had been Kulwicki, not Elliott, that Johnson had wanted to drive for him that season.

Kulwicki had his legion of fans too. Emphasizing the fact that he ran his own team on a much smaller budget than most of those he competed against, he had a decal of the cartoon figure Underdog plastered on the body of his Ford Thunderbird. Then, as always, many fans loved the underdog—and so as the race wound down, with Elliott in first and Kulwicki stalking him in second, the crowd of 165,000 cheered wildly for both drivers.

With about twenty-five laps to go, they were far enough in front that it seemed they would finish one-two unless they wrecked or one encountered a sudden mechanical failure. Kul-

271

wicki and his crew chief Paul Andrews calculated that they did not necessarily need to win the race to clinch the points championship; they only had to lead the most laps and finish second.

"You've led one hundred three laps today. The best he can do now is lead one hundred two. Save yourself and the car. Make sure you at least finish second and we'll win the championship," Andrews told Kulwicki as he roared around lap 310.

Kulwicki backed off, letting Elliott maintain the lead without challenging him over the last eighteen laps; Elliott won the race and collected 180 points. Kulwicki, who had entered the day with a slim ten-point edge over Elliott and even less of an advantage over Davey Allison, also received 180 points because he earned 175 for his runner-up finish and a five-point bonus for leading the most laps.

Kulwicki and Allison stayed at the track long after the race was over that day, as if they were lingering for a reason even they could not understand. A grinning Kulwicki, in fact, joined Elliott in Victory Lane to celebrate his championship, even though Elliott had won the race. Allison waved good-bye to an appreciative Atlanta crowd, smiling despite his disappointing finish on a day that had begun with much promise.

Those happy images of two drivers who were thought to be the future of their sport that afternoon haunt many who remember them to this day. Neither Kulwicki nor Allison would live through the following season.

Winning the championship strengthened Kulwicki's sponsorship deal with Hooters, the restaurant chain featuring scantily clad waitresses, which had been his primary sponsor for the 1992 Hooters 500. Coupled with the fact that he was now Winston Cup champion, his personal appearance schedule suddenly was crammed with more events than ever. On April 1, 1993, he was flying with Mark Brooks, son of Hooters CEO Robert Brooks, and two others in a private plane from an autograph session at a restaurant in Knoxville, Tennessee, to that weekend's race in

Bristol. On the approach to Tri-Cities Airport, the six-seater crashed—killing all four men.

The NASCAR community had not yet recovered from that tragedy when another one struck just over three months later. Davey Allison, a devout Catholic who had commented to friends and colleagues that maybe he hadn't won the championship in 1992 because the fate of death had awaited the Cup champion, was flying a jet helicopter from his hometown of Hueytown, Alabama, to Talladega to watch a practice session. Although he was considered an expert pilot of fixed-wing aircraft, Allison was inexperienced in the type of helicopter he was flying that day after having only recently purchased it. He crashed in the Talladega infield and died the next morning of severe head injuries.

The two designated stars of the immediate future were gone almost overnight. Someone else would have to rise from anonymity to fill the void left by their deaths.

Going virtually unnoticed in the 1992 Hooters 500 was Jeff Gordon, a boyish-looking driver who finished thirty-first. He didn't look like much; in fact, he didn't look like he was old enough to possess a legal driver's license.

But he had, in fact, been groomed to race from the age of five by his stepfather John Bickford. As a kid he had a stable of eight or nine quarter-midget cars that he would race all over the country, every week, without fail. When he was just fourteen, his parents packed up and moved from California to Pittsboro, Indiana, to give young Jeff's sprint car racing career a boost.

When Gordon was just twenty and racing in the Busch series as a prelude to crashing the Winston Cup party, team owner Jack Roush called up Gordon's stepfather and said he wanted Jeff to begin racing for him at NASCAR's highest level.

"We think your kid could be great, and we think he's ready. We'd like to hire him now," Roush said.

"That's a huge compliment, Jack. But I want to be clear on this.

If Jeff comes, so does Ray Evernham, his crew chief. Jeff and Ray are a package deal," John Bickford replied.

"Wait a minute. You don't understand. My drivers do not select their own crew chiefs," Roush said.

"Well, then I appreciate the call. Have a really nice day," said Bickford, who then hung up.

The phone rang again a moment later. It was Roush calling back.

"Why did you hang up on me?" Roush asked.

"Look, you've made your decision that you're not going to allow the driver to pick the crew chief. The crew chief for Jeff Gordon in Winston Cup will be Ray Evernham. It's not an option. It's not a negotiable point. That's the way it will be," Bickford said.

This time, a puzzled and defeated Roush hung up. If this kid didn't want to cash in on his ticket to the big time, so be it.

Not long thereafter, Gordon raced in the 1992 Hooters 500 with Ray Evernham as his crew chief and Rick Hendrick, not Roush, as his car owner. It would prove to be a formidable triumvirate that quickly took the Winston Cup circuit by storm, despite their inauspicious start in that first race.

At first glance, Gordon and Evernham seemed to be like the Odd Couple. Neither originally hailed from traditional racing communities. Gordon was a West Coast kid who had lived in the Bay Area near San Francisco before making the move to Indiana as a teenager, while Evernham grew up in the shadows of New York City.

Evernham angered some of his high school teachers by turning down a college art scholarship to race in open-wheel modifieds in New Jersey, Long Island and Connecticut. When he wasn't driving, he was working as a mechanic wherever he could to learn more about the sport and how the cars ran. For a time, he worked as a mechanic for cars running in the International Race of Champions series during the week and continued to drive modifieds on weekends.

But after a traumatic accident during a race on a track in Flemington, New Jersey, in 1991, Evernham suffered a brain-stem injury that affected his memory for a while and altered his depth perception forever; his driving career was over. He was by then already somewhat familiar with Gordon, having worked briefly as the chassis man on a crew thrown together in 1990 for Gordon's first venture into NASCAR's Busch series. Gordon remembered being impressed with Evernham because at the time he was still racing.

"He knew the cars better than I did mechanically, yet he could still relate to me as a driver," Gordon said.

When Evernham's career as a driver abruptly ended, he didn't immediately hook up with Gordon. The first full-time job available in NASCAR, where Evernham decided he belonged, was an opening for a chassis specialist for Alan Kulwicki. Like Kulwicki, Evernham also took a very cerebral approach to racing and had a background in mechanical engineering. He thought Kulwicki brilliant, even labeling him "a genius," but admitted that "his personality paid for that."

Kulwicki was as impatient as he was tough and demanding, refusing to suffer fools who failed to keep pace with his brilliance; this proved to turn a number of crew members against him quickly, and Evernham was no exception. The two engaged in a shouting match in the garage area at Daytona in February of 1992, and Evernham announced that he was quitting on the spot.

Still angry over the dispute, Evernham wanted to collect his thoughts and carefully decide what he ought to do next after storming out of the Kulwicki garage, but didn't make it out of the area before Ford engineers intercepted him and recruited him to work full-time on Gordon's Busch team. He only later discovered that he was hired despite the objections of Bill Davis, the owner of the Busch team.

"Ford agreed to pay my salary because Jeff said he wanted me," Evernham said; the two already were forming an unusual bond.

Kulwicki went on to win the Winston Cup that season, and that further motivated Evernham, who wanted to prove to Kulwicki and the rest of the racing world that he was "good enough and smart enough."

Gordon and Evernham won three Busch races on a limited budget in 1992, which led Hendrick to call Bickford and readily accept the package deal that Roush had already turned down. Upon his arrival at Hendrick Motorsports in 1993, the ambitious Evernham posted a huge checklist on the main workroom floor that would remain in place for the next several years. It read:

FROM NOBODY TO UPSTART
FROM UPSTART TO CONTENDER
FROM CONTENDER TO WINNER
FROM WINNER TO CHAMPION
FROM CHAMPION TO DYNASTY

Evernham began working a minimum of twelve hours a day seven days a week, largely ignoring his home life, despite the fact that his young son Raymond John (nicknamed Ray J., after driver A. J. Foyt) was diagnosed with leukemia shortly after he took the new job. Evernham described himself as being on a mission to prove he could be the best of the best at the Winston Cup level. Nothing was going to stand in his way.

He set about assembling a race team that he envisioned being more like an NFL coaching staff than the traditional NASCAR crew, once telling *Sports Illustrated:* "This is a professional sports franchise no matter how you look at it, and in some ways it's tougher. We play a lot more games. There's a mechanical factor. There are rules changes. I hired a lot of smart people. We hired engineers before any other Winston Cup teams had them."

Virginia Tech graduate Brian Whitesell left an engineering position with Mack Trucks behind to sign on as the Gordon team's truck driver until Evernham could get additional money budgeted for another full-time engineering job. Evernham eventually got the money and placed Whitesell in a post he likened to an offensive coordinator in football, saying that Whitesell's job was "to make the car go fast." Ed Guzzo, who came from a New Jersey car dealership, was hired as chief mechanic but Evernham saw him as the "defensive coordinator" to make sure stuff on the car wouldn't break down as often as others.

The pit crew was another priority for Evernham. He envisioned "the guys who go over the wall" on pit stops as a well-coordinated, well-conditioned group of muscular athletes akin to offensive linemen firing off the ball. They needed a coach, so another early Evernham hire was Andy Papathanassiou. Not by coincidence, Papathanassiou was an offensive guard for the Stanford University football team in the late 1980s and owned a master's degree in organizational behavior. Evernham made him NASCAR's first-ever "pit crew coach" and that is precisely how Papathanassiou approached the job.

After college, Papathanassiou toured Australia as a member of an American rugby team. But after returning to the San Francisco area, he went to a Winston Cup race at Sears Point in Sonoma, California, and started asking around the garage area if anyone needed help. He was hired by driver Derrike Cope's crew, sweeping floors, waxing the cars and "doing whatever they told me to do." Eventually, he worked his way up to being named the jack man on race days; after his promotion he approached the other crew members with a question.

"Okay, when's practice?" Papathanassiou asked.

They all looked at him as if he had two heads.

"Practice? What practice? We don't practice," they told him.

Years later, Papathanassiou said of that very moment: "That was it. That was the lightbulb. I knew then that there was a way I could make my mark in this business."

He later ended up working on Alan Kulwicki's team at the same time as Evernham. Their philosophies meshed, and once reunited at Hendrick Motorsports they set about forming a pit crew that would come to be known as "the Rainbow Warriors" in honor of the multicolored paint scheme on Gordon's No. 24 Chevrolet sponsored by DuPont. They even developed their own motto, which was Refuse to Lose.

Papathanassiou required all of his crew members to be outstanding athletes. He had them run and lift weights regularly, which no other teams were doing at the time. The tire changers had to be small, quick and agile enough to get up and around the car with their impact wrenches in minimal time. The tire carriers needed to be bigger and more muscular so they could handle the seventy-five-pound tires as if they were Krispy Kreme doughnuts.

And then he held practices.

"I remembered in college we'd have a two-hour practice, and it would get gridded and broken up in five-minute increments. There would be a horn that went off every five minutes, and you had better know where you needed to be when the horn went off because it's that fast," said Papathanassiou, snapping his fingers.

"We don't work with quite the same degree of organization because I don't have as many people to work with, but the idea is the same. We break things down into very, very simple steps. And we try to execute each step and put the steps together."

On Sundays, then, it became Evernham's job—his mission— to put all the steps together in such a way that all Gordon had to do was let his talents as a driver come to the forefront. He would have nothing else to worry about although, like all drivers, there were times when he was concerned with more than just driving. But Gordon could vent to Evernham about anything, even talk in ways that seemed foreign to others who might be monitoring their race day radio traffic, and the two quickly developed a deep understanding for what the other was saying.

The special chemistry started paying dividends almost immediately, as did the closeness and teamwork of the Rainbow Warriors, who got their times for a four-tire, full-gas, green-flag pit stop down from an average of roughly twenty to sixteen seconds. Those precious saved seconds, especially on days when the crew was consistently cutting their driver's time in the pit, repeatedly translated into improved track position as Gordon's career began to soar.

There were no victories in 1993, their first year together on the Winston Cup level, but they did register two second-place and eleven top-ten finishes in thirty starts; two wins and fourteen top tens followed in 1994. By 1995 the NASCAR world knew who the new driving star was, as Gordon won seven times, finished second on four occasions, third on five and had a remarkable twenty-three top-ten finishes in thirty-one starts to register his first Winston Cup championship.

He was only twenty-four years old, but Jeff Gordon had arrived, thanks to his own prodigious talent and Ray Evernham's revolutionary approach to building and maintaining a team.

At twenty-four, Jeff Gordon wasn't racing on small dirt tracks for grocery money like Dale Earnhardt had at that age. He was a Winston Cup series points champion, and Earnhardt fans began loving to hate him. Some of the animosity had to do with Gordon's perceived arrogance; Earnhardt himself had dubbed him Wonder Boy, and the derisive nickname had stuck. A kid with boyish good looks, a former beauty queen for a wife, the best crew chief in Ray Evernham, the richest car owner in Rick Hendrick, he seemingly had it all before paying his dues. At least that was the way many old-school NASCAR fans saw it.

Sure, Gordon had learned how to drive a race car—and even his most vocal critics could not deny that he was very skilled. But he had done it in Indiana and California, of all places, and it seemed as if his whole life had been programmed. He couldn't be more different from a good ol' boy like Earnhardt, the reincarnated Confederate soldier, or Bill Elliott, descendent of the moonshine mountain culture.

Gordon didn't care, and neither did Evernham. They heard the boos and saw the middle-finger salutes at every track they went to; but they were winning over their share of fans too, simply by winning more races than anyone else. In their first five years together they piled up twenty-nine wins and two points championships, with a second-place finish in the points chase sandwiched in between.

Meanwhile, Earnhardt had hit a dry spell that had many wondering if he was beginning to lose it—or worse yet, at age forty-five, already had. He won seventy races between 1979 and 1996, a staggering total; but he went winless in 1997 and entered the season-opening Daytona 500 in 1998 carrying the heavy burden of a fifty-nine-race winless streak. Coupled with the fact that the one major hole in his lifetime racing résumé was that he had never won NASCAR's most prestigious race, it wasn't as if he had just a monkey on his back; it was more like a one-thousand-pound gorilla.

Earnhardt knew he could win at Daytona International Speedway. During one stretch in the 1990s, he would win an unbelievable ten 125-mile qualifying races in a row. He had won the Pepsi 400, previously known as the Firecracker 400 and then the Pepsi Firecracker 400, twice. But the biggest event in stock car racing wasn't run for one hundred twenty-five miles during the week or for four hundred during July. It was run for five hundred miles on a Sunday afternoon in February.

There were several times when Earnhardt had been painfully close to winning the Daytona 500, only to have it slip from his grasp at the very end. He was leading late in the race in 1986 when he ran out of gas, leaving the door open for Geoff Bodine to win instead. In 1990, he was leading on the last lap when he ran into some debris along the backstretch, which jammed up his radiator and cut a tire, relegating him to the purgatory of a disappointing fifth as Derrike Cope pulled out the victory. Afterward, Earnhardt joked that maybe he had gotten a chicken bone that some disgruntled fan had thrown onto the track caught in his radiator. Some reporters ran with his facetious remark, but in truth, it had been debris from another car that had done him in. On another occasion, Earnhardt again was running up near the front when he slammed into a seagull—a seagull!—along the same backstretch, finishing his chances of winning that day.

While the diminutive Gordon, five foot seven and 150 pounds, was gaining in the career wins column, the swarthy Earnhardt, who went six one and a solid 185 pounds, was getting steamed, and so were his fans. Gordon was winning more than anyone at the time and was such an atypical NASCAR hero that he became the target of their considerable abuse. It especially annoyed them that Gordon had added his first of what figured to be many Daytona 500 triumphs in 1997 before turning twenty-six—en route to his second points championship. One of the Earnhardt legion's favorite battle cries, usually scrawled with a black magic marker on a makeshift piece of cardboard and accompanied by a picture of Earnhardt's black No. 3 car, was: I'M GONNA KICK JEFF GORDON'S SKINNY LITTLE ASS! It may not have been all that creative, but it was to the point. As subtle as the Intimidator himself.

Asked about Gordon once, Earnhardt shook his head and said: "We just don't like the same things. I like to hunt and fish. He likes them video toys."

When Gordon wept openly at the Winston Cup awards banquet in 1997 after picking up his second points championship, Earnhardt was spotted smirking in the crowd.

But at Daytona in 1998, it was Earnhardt and not Gordon who had a date with destiny. Gordon, who had won NASCAR's biggest race in 1997 and was looking to repeat, had led much of the race before he hit a piece of debris that fouled up the way his car was handling and removed him from the hunt. Earnhardt charged hard the rest of the way and finally filled the Daytona void on his résumé.

In an uncommonly public display of deeply felt respect seldom seen in NASCAR, drivers, car owners and pit crews lined up along pit road to salute Earnhardt's historic victory. Afterward, the eighth-grade dropout did doughnuts in the infield, trying to scrawl the number three in the dirt. "I'm pretty good at writin', huh?" he told writers in the press box, pointing to his infield handi-work. And when he first climbed onto the platform for the winner's interview with the media, the beaming Earnhardt reached behind his back and flung a stuffed toy animal at the throng of reporters as he shouted: "I'm here! And I've got that goddamn monkey off my back!"

It would be Earnhardt's only victory in 1998, though. Gordon went on to post thirteen, tying Richard Petty's "modern-day" record set in 1975 after the Winston Cup race schedule had been reduced to slightly more than thirty races per season, giving Gordon and Evernham forty-two victories and three points champion-ships in their first six seasons. Seven more wins followed in 1999, but Evernham stunned Gordon and the entire NASCAR inner circle by announcing at midseason that he was leaving to pursue new challenges as the head of his own Evernham Motor-sports enterprises, which had been charged with reintroducing Dodges into NASCAR to challenge Ford, Chevy and Pontiac.

Among those who wondered what it would mean long term to Gordon's No. 24 team was the always outspoken Darrell Waltrip.

"You take Ray Evernham away from Jeff Gordon, and what do you have?" Waltrip asked, and he wasn't the only one asking. "You've got to have that relationship and that chemistry."

Meanwhile, the growth of NASCAR continued to soar through the sport's fifty-year anniversary and on into the new millennium. By 1994, stock car merchandise sales surpassed $200 million. *Forbes* magazine estimated that the combined annual in-come for NASCAR, speedway owners and race teams was about $2 billion. Television numbers continued to jump, with an esti-mated two million fans viewing at least one Winston Cup race by 1994 and with the number increasing to 2.6 million in 1995 and surpassing three million in '96 and '97. By 1998, races were being held in seventeen states, from New Hampshire and Michigan in the North to North Carolina, Georgia and Florida in the South to Arizona and California in the West. There was a new superspeedway opening in Fort Worth, Texas, just outside of Dallas, and there were plans for similar venues already under way near Lexington, Kentucky, and in big cities like Chicago and Kansas City. There was even a series of exhibition races held in Japan as the sport attempted to establish an international following.

Dale Earnhardt, of all people, was invited in April of 1998 to address the National Press Club in Washington, D.C.; the same prestigious organization that had previously hosted prominent world leaders, including Indira Gandhi and the Dalai Lama.

The Intimidator opened his speech by telling the gathering: "I worked hard yesterday on the farm trying to get tired. But I didn't sleep anyway. I'm pretty intimidated to be here."

That he was invited at all clearly indicated that Winston Cup racing and NASCAR had come a long, long way, baby.

"I didn't get much of an education," the eighth-grade dropout admitted. "But if you want to talk racin', I can tell you where we've come from and where we're goin'."

But despite all the newfound notoriety and popularity, no one should forget NASCAR's colorful, moonshine-stained roots.

Donnie Allison, Bobby Allison and Cale Yarborough returned to Daytona in 1999 and were asked to do a credit card commercial making light of their fight twenty years earlier that helped popularize the circuit. The director asked Donnie Allison to admit that he lost the race when he ran into Yarborough.

"But I didn't run into Cale. He ran into me," Donnie said.

"Well, just say it the way I want for the commercial," the director implored.

"No way. That wasn't how it happened. He ran into me," Donnie insisted.

"No, no, no," Yarborough interjected. "It wasn't my fault. It was his—and Bobby's for blocking us in the first place, if I remember right."

For a moment, bystanders wondered if three ex-drivers, now well into their sixties, might come to blows again—twenty years after the fact. It was another of those unscripted, unpredictable moments that endears NASCAR to the public, and the director eventually was forced to find another way to film his commercial, proving that drivers can have long memories in NASCAR.

Nonetheless, the commercial shoot was further evidence that NASCAR had emerged from the hills and hollows of North Carolina, Virginia and Georgia to deliver the goods again. Only this time it wasn't moonshine they were bringing to the public. It was big-dollars entertainment.

To illustrate what it all meant, consider this: in 1973, Darrell Waltrip competed in nineteen races and won a total of $33,466 as a NASCAR rookie, $2,434 less than his take for finishing forty-third in the inaugural Interstate Batteries race at the new Texas Motor Speedway in 1997.

Triumphs and Tragedies

It's a balmy Saturday night in May 2000, and 130,000 people from all walks of life are making their way to Charlotte Motor Speedway to see a spectacle like no other in professional sports: the Winston, stock car racing's version of an all-star game. The speedway, an immense structure that could accommodate 40,000 more than the 130,000 on hand (and will when the Coca-Cola 600 is run there in eight days), isn't actually in Charlotte, and technically isn't the Charlotte Motor Speedway any longer, proving once again that nothing is ever what it seems to be in the sport affectionately nicknamed "redneck racin'." Located on the city's outskirts in Concord, the track's ownership recently outraged many of the locals by following the lead of other professional sports and changing the venue's name for the right price, accepting several million dollars from the Lowe's Home Improvement corporation to rechristen the venue Lowe's Motor Speedway. It is ironic that the agreement to switch the name so offended racing's so-called purists; this is, after all, the same sporting subculture that plasters sponsors' logos all over its cars and the drivers who man them. NASCAR is an emphatically corporate sport, far removed from its moonshine roots in some ways, still clinging to them in others.

Outside the track, fans finally have moved away from their

grills, campers and recreational vehicles and begun to gravitate toward the massive facility. Some have been partying for days, others only for hours, and it is not necessarily the crowd that NASCAR novices might expect. There are plenty of beer-guzzling rednecks, to be sure; but there are also lawyers and doctors, accountants and insurance adjusters—college graduates all. There are fans that have been attending races for three decades, and fans who haven't yet reached their tenth birthday. There are mothers and fathers and children, fans of Gordon and Earnhardt, Marlin and Martin. There are even a few African-American fans in attendance, despite the perception that they are unwelcome.

There are fans in fancy jackets or shirts advertising their loyalties, and there are fans wearing white T-shirts with black No. 3s crudely spray-painted on them, signifying their undying allegiance to Dale Earnhardt. Better yet, fans these days get two Earnhardts for the price of one. Dale's son, Dale Jr., is among the crowd favorites too, and not just because he drives cars sponsored by Budweiser.

Little E, as he has come to be known, is bringing in new fans to the sport in droves. If his father is best described as a walking country & western song, then the younger Earnhardt is all rock'n'roll. He's the only NASCAR driver ever to be featured in *Rolling Stone,* where he admitted to being a hard-core fan of the alternative rock band Nirvana, among others. The interview for the article took place in the basement of his home in Mooresville, North Carolina, in a homemade bar unlike any other. As he talked, a framed poster of Kurt Cobain—the troubled lead singer of Nirvana who eventually committed suicide—and a cooler large enough to hold eleven (eleven!) cases of ice-cold Bud loomed behind him in the background. Little E affectionately calls the place "Club E."

That Dale Earnhardt Jr. is an enormously talented race driver no one doubts, but he's still just a kid, only twenty-six, and is the first to admit that there are days when he gets to the racetrack and longs to get back home so he "can fuck off." Sometimes Dale Jr. just wants to hang out in Club E, listen to Pearl Jam or surf the Internet and play video games on his computer. Remember, in 1997 Dale's father had derided Jeff Gordon for "liking them video toys." Now Junior drives for dad, or Dale Earnhardt, Inc.

Little E was born in Concord, near the track, but his parents separated when he was about three years old and he and his sister Kelly went to live with their mother for a while. One day, when he was about six, he awoke to discover a fire in the kitchen. Everyone ran out of the house, which promptly burned down; his mother subsequently handed over custody of the kids to Dale Sr. (who hated to be called "Dale Sr.") and moved to Norfolk, Virginia, changing Junior's life forever.

It was early 1980, and Dale Earnhardt had just captured Rookie of the Year honors on the Winston Cup circuit.

"Your dad's doin' good," Junior's mother told him. "He can put you in a good school. This is the best thing for you."

Dale Jr. looked at his mother, wanting to know just one thing.

"Are my toys coming with me?" he asked.

Thus, Dale Jr. entered the world of his father, the reluctant Dale Sr., which was dominated by Winston Cup racing. They didn't communicate much as Junior grew into a young man; the elder Earnhardt was usually off racing somewhere or making some other kind of public appearance as he got more and more popular, and when he was home Junior mostly remembers his father sitting in a recliner in front of the television.

"He'd be sittin' there watchin' TV in the recliner, and you ask him a question and he wouldn't hear you. You rarely even get a response," Little E told *Rolling Stone.* "He was so in his racin' thing, you could hardly sometimes have a conversation with him."

In time, Junior would get into it pretty deep too. While his father was building a racing empire that includes "the Garage Mahal," an impressive facility in Mooresville that redefines the term *race shop* and his own Dale Earnhardt Monopoly set, Junior was off getting a degree in automotives from Mitchell Community College in Statesville, North Carolina. He later worked at his father's auto dealership for $180 a week, progressing to the point where he could proudly perform an oil change in precisely eight minutes.

Eventually, he raced late-model stock cars and started to get hooked on the sport, although he's hardly consumed by it as his father once was.

"I'm a little more three-dimensional than, 'Oh, drivin's kick-ass.' Drivin' is fun, but it's not the ultimate high," he told *Rolling Stone.*

He has proven good enough at it—and carries such a marketable name—that Budweiser signed Little E to a sponsorship deal worth $50 million prior to the 2000 Winston Cup season. He has inherited his father's hard-driving competitiveness and wants to prove that he is worth the notoriety and enormous contract. He is a New Generation driver for a new breed of fans who are flocking to the nation's fastest-growing professional sport.

On the way into the Winston, fans can purchase just about anything they could possibly need. They can buy hats and T-shirts, grilled chicken sandwiches and chewing tobacco. They can even purchase a scanner for $250, then for another ten pick up a list of the racing teams' radio frequencies so they can monitor them for the evening.

Coolers are everywhere; this is one of the few places left in America where fans are allowed to bring in their own food and beverages, with the emphasis this night decidedly on the latter. The only stipulations are that the coolers be no more than fourteen inches high so they can fit under the seats, and that they carry no glass items. And fans are asked not to throw any leftover chicken bones or other debris onto the track. There is a North Carolina state law against that on the books.

As the crowd moves toward the gates, ushers use wooden sticks to investigate a selected number of coolers while letting most drift past without a poke. A jar of pickles is purged.

"Oh, man. Those were Claussen dills," the offender moans as he picks up what is left of his stash, about two cases worth of canned beer, and moves on.

Those who forget to pack a cooler need not fret. A twenty-four-ounce can of beer can be had inside for five dollars.

It is a place where folks come to have a good time.

"This is truly America," says one fan. "You can wear a cigarette company's logo on your head and nobody cares. You can bring your own stuff to eat and drink and do it without going broke. It's the last bastion in this country where you can enjoy yourself without being looked down upon for not being politically correct."

Perhaps that is why Dale Jr. is so wildly popular—because he will admit to being politically incorrect. It also helps that he's damn good at what he does for a living these days.

Dale Jr. is in this event because he has already won two races, becoming the first multiple winner on the Winston Cup circuit in the 2000 season, accomplishing that feat in only sixteen races; faster than Jeff Gordon or his father or dozens of other star drivers ever dreamed of doing it as Cup rookies. Another young standout in the field, the talented and temperamental Tony Stewart, set the Cup record for rookie victories the previous season with three.

When the real racin' begins—there are a number of preliminaries before a series of short races between the Winston Cup all-stars that constitute the main event—Dale Jr. takes over the show, delighting much of the crowd, which alternately chugs Budweisers in his honor and flips Gordon's No. 24 car the bird every time it whizzes by because, well, he's Jeff Gordon. In truth, Gordon is a likable person who has little in common with both Earnhardts, which is enough to make their fans and those of other "old-school" drivers dislike him intensely.

At one point, Earnhardt Jr. calmly tells his crew over the radio that, "This has been pretty easy so far. Give me four fresh tires and I'll go win this damn thing."

He does it by driving past defending Cup champion Dale Jarrett, Ned's son, and his own father, who does not look like the Intimidator on this night, thanks to a wild, rainbow-colored, one-night paint scheme that makes his car look more like Gordon's than his own. Maybe the two racers aren't as different as they would like everyone to believe after all.

After winning the Winston, Earnhardt Jr. asks for a Budweiser before getting on with his news conference, during which he mentions that the cooler at Club E will be filled and ready to go in celebration of this victory. Little E, very much unlike his father, is young, happy to be alive and ready to party.

"Everybody is different," fellow Winston Cup rookie Matt Kenseth says of Junior. "He just gets away with being himself more than the others dare do. And I applaud him for that."

So does Stacy Compton, another Winston Cup rookie who sometimes watches Dale Jr. and can only shake his head and smile.

"He's not typical," Compton said. "That's what this sport needs."

As for Dale Jr. himself, he says that the key to his existence is not to care too much about what others think of him. In that respect, he is his father's son.

"I don't know how I'm perceived. I just know what I like, and if that's not what everybody else likes, I guess that is new," he shrugged a few days after winning the Winston and before winning the pole for the subsequent Coca-Cola 600. This was after reporter David Newton of the *State* newspaper in Columbia, South Carolina, spent two days trying to track him down, only to have Junior blow him off to slip away to a nearby mall to hang out less than two hours before he set a qualifying record for the 600. Could anyone imagine his dad heading to the mall to hang out ninety minutes before trying to qualify for a big race?

Asked what he's doing with all the money he's suddenly winning, and Earnhardt Jr. breaks into a grin.

"I bought a twenty-five-foot boat on Lake Norman [near his Mooresville home], but it ain't nothin' special," he said. "I bought a new truck and paid cash for it. That was cool. I bought it from my dad, and he gave me a pretty good deal, I think.

"I'm making a real good living, but all I wanted to do was to be able to hold down a job. I look at my peers and see what they've accomplished and what I've accomplished, and I think I've done enough to stick around."

Race week in Charlotte is unlike any other. In a one-week span, drivers run in the Winston, hold a spirited Pole Night of qualifying and then run what now is known as the Coca-Cola 600.

This is the track brought back to life in the mid-1970s by Humpy Wheeler and Bruton Smith, a pair of old-time promoters who form a formidable good cop-bad cop routine. Wheeler is the schmoozer, the master marketer who loves to blow things up before a race, using apparently every bit of the considerable military personnel available within a one hundred-mile radius. The balding, squat, septuagenarian Smith, a former paratrooper who employs a retired U.S. Air Force general as an advisor, is the behind-the-scenes money man who knows only one way to get things done: bullying whoever dares to stand in his way.

He isn't popular and doesn't care; he isn't out to win friends. He's out to make money and promote racing, the only sport he truly loves. The trouble is that he can't even get along with very many people in the racing world, frequently feuding with Bill France Jr. and the rest of the folks who control NASCAR's governing body.

Pete Wright, the longtime NASCAR mechanic who in the year 2000 was working with driver Ken Schrader's team, remembers when Lowe's Motor Speedway improved its lighting system years ago.

"They were having this big ceremony, the turning on the lights," Wright recalls. "Bruton stood there and he made this big speech about putting it under the lights, and then he turned around to flip the switch on. But when he flipped the switch on, sparks flew everywhere. I mean, it was like a big fireworks show or something. You could smell the electrical ozone.

"When he did that, all that stuff come down on his head. You could see him just brushing it off. He walked over to get away from it for a minute, and when he did you could just see the smoke coming off his head. I know it had to burn his head. That was funny, because everybody wanted to see him get burned."

It was Smith who offered $90,000 condominiums overlooking the track in the late 1970s, prompting jokes on Johnny Carson's *Tonight Show;* no one was laughing as the millennium approached. Some of those same condos were selling for $500,000 to corporations that had matching logos painted somewhere on the cars that were whizzing by outside their windows at nearly two hundred miles per hour: Kodak, Pepsi and Coke, McDonald's, MCI and BellSouth, Kellogg's, Home Depot and Lowe's.

Wheeler and Smith were also among the first to recognize that their audience wasn't just a bunch of Bubbas brought up on Budweiser; there were women coming to their races too. Marketing estimates now indicate that nearly 40 percent of racing fans are women.

"In 1975, fifteen percent of the people coming to races in Charlotte were female," Wheeler said. "I would say that was pretty indicative of the circuit as a whole. We set out to purposely change that by marketing to bring the females in, realizing that we needed to find a much broader range of fans to weather the bad times.

"We took a cue from the oil industry during World War Two when they were trying to get women who were suddenly driving the family car to stop in and pump gas at their service stations. What they did was clean up their stations and make sure they had a decent women's restroom."

Wheeler remembers years ago when Crisco, the company that makes cooking oil and shortening, wanted to sponsor Buddy Baker's car because its officials said that it wanted to protect what was at the time its largest regional market per capita in the world.

"That really got us thinking," Wheeler said. "Men don't buy Crisco, unless they're a chef at a restaurant. That is a heavy female buy. Then we started getting some very strong allies with the people at Tide, Folgers and Hardee's."

By 2000, the women were not only coming to the races but by

their mere presence were helping sell the sport to a growing number of advertisers who years earlier never would have considered venturing into NASCAR sponsorship. Ed Hardin, columnist for the Greensboro *News & Record* in North Carolina, grew up around racing and at one time lived down the street from the famous Petty family. He remembers going to races when he was young, but it wasn't for the whole family.

"Mom and Sister just weren't invited," he said. "I don't remember there ever being a discussion about it."

Not that his mother wanted to go anyway.

"My mom was horrified by it...sunburnt men walking around with no shirts, sweating and drinking all day," Hardin added.

At least that had changed by the time Race Week arrived at Lowe's Motor Speedway in 2000. But while women were increasingly welcome, some others still largely weren't.

Al Shuford, a professional athletic trainer who works in the infield care center, feels at home once he's inside the track. But coming into the place can be a little unnerving. Shuford is an African-American who happens to have fallen in love with racing; not all the rednecks who come to the track have responded positively to his presence.

In 1996, when Shuford was working as an assistant trainer with the Carolina Panthers of the National Football League, he and a colleague of Mexican descent, fellow assistant trainer Dan Ruiz, were walking through the infield at what was then known as Charlotte Motor Speedway. Suddenly, a group of infield regulars closed in from behind them.

"Oh, we're lettin' y'all in here now too, huh?" they snorted.

Shuford and Ruiz ignored them and pressed on. But they got the message.

"Was I surprised? Yes. I think about that every now and then," Shuford said. "But I think the role is changed when you're a health care provider versus Joe Schmoe just trying to sit in the stands, somebody who is just an average person who has come to watch the race. I'm there offering assistance. It's totally different. They are much more accepting, much more tolerant of someone who is giving back something.

"When I'm there, I've got an official pass in the window. There is not a question asked, not the blink of an eye. . . . But, yeah, I think about it when I see the [Confederate] flags flying and things like that."

Make no mistake about it; there may be a controversy about the presence of the Confederate flag formerly raised over the South Carolina state capitol building, but there is no controversy about it flying in infields at NASCAR tracks throughout the country. In the infields, it stays; if you don't like it, you can go. Better yet, if you don't like it, don't come in the first place.

That may not be politically correct, but that's the way it is. As NASCAR moves more into the American mainstream, it's time for the circuit to address the latent racism apparent in the sport. How to address it remains in question.

Shuford would like to believe that it can change and it will. He talks about what a great sport stock car racing is, and about the many people involved in it that he has grown to respect. He has become close to driver Bobby Labonte and does a great deal of work for the Joe Gibbs–owned teams that Labonte and Tony Stewart drive for; Shuford also has worked extensively with John Andretti, who drives for the Petty Enterprises team, and for the teams owned by Rick Hendrick.

During one of his visits with Andretti, Shuford sat down and talked at length with Dale Inman, Richard Petty's former crew chief.

"I had never met Dale before, and I sat there and talked with him for three hours. We covered the 1950s through to the year 2000. He told me what racing was and what it used to be like, going to races across the country and [how different] it is now," Shuford said. "He understood my role and I understood his from what it used to be, and he admitted some things could have been different from his perspective over the years."

Inman told Shuford: "Al, I've had to change over the years. Richard and I have been together for fifty years. He's my second cousin. We were born in the same cradle. We grew up together. What we knew was what we knew back then."

Shuford later said: "I asked him specifically about acceptance of minorities into racing. He said, 'I've had to change.' But he was a great guy, an unbelievable guy. He had me crying for three hours, telling me stories about NASCAR's history.

"He had to be more accepting of the future, as it changed. He named a couple of [minority] drivers . . . Willy T. Ribbs, Wendell Scott . . . but he said what kept those guys from not being good, in his opinion, was sponsorship money—which applies even to today's standards—and their age. They were a little bit older when they got to the Winston Cup level, and that kind of prohibited them from doing what they had hoped to do.

"Look at some of these guys now. Adam Petty was driving, when? I remember him driving at seventeen. Earnhardt Jr. is another one. They're starting earlier and they have the backing. [Inman] credited that with being the biggest difference from then until now, and that's what kept the black drivers off the circuit longer. It wasn't ability, because he said those guys were as good if not better than anybody around. But they didn't have the tires and they didn't have the transmissions and they didn't have the motors.

"All those things, when you start putting the pieces together and talking about the 1950s and the 1960s, those were turbulent times for America. It was changing. The Vietnam War was going on. Everybody was looking for an identity. It was the same with them. You can't hold it against them, because that's just the way it was."

But that isn't the way it needs to remain. Like everyone else, Shuford is grasping for answers about how change can be kick-started.

As Shuford drove through a vast campground just outside Lowe's Motor Speedway on his way into the infield care center for the 2000 Coca-Cola 600, he couldn't help but notice a plethora of Confederate flags and redneck fans saluting him with raised middle fingers. And when Shuford subbed as the starter who flagged Happy Hour before the Coca-Cola 600 in 1998, he got more than angry stares while working in the tower above the start-finish line.

"Where I'm going with my story is not how I was perceived by the drivers, because I was the guy with the flag," Shuford said. "I started 'em and stopped 'em. I was the guy controlling things. It was the people sitting behind me at the start-finish line, throwing chicken bones and booing, because it was something new for them. They had never seen a black man standing up in the tower like that, flagging Happy Hour. Nothing bad really happened, but you got the pointing and the looks and things like that."

Still, he took heart from longtime starter Doyle Ford's approach to the situation. Shuford had consulted Ford, who was getting ready to retire, about climbing up in the tower. Ford supported him and even went so far as to get permission from Bill France Jr., head of NASCAR, to put Shuford there.

"I blocked all the other stuff out because there's forty-three cars out there," Shuford said. "Doyle was telling me, 'Al, don't drop the flag on the track—and pay attention to what you're doing. Don't worry about nothing else.' I had headphones on so I could listen to the spotters and all that, and I just kept saying to myself, This is what matters right here. And Doyle was so calming, so reassuring that he made it different for me. And Doyle had been around in NASCAR for thirty years. He never even gave it a blink to have me up there.

"So yeah, I think it is changing and it can change."

But is it changing fast enough? Will it ever progress to the point where Shuford can take his young son to a race without fear of how they will be treated?

"I don't know," Shuford candidly admits. "As long as you have owners and drivers who want to be the best, no matter where you get the best from, I think it will. But the people are the grass roots of NASCAR."

Shuford is talking about the fans who buy the tickets and millions of dollars' worth of NASCAR merchandise each year, not to mention the products that are advertised on the cars driven by their exclusively Caucasian heroes each Sunday. These are many of the same people who make up the infields where Shuford does not yet feel welcome.

"You're talking about changing the grass roots. I'm not so sure the sport is ready to get away from the people who helped build NASCAR," Shuford said. "We all have to be more tolerant and more accepting, go with the flow a little bit better. I think we have, and the people can change. The drivers, the owners and the crews can change it tremendously."

This is where NASCAR stands in the year 2001, as it reaps the cash from the new television contract reached with FOX, NBC and TBS, the networks that will pay a staggering $2.8 billion over the next six years to televise the circuit's races. That averages out to more than $466 million per year. By comparison, NASCAR received $3 million fifteen years earlier for the TV rights to twenty-eight races during the 1985 season.

It is an exciting, growing sport in desperate need of serious self-examination; NASCAR requires more diversity and a heightened sensitivity to discrimination, and must also address legitimate safety concerns—two issues it has long struggled with and likely will continue to confront for years. How NASCAR handles them will go a long way to determining whether it sustains its current level of popularity and slowly begins to build on it, or if it peaks and begins to withdraw back into its deep southern regional roots.

Automobile racing is different from all other professional sports because death lurks in those corners that its drivers barrel into at breakneck speeds; corners that spare not even the grandchildren of legends, nor the legends themselves.

Adam Petty was supposed to be the future of Petty Enterprises. His father Kyle used to joke that Adam had more talent in his little finger than Kyle had in his entire body when it came to driving race cars. "The genes for that skill must have skipped a generation," he would wryly observe.

As the 2000 season began, Adam Petty was planning to run a full schedule in the Busch series and a limited schedule of five races at the Winston Cup level—enough events to gain some valuable experience without compromising his rookie status for the 2001 season, during which he intended to move to the big stage full-time. It was the same path that had been plotted for Dale Earnhardt Jr. and Matt Kenseth, the best rookie drivers in 2000.

Though only nineteen, Adam Petty truly was the great hope for Petty Enterprises, the family-owned operation that had been a staple in NASCAR since the very beginning. He began driving motor bikes at age three and race cars at age six. He was a fourth-generation Petty, and he was born to race.

In January of 2000 Adam Petty talked about fulfilling the family legacy. "My goal is to run Winston Cup full-time in 2001," he said, flashing an infectious smile that immediately reminded everyone of his father and grandfather. "I don't know if we will, but that's my goal. That's why we're planning to run the five Cup races this year—to see how we like it . . . to see if I can do it. I'm not being cocky or anything, but I think I can go out there and drive a Winston Cup car. But this year, I just want to learn as much as I can."

He considered being a rookie named Petty in the Winston Cup series, which marks its rookies' cars during races with a yellow stripe on their bumpers.

"I think with that yellow sticker on your bumper comes a lot of hype. With my name too comes a lot of hype," he said. "I hope I can live up to the hype."

Adam Petty knew the hallowed place the family name occupied in the sport. Unlike Dale Earnhardt Jr., who seemed to be a rebel, the younger Petty seemed more appreciative and more respectful of his legacy. He also admitted that carrying the Petty legacy with him was at times a heavy, but necessary, burden.

"Looking back through all the years, you see what my great-grandfather did and what my grandfather did for the sport, and you realize that you do have big shoes to fill," Adam Petty said. "But you know, I've always had it in my mind just to go out week in and week out and just do the best that I can. That's all I've ever done. If I finish thirtieth and that's the best I could have done, then I'm happy with myself. And my grandfather and my dad are happy with that.

"They don't put any pressure on me at all. Sure, there is going to be pressure on you. There was a lot of pressure on me last year to go out and do what Dale Earnhardt Jr. did during his freshman year [in the Busch series, when Little E won that circuit's championship]. But it doesn't always happen that way. You just do the best that you can."

Asked if he frequently gained advice from the elder Pettys, Adam, still smiling, thought for a moment and replied: "A lot of that goes on. Me and my dad are really, really close. Every day after practice, I'm probably in his garage for thirty minutes, telling him everything my car is doing. Then I get feedback from him on what his race car is doing, and we can help each other out.

"My grandfather has been out of it for awhile. I'm not going to say he's lost his touch or anything, but it's a little bit different than it was a couple years ago. He's always there for advice about anything I want to ask him. But over the last couple of years, my dad and I have become really, really close and we're the ones that talk the most."

They talked a great deal after September 7, 1998, when the younger Petty was introduced firsthand to the dark side of racing. Adam was behind the wheel when a tragic accident occurred at the Minnesota State Fairgrounds during an American Speed Association race (a circuit that is considered a proving ground for up-and-coming drivers). During what appeared to be a routine pit stop, Adam's crew chief, forty-year-old Chris Bradley, jumped under the car to adjust a sway bar. Bradley did so apparently without warning either the driver or the rest of the crew of his intentions. So as soon as the jack dropped after his tires had been changed, Adam Petty did as he had been taught by his father, grandfather and great-grandfather since he was a small boy.

He hit the gas pedal and got moving.

Chris Bradley was still under the car. He died almost instantly as Adam Petty ran over him.

In the aftermath, Adam Petty had a difficult time dealing with the death of a man he considered a family friend. He said that he found the most consolation by seeking the counsel of his grandfather, the King, who told Adam of the similar incident that stained his career in 1965 when Richard lost control of a dragster in Georgia and the car soared into the crowd, killing an eight-year-old boy.

Richard Petty told his grandson that he had to pick up and move on. He didn't have to mention that he picked up the pieces and went on to become NASCAR's all-time winningest driver after his own fateful day in Georgia more than three decades earlier.

Yes, someone had died. But the racin' had to go on. It is a family mantra and a way of life that Adam Petty believed in but had difficulty coming to grips with in the wake of Bradley's death.

"People in racing have told me that I went to Minnesota a boy and came back a man," Adam Petty told Rick Bonnell of *The Charlotte Observer* of the incident. "I always used to think when you buckled into that car and put your helmet on, you were the only one in danger. Now I realize [Bradley] gave his life trying to help me win a race. That's what gets me shaken up."

Ultimately, though, Adam Petty was determined not to let the lingering psychological damage from the incident wreck his budding career or his predetermined place as the next in racing's first family's lineage.

"I can't let that one day get to me so that my racing career is ruined," he told Bonnell.

So he picked up and moved on. Shortly before the start of the 2000 racing season, his grandfather was asked about Adam's future in the sport.

Richard Petty admitted that Adam did seem quite a bit different from his own son Kyle. He likened Kyle to Adam's brother Austin, younger by one year—quick to point out that different didn't in any way mean better or worse. He was only referring to racin' genes.

"Adam's always had a commitment to it," he said. "I don't know if he got blowed away from growin' up around it all the time, seeing all the heroes or just the competition, or what. I don't know. But he's always been obsessed with it. Austin, every time you see him, he's on a different kick. He's got an airplane, and he's flying it one week. He's got a boat or wants a boat the next week, or a motorcycle. He's more like Kyle.

"Austin has never really settled down to one specific thing, whereas Adam, a long time ago, said racing was it. He wasn't never into football or basketball or baseball. Since he was ten years old, he's been that way. And even before that he was always in go-carts and wanting to ride a motorcycle, whatever."

Asked what his expectations were for Adam's initial foray into Winston Cup racing, the King replied: "We'd like for him to win, of course, but we'd like him to get that seat time, so when the time comes, his education is finished."

Tragically, Adam Petty never got to finish his education. The first fourth-generation driver in NASCAR history died of head trauma on May 12, 2000 during a practice session at New Hampshire International Speedway in Loudon, New Hampshire, when his No. 45 Sprint PCS-sponsored Chevrolet Monte Carlo crashed head-on into the turn three outer wall.

News of his death shook the NASCAR world to its core. Only six weeks earlier, the Pettys had lost great-grandfather Lee, but he had been eighty-six and passed away quietly after complications from stomach surgery. Adam Petty was only nineteen, still a teenager.

At Adam's funeral, his brother Austin, only eighteen himself, spoke of the passion Adam had held for stock car racing.

"From the time he was a little kid, I can remember that all he wanted to do was race," Austin told the family's pastor Douglas Carty and others in attendance at the service. "He wanted to grow up and be a race car driver just like Daddy."

Twelve days after the terrible accident, Richard Petty strode into the garage area at Lowe's Motor Speedway in Charlotte and made a state-of-the-first-family address to the media. It was an emotional gathering. Behind his trademark dark glasses, hiding bloodshot eyes showing the strain of an incomprehensible loss, the man known to auto racing fans around the world as the King touched on the special relationship he had with his grandson. He talked about how at first he felt some guilt for having ever introduced Adam into a sport that could take his life in this fashion, but then discussed how he came to grips with that awful notion.

"I was thinking the other evening and, man, I felt bad. I was thinking if I hadn't of been in racing, hadn't of pushed Kyle or if I'd stayed away from Kyle or hadn't of worked with Adam, then maybe this wouldn't have happened," the King said. "Then I read in the paper—the first thing I done Monday night [two days after the wreck] was pick up a paper—where a boy seventeen and one fifteen drowned. Different places, just swimming, just having fun. That just lifted a cloud off me.

"We just look at it that part of living is dying. Adam just got it a little bit earlier than when we wanted him to. But I think you see very few nineteen-year-old kids that have affected as many people, that have touched as many people, as Adam has. I think he was too young for anybody to really evaluate what his career was going to be. But I think the majority of the people who have ever met him remember his smile, patting them on the back, joking with them or whatever. I guess that's probably the best memory that anybody could ever have of anybody, the memory that he was a pretty good kid."

But only a kid.

Kyle Petty was especially devastated by Adam's unexpected and sudden loss. Yet he too had the class and dignity to meet with the media and discuss the impact of Adam's death on his life and on racing's most famous family, doing so at Dover Downs International Speedway in Dover, Delaware, less than a month after the incident. Discussing the first trip he and his wife Pattie took back to their son's race shop in North Carolina, he said, "It was incredibly hard for Pattie and I to go back to Adam's race shop," he said, his voice cracking. "You'll never know how hard it was to walk through those doors and see those cars sitting there with his name on them; to see his seats in the cars and his uniforms and stuff like that."

He talked about how he wanted to, maybe needed to, get back to racing, and announced that he would drive his son's No. 45 Sprint-sponsored Chevrolet in the Busch Series race that weekend at Dover.

"It never crossed my mind to quit," Kyle Petty said. "This is what the Petty family has always done, as a family. You don't quit. You just keep plugging along. We're like a bunch of farmers. Just because things have been bad, you don't quit." Richard Petty had said virtually the same thing just a few weeks earlier, employing the same metaphor.

"Petty Enterprises will go on," the King had said. "Racing is what we know, and that's what we'll be doing. We've got to make a living, man. We're like farmers. Even though there's a drought one year, he plants again next year. Well, we do the same thing."

The racing, as always, had to go on. And so on it went.

The racing went on without a victory for Michael Waltrip through the 2000 season, but that surprised no one. Darrell's younger brother by sixteen years, Michael had been racing at the Winston Cup level for seven years without winning a single points event (he had captured the Winston, the non-points all-star event, in 1996). It was a streak he had figured on breaking in 2000.

"I have to prove something every day. You don't run four hundred and twenty-some races and put a zero in the win column and not have to prove something every day," he said prior to the season. "It doesn't matter what I accomplish short of winning a race. People will always think, 'Why does he deserve to be here? How can he win ten or twelve million dollars and never win a race?'

"But I know I'm a better race-car driver than most, and I know I can do the job. I have to listen to a bunch of crap when it doesn't all work out right. But I've got broad shoulders and I love to drive race cars. So as long as I'm good enough to play a competitive part, I'm going to be around."

A gangly six-foot-five and 220 pounds, the younger Waltrip possessed a quick wit and a charming smile. But his winless streak had stretched to 462 races by the end of the 2000 season and his growing number of critics were beginning to openly question if he would ever reach Victory Lane.

Dale Earnhardt, however, was not one of Michael Waltrip's critics. Stunning many in the racing community, Earnhardt offered Waltrip a new ride for the 2001 season, adding a third team to the operation at Dale Earnhardt, Inc. (DEI). The other two cars would be driven by Dale Jr. and Steve Park as the elder Earnhardt continued to honor his longtime commitment to friend Richard Childress by driving for one of the two teams fielded by Richard Childress Racing. Of course, all the teams involved in both DEI and RCR swapped information and equipment, making them formidable both as a group and individually.

Why give Michael Waltrip one of these coveted rides when he had never won a race? Earnhardt told anyone who asked that it was because he believed Waltrip not only could, but would, win. And soon if given the right opportunity.

Meanwhile, the elder Earnhardt had given Dale Jr. a little advice toward the end of the 2000 season. As time passed and Dale Jr. began taking those halting, tentative steps toward maturity that sooner or later all men must, the two who had for years not been particularly tight grew increasingly closer. The father pulled the son aside shortly after countless news stories trumpeted Little E's arrival in the big time, and the younger Earnhardt was reveling in his growing reputation as a party animal and rock'n'roll race-car driver.

"You're going to regret telling all them reporters about Club E and all that other stuff," the elder Earnhardt warned Dale Jr.

"Why?"

"Keep 'em guessin'. The less they know about your personal life, the better."

Dale Jr. at first disregarded the advice, as most young men who are still feeling their way in their relationship with a father would. He filed it away and kept on living his life as he had been.

Then, late in the season, after some minor feuds with members of his crew and a drought on the track, Dale Jr. woke up one day and thought again about his father's words. He admitted to himself, and in subsequent conversations with Associated Press reporter Jenna Fryer, that he had been getting full of himself and had been enjoying a little too much of his sponsor's product. On several occasions, Little E had partied late through the night and into the early-morning hours, only to arrive late and hung-over to appearances mandated by his sponsorship deal. He finally had to admit that maybe his father was right. Maybe he needed to keep a little more of his private life private. And maybe he had to start concentrating more on what really mattered: his career on the racetrack.

Dale Earnhardt was a master at keeping the proper distance between his private family life and his adoring public, all the while devoting most of his energy to the task of performing at a high level behind the wheel.

Once, Earnhardt somewhat reluctantly took a television crew wanting to experience a day away from the track with the Intimidator with him on a hunting trip to Alabama. Shortly after boarding a private Learjet that Earnhardt routinely used for such getaways, the Man in Black started serving his guests cocktails, making sure to pour one for himself. When the plane landed, the party was met on the tarmac by an Earnhardt acquaintance who stepped out of a Chevy Blazer and threw the keys to the famous driver. Earnhardt flashed his mischievous grin and slid behind the wheel, after which he proceeded to scare the living daylights out of the television folks. Driving at high speeds down a private and secluded country lane of dirt and loose gravel, he soon commanded one of his companions to hand him a hunting rifle. Then, without slowing any, he began firing out the window at deer he supposedly spotted along the way. This terrified the TV crew, who were none too pleased when they arrived at Earnhardt's "hunting lodge" to find it rather primitive and not quite befitting the luxurious digs they had envisioned sharing with the multi-millionaire driver.

But the simple accommodations suited Earnhardt just fine, and the trip served its purpose. Those media types were so frightened by the experience in the Blazer and so sobered by the simple shack they were forced to camp out in that they never asked to come along again.

While intensely private and seemingly distant to many, Earnhardt did have a softer side that the few in his inner circle were privy to, and was also a notorious practical joker with the other drivers. One time, in response to a joke that had been pulled on him by Rusty Wallace (who had hidden Earnhardt's steering wheel just before the beginning of a race), he planted on open can of sardines underneath Wallace's seat on the day of a hot, long race at Rockingham. The resultant stench nearly drove Wallace crazy.

In April of 1999, outdoors writer Bryan Brasher of the *Columbus Ledger-Enquirer* in Columbus, Georgia, received a phone tip that Earnhardt was in the area doing some turkey hunting. If he wanted to do a brief interview, he was to come to nearby Phenix City, Alabama, that evening.

Brasher listened that night as Earnhardt passionately delved into his tales of turkey hunting for some forty-five minutes. Then they went to get something to eat. As the talk around the table turned to Learjets, Brasher felt somewhat left out. Earnhardt sensed this and turned to him.

"What's your profession?" Earnhardt asked.

"I'm an outdoors writer," Brasher replied.

"Good. I thought you might have been another NASCAR punk." Then Earnhardt grinned.

"I told [longtime friend and hunting companion] Bill [Jordan] on the way to the restaurant that you were one of the best writers I'd ever met, because I'd been around you forty-five minutes and you hadn't asked me a question yet."

Next it was Brasher's turn to be honest with Earnhardt. He told him he had been tight-lipped because he was scared of suffering the same fate as reporters he had seen "crash and burn" with Earnhardt on television.

Again, Earnhardt smiled.

"Plus, when you started talking about Learjets and all that, I didn't have much to say. I was going to tell you guys that I changed the starter in my truck the other day, but I didn't think anyone would care," Brasher added.

"Man, I'm just like you," insisted the Intimidator, at last putting Brasher at ease.

Later, as Brasher listened to Earnhardt talk some more, the writer thought to himself: "He is indeed a lot like me—and probably more like a lot of other common folks than they've ever realized."

These were the types of stories that helped the average fan identify with Earnhardt, who was still running hard by the time the 2001 season was set to open with the Daytona 500, billed as the Great American Race. Earnhardt said that he was gunning for his eighth points championship, and no one doubted that he very well might bag another title. David Poole, racing writer for the *Charlotte Observer*, even predicted it on the eve of the race.

The weekend marked the dawning of a new age for NASCAR, one in which it was planning to cruise even further into the American mainstream. In one indication of progress, Willy T. Ribbs had driven two days earlier in the NASCAR Truck series race, having finally received a call back from someone in the sport when Winston Cup driver and truck series team owner Bobby Hamilton phoned the previous offseason to offer the veteran African-American driver a shot at a ride.

Furthermore, this Daytona 500 was the opening gambit in the new NASCAR television sweepstakes. Viewership for the Bud Shootout, a non-points event run the weekend before the 500, was up twenty-six percent over the previous year and the FOX network, led by respected play-by-play voice Mike Joy, former Earnhardt crew chief Larry McReynolds and newly-retired driver Darrell Waltrip in the broadcast booth, was ready to strut its stuff before the nation. Bobby Labonte began the race as the defending Winston Cup points champion, but no one was a bigger star on the starting grid than Earnhardt in his black number three Chevrolet Monte Carlo with the familiar Goodwrench sponsorship decals plastered all over it.

To heighten the spectacle, NASCAR had consented to new aerodynamic rules that supposedly would allow for more of the sort of side-by-side racing that purists, including Earnhardt himself, had been clamoring for over the last year or longer. So what if the side-by-side jostling would take place at speeds in excess of 180 miles per hour? It would make for a great show.

It also made for great danger, as evidenced by a horrifying nineteen-car crash on lap 174 of the two-hundred-lap event when Robby Gordon tapped Ward Burton from behind in a pack of cars and set off a chain reaction that resulted in Tony Stewart's car tumbling through the air. Stewart's Pontiac at first landed on Jeff Gordon's Chevrolet, bounced and barrel-rolled before going airborne again and landing on top of teammate Bobby Labonte's Pontiac. A hush settled over the crowd as fans flashed back to the nightmares of the previous season that had claimed the lives of NASCAR drivers Adam Petty, Kenny Irwin and Tony Roper. Miraculously, Stewart emerged relatively unscathed with only a concussion and a minor shoulder injury, and the race quickly resumed as he was shuffled off to the nearby Halifax Medical Center to undergo a battery of precautionary tests.

The restart of the race came with twenty-one laps remaining. On lap 184, Michael Waltrip took the lead from none other than his new boss, Dale Earnhardt. It was the forty-ninth lead change in a race that was shaping up to be as competitive and as exciting as the fans, television executives and race officials could have hoped for. On the track, though, it was harrowing. The drivers were not enjoying themselves, especially after Stewart's wreck.

As the laps wound down, Earnhardt Jr. moved into second. His father settled into third behind the front-running Waltrip, and the Intimidator curiously began playing a different kind of role, attempting to block Sterling Marlin's Dodge so that his son and Waltrip could continue to stretch the lead out front. It was the first time anyone could remember the elder Earnhardt not running to win.

Recalling that it had taken himself seventeen tries to win the Daytona 500, Darrell Waltrip was openly cheering his younger brother on in the broadcast booth.

"'You got it, Michael! You got it!" the elder Waltrip shouted to millions as his brother charged down the backstretch of the 2.5-mile trioval on the final lap, with Dale Jr. nipping at his rear wheels but apparently content to settle for second place behind his new teammate. They zipped through turn four and headed for the finish line and the checkered flag, as the black No. 3 and Marlin's fast Dodge battled furiously for third place behind them.

Suddenly, there was contact. Marlin's car brushed Earnhardt's and as the Intimidator tried to maintain control, his Chevrolet turned head-on into the outside wall in turn four and slammed hard after being hit from behind by Ken Schrader's car.

"That's a bad wreck. When you hit the wall head-on like that, it hurts. TV doesn't do it justice," Darrell Waltrip observed, even as he began to celebrate his younger brother's first triumph in 463 Winston Cup starts.

Yet neither Waltrip realized at that moment how bad a wreck it really was. Even as Michael Waltrip crossed the finish line and took the checkered flag, Dale Earnhardt, racing icon and driver of the most famous car in all of motorsports, was dead at age forty-nine. Doctors later would determine that he died instantly of head injuries at impact, setting off a furious debate over safety in a sport that has already proven that it will never be totally safe.

The NASCAR family had been within seconds of trumpeting this Daytona 500 as one of its greatest ever in front of record numbers of fans. Now the stock-car racing world sat in stunned silence, not knowing the fate of its biggest star.

As Michael Waltrip celebrated in Victory Lane, failing to realize what had happened to his friend and car owner, rescue workers tried desperately to cut Earnhardt from his car and revive him. Eventually he was rushed to the same Halifax Medical Center where Stewart had been taken less than an hour previously, but efforts to revive him failed. He was pronounced dead at 5:16 P.M.

At 7 P.M., NASCAR president Mike Helton relayed the dreaded news.

"This is undoubtedly one of the most difficult announcements I've ever had to make," Helton said. "But after the accident in turn four at the end of the Daytona Five Hundred, we've lost Dale Earnhardt."

His voice breaking with raw emotion, Helton then read a statement from Bill France Jr., Big Bill's son and the former NASCAR president who remained chairman of NASCAR's board of directors.

"Today NASCAR lost its greatest driver in the history of the sport," France said in the statement.

In the days and even weeks that followed, the questions came endlessly. Would it have made a difference if Earnhardt had been wearing the new HANS (which stands for Head And Neck Support) device? Would "soft walls" (which Humpy Wheeler at Lowe's Motor Speedway has long been in favor of installing) have saved his life? And what about a seatbelt that appeared to have snapped? If it had functioned properly, could it have prevented this tragedy?

Of course, the answers were few and inconclusive. Helton dodged many of the safety questions, saying NASCAR already was doing all it could. But after four deaths in nine months, after the death of one of racing's first family and now this, there was an outcry in the media and among fans. Somehow, somebody needed to start doing more.

They knew they couldn't get in, but they came anyway.

Jim and Sheri Rayner came all the way from Caldwell, Ohio, just to stand outside Charlotte's Calvary Church in the freezing rain and pay homage to Earnhardt, their fallen hero who was eulogized inside during a brief but emotional memorial service attended by many of NASCAR's biggest names from the past and present.

"We drove through snow and ice and freezing rain. Plus we got lost. You don't even want to know how long it took us to get here," Jim Rayner said.

Getting lost, though, turned out to be a blessing in Rayner's book. Somehow he and his wife and friend Shawn Wiley ended up in Welcome, North Carolina, home of the Richard Childress Racing shop that was home to the cars Earnhardt raced.

"We stopped and went to the museum at the shop and someone there told us we had just missed the caravan that left for the service. Then we came straight here," said Rayner, adorned in a Goodwrench jacket that displayed Earnhardt's signature.

At the twenty-two-minute memorial service inside Calvary Church, chaplain Dale Beaver of the Motor Racing Outreach ministry delivered a eulogy that again illustrated a softer side of the hard-driving Earnhardt. Beaver told the story of his first apprehensive meeting with the legendary driver, recalling a time when the chaplain had asked the elder Earnhardt to sign a permission slip allowing his daughter Taylor to attend a youth camping trip in the Poconos.

"I half-expected to find a man eating a bear, tearing it apart with his bare hands. I thought, 'He's eating bear and I'm going to be dessert.' " Beaver said.

Instead, Beaver said that he walked into Earnhardt's transporter and came upon a very different kind of person.

"I saw a man eating an orange, who with a very warm demeanor welcomed me into his presence," Beaver said. "I didn't come into the presence of a racing icon or an intimidating figure. I came into the presence of a dad, a father, who was concerned about his daughter."

Beaver also talked about sensing that he was in the presence of "greatness" and recalled how he prayed with Earnhardt and his wife, Teresa, for a safe race prior to the fatal accident.

"Most of the time, God grants us that request," Beaver said. "Sometimes he doesn't."

Bracketing a scripture reading by Reverend John Cozart of St. Mark's Lutheran Church in Mooresville and Beaver's eulogy were a pair of songs performed by longtime Earnhardt friend Randy Owen, a country-music star with the band Alabama. The first song, "Goodbye (Kelly's Song)," included the line: "Goodbye. That one word hurts so bad when you lose a friend."

Following Owen's second song, "Angels Among Us," Teresa Earnhardt climbed onto the altar, appeared to briefly kiss a bouquet of flowers arranged to look like a large No. 3 and then turned to the crowd of about 3,000 to mouth the words "thank you" and blow a kiss. Then she quickly stepped down off the altar and began the family's procession out of the sanctuary.

Among those attending the service were most of NASCAR's current drivers and several older retired drivers such as Richard Petty, Junior Johnson, Darrell Waltrip, Bobby Allison and his brother Donnie. Other NASCAR figures such as Bill France Jr., Mike Helton and Bruton Smith, chairman and CEO of Speedway Motorsports, also were in attendance.

The invitation-only service kept most of the general public away, but the media was there in abundance, and it was also broadcast to millions on FOX Sports Net.

After the service, Smith said that in a strange way, the sport of stock car racing stands taller than ever in the wake of Earnhardt's passing.

"The sport has lost great drivers before, but I think this has brought attention to our sport in a way that is unbelievable. If you're not an avid race fan, you've heard about our sport now—and maybe it is an awakening," Smith said. "Maybe, even in death, Dale Earnhardt is going to continue to build our sport. That's the way I look at it.

"This has been such a major, major shock. But it's brought a bigness to our sport that I never realized was there. We're going to miss him, but we will go on. We've exposed our sport internationally now, maybe in a way that we never could have. I guess the only way I can put it is that this reminds me a great deal of when Elvis [Presley] died. It makes me wonder if Dale Earnhardt will have the same impact on his world that Elvis did on his. That could happen easily. I didn't realize how many millions of people knew, or thought they knew, Dale Earnhardt."

In the days following his death, they came by the thousands to the racing headquarters of Dale Earnhardt, Inc. in Mooresville, North Carolina, constructing makeshift memorials that grew in size exponentially every day. State police reported that crowds from dawn to dusk numbered at about 10,000 daily for much of the week following Earnhardt's passing. Folks came from as far away as Canada, Iowa, New York, Wisconsin, New Jersey, Ohio and Texas. Many drove straight to Mooresville from Daytona Beach, where they had watched their hero meet his demise.

One anonymous fan placed a poem at the gates of the place they call the Garage Mahal. It read:

WHEN GOD PUT YOU ON THIS EARTH, HE KNEW WHAT YOU
    WOULD BE.
YOU WOULD BE THE DRIVER OF THAT BLACK NUMBER THREE.
NOW YOU DRIVE IN HEAVEN, RACING FOR THE LORD.
I ONLY HOPE THAT GOD DIDN'T PUT YOU IN A FORD.

Another fan placed a clock sporting Earnhardt's face on it with the hands frozen in time at 5:16, the exact time that he had been pronounced dead. Still another wrote a note that cried, "There will always be a number-three-shaped hole in my heart."

Over the next seven days, memorials were staged in cities throughout America. President George W. Bush sent a delegate to the memorial in Charlotte and dropped a telegram to Teresa, mourning the loss "of an American icon."

The media came too, and not just the racing media. In the week that was to follow, Earnhardt graced the cover of *Time* magazine and was remembered in virtually every publication from *USA Today* and *The New York Times* to the *Winston-Salem Journal* and other southeastern newspapers whose readers felt they had gotten to know the man through the years. The electronic media descended in full force as well, from CNN/SI to ESPN and FOX Sports Net to the major news networks.

Outside Calvary Church after the memorial service, Junior Johnson stopped to talk about Earnhardt's legacy—and the wreck that led to his death.

"You've got to feel lucky to come out of one of those things in good shape," Johnson said. "Dale had some serious, serious accidents that he walked away from through the years. It caught up with him, I guess.

"I've never seen this many drivers and race fans at another driver's funeral. It shows that everybody had a lot of respect for Dale, and that they'll miss him. Racing will go on with a sad heart for a little while. But then things will pick back up and go their own way. At the same time, Dale won't ever be forgotten."

Johnson was asked if the sport had grown even more dangerous in recent years with the increase in speeds.

"I think it's as safe as it's ever been. They'll work on anything and everything they can to make it safer. That's what they do," Johnson said. "The sport has always been life-threatening, and a lot of other sports are the same way. You can get killed on a horse or anything of that nature."

Horseback riders don't slam into walls at 180 miles per hour, however, and the general contention of NASCAR advocates that someone could get killed walking across the street to get a newspaper trivializes the seriousness of the safety issues facing the sport. Several drivers, who in the past have repeatedly been rebuffed when they've attempted to organize in any way as a separate entity, have in the wake of the Earnhardt tragedy openly suggested the need for a safety review board that operates independently of NASCAR.

"It is a dangerous sport, but I also feel like we focus a lot on safety," Jeff Gordon said. "Here recently things have happened to catch our attention when it comes to safety. Who's to say we can't make it safer? I think we can.

"Overall, we have very safe race cars. But along the way, you can always make things safer. It's not just Dale. This goes back to when all of these things started, with Adam [Petty] and Kenny [Irwin]. Dale's accident is making us all look at it just a little bit harder."

Yet many drivers are reluctant to try new safety devices. Immediately after Earnhardt's death, much debate began anew about the HANS device, a revolutionary head-restraint system designed to prevent precisely the types of head injuries that killed Adam Petty, Irwin and truck series driver Tony Roper during the 2000 racing season. Regardless, only twenty-one Winston Cup drivers had purchased the $1,275 HANS device by the morning of the 2001 Daytona 500, and fewer still actually wore it during the race. Many said they simply were not comfortable wearing the device, and others questioned whether they would be able to remove it quickly enough if they were in an accident and had to escape from their car as fast as possible.

Driver Mark Martin epitomized the skepticism of many in his profession when he said: "I won't wear one of those devices for anything. I can tell by looking at it that I wouldn't wear it. I've been racing for twenty-five years. I'll keep my fingers crossed. I've got a few more years left. I'm not going to tinker with that thing. It just doesn't look like something I could wear."

Dr. Steve Bohannon, the emergency room physician at Halifax Medical Center and director of Daytona International Speedway's emergency medical services, said that he did not think the HANS device would have saved Earnhardt. He also initially said that he didn't think the fact that Earnhardt wore an open-faced helmet rather than a full-faced model contributed to the driver's death—although he later would reconsider that comment in light of the revelation that the left lap belt in the five-point seat-belt harness system worn by Earnhardt had broken.

Another proposal that needs to be explored further (and NASCAR could have moved more quickly to develop) is the installation of "soft walls." Instead of crashing into concrete at 180 miles per hour, Earnhardt could have perhaps hit a soft wall that would have absorbed and dissipated some of the impact's force. Though sure to help in the event of head-on collisions, race officials differ on what types of soft walls might work, and have legitimate concerns about what might result if a car were to brush a soft wall and snag on it, causing it to spin.

When Humpy Wheeler, president of Lowe's Motor Speedway in Charlotte, ran a test in 2000 by dropping a Cadillac from a crane onto one version of a soft wall, NASCAR officials privately scoffed and dismissed it as a publicity stunt. Wheeler, however, continued to insist that more could be done to make tracks safer—an issue he has championed since three spectators were killed during an Indy Racing League event at his track only a year earlier. In October of 2000 Wheeler installed what he called "our version" of soft walls at the track's supposed trouble spots, inside turns two and four, placing encapsulated polystyrene barriers—material originally designed for use in building boat docks—inside the turns.

"Something is going to come out better than what we've come up with, but we wanted to do something," Wheeler said at the time.

Earnhardt himself had addressed the seemingly meaningless concern held by some that soft walls would fragment upon impact after a crash and therefore could cause a mess that would delay Winston Cup races.

"I'd rather they spend twenty minutes cleaning up that mess than be cleaning me off that wall," Earnhardt told reporters.

Finally, there was talk of slowing the cars down. Frankly, there may be no other way of making NASCAR events safer. Proponents argued that good races could still result even if speeds were slowed by an average of ten miles per hour or more per race, while others were quick to protest that the point of the sport all along has been to go as fast as you can, period.

Certainly that is how Junior Johnson always approached racing. And Earnhardt, too. Yet even the resilient, optimistic Johnson wondered aloud along with the rest of a nation how the sudden and incomprehensible loss of Earnhardt would affect the sport at this critical juncture in its existence.

"This loss is as deep as it can possibly be," Johnson said. "I've never seen any race-car driver since I've been in racing create this kind of a stir—and I've seen Fireball Roberts and Joe Weatherly and Curtis Turner all pass away. None of 'em created the multitude of heartbreak that Dale's passing has. It's been a devastating thing for the sport. It's one of the worst happenings that I've ever seen in auto racing."

The Rayner's couldn't have agreed more.

"I guess we built him up bigger than life," said a red-eyed Shari Rayner, wearing a black Earnhardt jacket outside Calvary Church the same dreary afternoon. "The thing is, what do you tell your three young sons? They're all Earnhardt fans too, and they still think he's coming back."

Jim Rayner gazed at the church and watched as Teresa Earnhardt climbed into a long, black limousine and sped from the premises after the service. He had a seven-hour ride back to Ohio ahead of him, but he and his wife weren't yet ready to hit that road.

"We're going to go by his shop in Mooresville first. Fate already took us to the Childress shop in Welcome," Jim Rayner said. "We had to come. We had to do this. We felt like he was one of us. This helps us get some closure, or at least some understanding."

Shari Rayner agreed that she and her husband had one more stop to make.

"We brought flowers. And a card that our three boys made. We have to go by his shop to pay our last respects. We just have to," she said.

Then they turned to go, a cold mist dampening the air and their eyes.

The boys went racin' the following Sunday at Rockingham. But it wasn't business as usual. There was no way it possibly could be.

"As much as you want to hope it's business as usual, it's not." Gordon said. "There's definitely something missing and everybody is very aware of that."

Voicing the opinion of many of his fellow competitors, driver Stacy Compton talked about both the difficulty and the redeeming value of getting back to work so quickly after such a devastating incident.

"I think it does everybody good to come here," Compton said. "I think it does everybody good to get back in the swing of things and stay busy and stop watching TV and seeing the tributes to him. You sit there and you look at that, and it gets to you."

Discussing the emotional memorial service for Earnhardt he had attended less than forty-eight hours before qualifying began for the Rockingham race, Compton said: "Drivers and teams don't like going to funerals. It's sort of a cardinal sin. I've never seen a group of people come together as much as they did at that memorial service. . . . I think that brought some closure, and I think coming back to the track will help bring some closure as well."

Dale Earnhardt Jr. spoke briefly to reporters but did not take questions. Mainly, he wanted the world to know that he in no way blamed Sterling Marlin for his father's death—even though Marlin had received death threats from angry and misguided Earnhardt fans after the accident, which had occurred at least in part because Marlin brushed Earnhardt from behind.

"That's ridiculous, and it won't be tolerated," Earnhardt Jr. said of the accusation.

Tens of thousands came to the Rock to pay their last respects to the Man in Black and perhaps begin forging new allegiances that would sustain them and their beloved sport as it entered a new and unpredictable era.

The pole for the race was won by none other than Jeff Gordon, to so many the anti-Earnhardt figure. Gordon wore a black No. 3 Earnhardt hat as he spoke with the media about his hot qualifying run and the sport's future without the man with whom he had dueled so often.

"I thought I would always be racing against Dale Earnhardt in that black three car out there," Gordon said. "As much as we're going to miss Dale, though, the sport itself has a lot of stars, a lot of young guys coming up who can be superstars. I don't think the sport's ever revolved around one person. I think that we're all pretty grateful for that one person like Dale and for how much the sport grew because of him. But I think we all know that we've got to continue to go out there and just do our jobs as best we can and hope that the fans continue to support us."

Gordon fingered the Earnhardt hat on his head and added: "I can promise you I'm not wearing this hat so I can fill his shoes. Dale Earnhardt cannot be replaced in any way."

He paused to think and reflected on their rivalry and their relationship.

"We weren't fishing buddies. We weren't guys that called one another all the time," Gordon said. "But he was somebody I respected greatly and I learned a lot from him—more than he ever imagined."

Gordon was asked to name his fondest memory of Earnhardt.

"My first time racing in the IROC series (where competitors all have identical cars), we were out there practicing on the track," Gordon said. "I got side-by-side with Ken Schrader coming to the back straightaway. Dale was behind me. He thought he was going to push me. Of course we ended up going three wide. For some reason, I decided to look over. I look at Schrader and he's looking straight up. I look over at Dale and he was just beaming with a smile. He was having a ball.

"That's just the way he was. I think that smile meant that he was having fun, but he also knew he wasn't going to be the one that had to lift off the gas, that it was going to be me."

After seventy-six Winston Cup victories and a record-tying seven points championships, Dale Earnhardt could finally lift his foot off the gas pedal. He was, all his fellow drivers agreed, in a better place.

Prior to the start of the Dura Lube 400 at Rockingham, Darrell Waltrip spoke with reporters about Earnhardt. Like so many NASCAR legends before them, Waltrip and Earnhardt had been bitter rivals on the track—only to become close friends later on. "I thought we were going to grow old together," Waltrip said.

Waltrip discussed racing in general and what he had seen and thought as Earnhardt plowed head-on into the turn four wall at Daytona one week earlier, saying "It's like riding a bull. It tosses you around, and then eventually tosses you off. But when the bull rams you head-on into the wall, you don't get up. The thing is, I thought Dale Earnhardt could."

Everyone did. The prevailing sentiment in the garage area on this day, then, was that if it could happen to Earnhardt, it could certainly happen to anyone.

Waltrip talked about his younger brother, too. Finally a winner after all these years, and the victor of the sport's most prestigious race, Michael Waltrip was nevertheless feeling about as low as an individual could. Within a year, the Waltrips had lost their father and one of their most cherished mutual friends in the Intimidator, who had believed in Michael when others wouldn't.

Of Michael Waltrip, Darrell said: "He lost his father, lost his mentor. He's in a dark and lonely place."

So why continue to race? Why did any of them want to go on? Darrell Waltrip offered a simple answer.

"It comes down to risk versus reward. Are you willing to take the risk for the reward?" he said.

To a man, they are. And this is what they do for a living. That included young Dale Earnhardt Jr.

Tony Eury Jr., a member of Little E's crew, talked about how hard coming to the Rockingham track had been for the grieving Earnhardt.

"Today was probably the hardest day on him as far as his dad not being here and going to the drivers' meeting and stuff like that," Eury Jr. said. "We were just wanting to go racing. That's the only way we can really put it behind us—if we just go racin' and just remember the good times. That's what he would have wanted us to do.

"Dale Jr. and his father, they were the closest on race day. Dale Jr. would be in the coach and his dad would pick him up and they'd go to the drivers' meeting together and have their little father-son chats. That's kind of what he's missing today. But we're going to have to pick up and move on."

Before the race, Darrell Waltrip implored the crowd to offer a moment of silence for the fallen driver of the black No. 3. Silence settled over the track, interrupted only by the occasional sounds of someone sobbing. There didn't appear to be a dry eye in the house . . . not on pit road nor in the packed grandstands, where there seemed to be even more Earnhardt gear worn by fans than usual.

Then Waltrip trumpeted the beginning of another race.

"Why are we racing here today? Because Dale would have wanted us to!" Waltrip thundered over the public-address system.

But in a harrowing moment only seconds after the start of the race, Dale Earnhardt Jr. crashed head-on into an outside wall in a scene eerily reminiscent of the accident that had taken his father's life only one week earlier. Another hush came over the crowd, followed by a collective sigh of relief when Little E was able to hobble away with minor injuries and a clear resolve to race again as soon as possible.

Steve Crisp, another Budweiser team crew member, shrugged when asked about Little E's mood the morning of the race.

"He was fine. He was real focused this morning and he was ready to do it."

Crisp shrugged again when asked about the wreck.

"They've been wrecking them for fifty years. They'll wreck them for fifty more. It's a shame."

When the race at Rockingham concluded one week and one day after Earnhardt's death (because of a twenty-four-hour rain delay that followed Earnhardt Jr.'s wreck), Steve Park emerged the victor, which seemed a fitting conclusion. Like Michael Waltrip, the already forgotten winner of the Daytona 500, Park drove for Dale Earnhardt, Inc., and as he took his Polish victory lap the wrong way around the track, Park waved a black number three Earnhardt hat out the window. When he climbed from his car in Victory Lane, he wiped tears from his eyes.

"Dale's the one who taught me how to drive in this race. He told me to stay off the brakes. We stayed off the brakes all day and we won the race. Thank God for this," the emotional Park said.

Then Park promptly thanked all his sponsors.

Bibliography

Center, Bill and Bob Moore. *NASCAR 50 Greatest Drivers.* New York:
  HarperHorizon, 1998.

Fielden, Greg. *Charlotte Motor Speedway.* Osceola, WI: MBI Publishing Company,
  2000.

Golenbock, Peter and Greg Fielden. *The Stock Car Racing Encyclopedia.*
  New York: Macmillan, 1997.

Golenbock, Peter. *The Last Lap.* New York: Macmillan, 1998.

Howell, Mark D. *From Moonshine to Madison Avenue.* Bowling Green, OH:
  BGSU Popular Press, 1997.

Hunter, Don and Ben White. *American Stock Car Racers.* Osceola, WI:
  Motorbooks International, 1997.

The Official NASCAR 1999 Preview and Press Guide. Charlotte, NC:
  UMI Publications, Inc., 1999.

The Official NASCAR 2000 Preview and Press Guide. Charlotte, NC:
  UMI Publications, Inc., 2000.

Index

Photo Credits

"Menzer does a first-rate job of laying out the history of a sport which h
origins in the days of moonshine runners in the rural South and, today
industry that generates billions in revenue . . . a book which will be cher
by NASCAR fans."

—*Rocky Mountain*

In *The Wildest Ride*, Joe Menzer gives us a timely, comprehensive look
dramatic, rollicking history of stock-car racing in America, exploring bc
inauspicious bootlegging beginnings and the billion-dollar industry that
become. Menzer straps the reader into the driver's seat for a run th
NASCAR's history, revealing the sport's remarkable rise from rogue outfit to cor
darling. Menzer also profiles the many superstar drivers who have dominate
sport, men as unpredictable as they are fearless, including "The Intimidator,"
Earnhardt, whose ferocious driving made him NASCAR's signature persona
and whose tragic death at the 2001 Daytona 500 was mourned by millions.

Menzer expertly maneuvers through the tight corners and wide-open stra
aways of NASCAR's history, examining the circuit's attempt to distance itsel
its "redneck racin'" past without compromising its country roots. Simultane
rowdy and insightful, *The Wildest Ride* is a thorough and unfailingly honest ac
of NASCAR's amazing rise to prominer⎯⎯⎯⎯⎯⎯⎯⎯⎯⎯⎯⎯ a uni
American phenomenon.

"A thorough history of the fastest growing sport in America."

—*New York Daily*

"Insightful, energetic . . . an excellent, broad-ranging account."

—*Publishers W*

JOE MENZER is a sportswriter for *The Winston-Salem Journal*. His art
have appeared in *The Sporting News, Inside Sports, Hoop Magazine,* and *Bask*
Weekly. He is the author of *Four Corners: How UNC, N.C. State, Duke and V*
Forest Made North Carolina the Center of the Basketball Universe. He liv
Charlotte, North Carolina, with his wife and children.

A T O U C H S T O N E B O O
Published by Simon & Schuster New York

Cover design by Calvin Chu
Cover photograph by Getty Images

Register online at www.simonsays.com for more information on this and other great books.

ISBN-13: 978-0-7432-2625-7
ISBN-10: 0-7432-2625-9

06021500

U.S. $15.00
Can. $21.50